IMAGES
of America

Gainesville and Cooke County

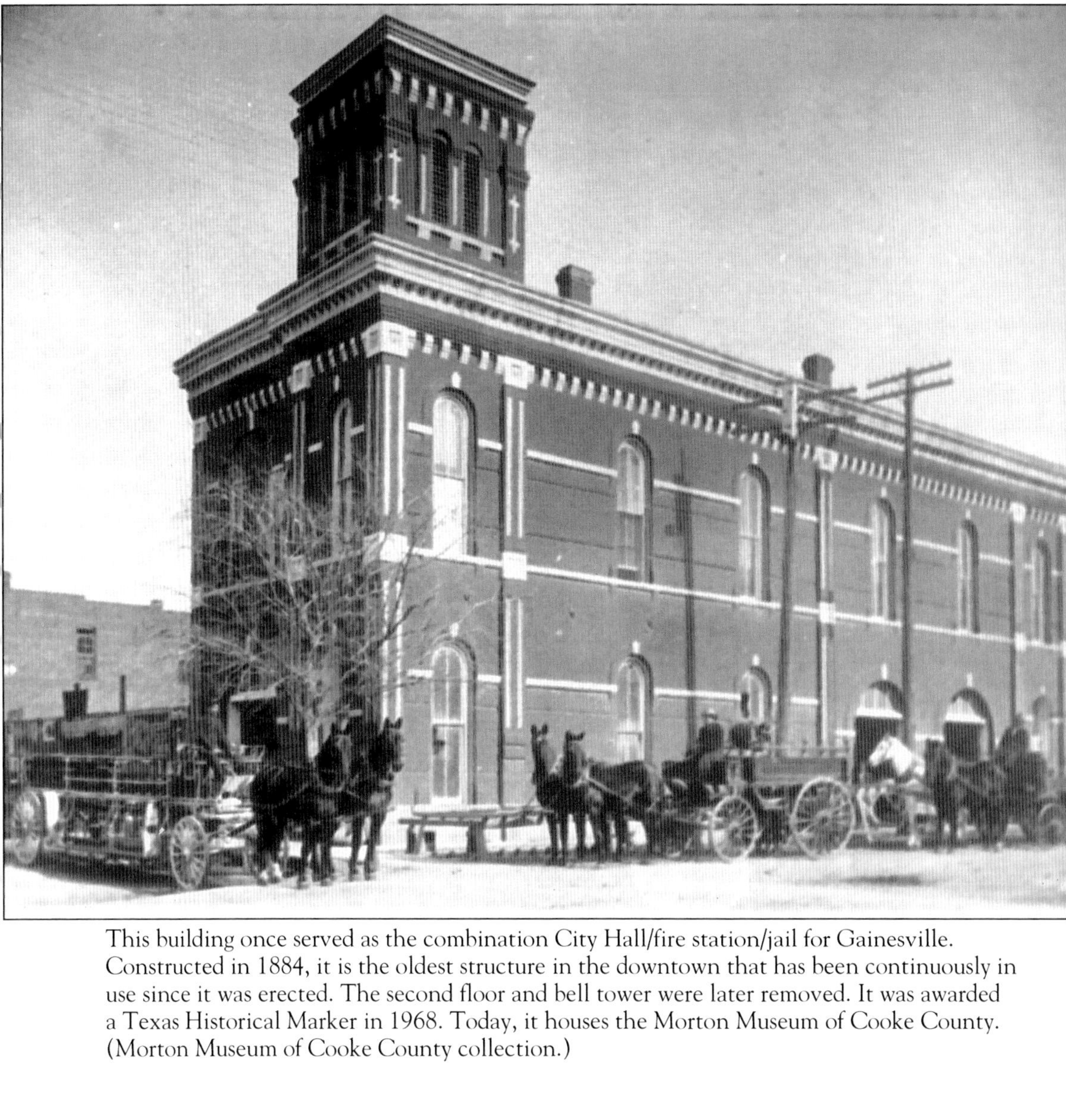

This building once served as the combination City Hall/fire station/jail for Gainesville. Constructed in 1884, it is the oldest structure in the downtown that has been continuously in use since it was erected. The second floor and bell tower were later removed. It was awarded a Texas Historical Marker in 1968. Today, it houses the Morton Museum of Cooke County. (Morton Museum of Cooke County collection.)

IMAGES
of America

GAINESVILLE AND COOKE COUNTY

Shana Powell

ARCADIA
PUBLISHING

ISBN 978-0-7385-0785-9

Published by Arcadia Publishing
Charleston, South Carolina

Printed in the United States of America

Library of Congress Catalog Card Number: 00-106914

For all general information contact Arcadia Publishing at:
Telephone 843-853-2070
Fax 843-853-0044
E-Mail sales@arcadiapublishing.com
For customer service and orders:
Toll-Free 1-888-313-2665

Visit us on the Internet at www.arcadiapublishing.com

Contents

ACKNOWLEDGMENTS

Many years ago F.M. Boyd moved to Gainesville, Texas and opened a photography studio. Later, Guy Breeding, also a photographer, arrived in town. The two joined forces and the Boyd & Breeding Studio emerged. Together, they chronicled several decades of Cooke County history. In time, the studio closed. After the Morton Museum of Cooke County opened in 1968, Mrs. Breeding donated thousands of prints and negatives from the studio to the museum. For more than two years, Mary Ann Arendt inventoried the collection. A majority of the images seen in this book are derived from the Boyd & Breeding Collection. I truly appreciate the loan of photographs from the following individuals for the volume: Jack Merrick, Paul Schad, Francis Wiese, Margaret Hays, Delsie Lillard Lance, Pat Winstead, Lisa Roberts and Butterfield Stage, and the *Gainesville Daily Register*.

I owe a debt of gratitude to Mary Ann Arendt for her perseverance in working with the Boyd & Breeding Collection, and to Billie Hood for creating a computer database for the collection. I also appreciate Arcadia Publishing for taking on this project.

I want to thank all of the people of Gainesville and Cooke County who have taught me so much about the rich history of this area. I also want to thank the Board of Directors of the Cooke County Heritage Society for its support over the years. A special thank you goes to Kathy Steed for all her work and encouragement during this project.

It proved impossible to include the photographs of everyone who made contributions to the history of the area, or of all the businesses, churches, organizations, and events without which Cooke County would not have been the same. This volume contains only a sample of the county's past and is by no means a comprehensive account. Hopefully, it will encourage others to collect other photos of the past and save them for future generations.

I dedicate this book to my husband, John Powell; my parents, Charles and Christine Longwell; my niece, Michelle McCray; and to all the individuals who came to Cooke County over the years and struggled to make living conditions here better for those still to come.

Finally, I dedicate this book in memory of my sister Sharla McCray, who would have loved to see Elvis Presley's performance in Gainesville in 1955.

Shana Powell
June 2000

INTRODUCTION

The first travelers who entered the Cooke County area in North-Central Texas—Native Americans, gold seekers headed for California, army officials, and others—discovered a raw, unspoiled land. Eyewitness accounts speak of "grass that was as high as a man's head" and "one of the most beautiful locations for farmers to be found anywhere." In 1841, W.S. Peters and associates signed their first contract with the Republic of Texas, "which provided that within three years they would bring 600 families into North-Central Texas" into what came to be known as the Peters Colony. In 1847, Ft. Fitzhugh, the first site of settlement in the region, was established. In the following year, the state legislature created Cooke County, named for William G. Cooke, a hero of the Texas War for Independence.

According to local folklore, one day Bob Wheelock rode up to a group of people standing at one of the two proposed sites for the as yet unnamed county seat of Cooke. Apparently, it looked as if they might choose a location along Wheeler Creek. Reportedly, Wheelock, the county judge, "picked up a jug of whiskey and shouted 'All in favor of putting the town here, come with me' and then rode to the Mary E. Clark site closer to Elm Creek which was finally approved." City residents called their new community Liberty, which proved short-lived, as a Liberty, Texas already existed. Eventually, a new name emerged—Gainesville. Ironically, Gainesville—seemingly founded as a result of the enticements of a jug of whiskey—voted in Prohibition in 1910.

The first hint of prosperity arrived with the Butterfield Stagecoach in 1858. Bringing freight, passengers, and mail, it literally put the county on the map. The Civil War was a difficult time for everyone, and the residents of Cooke County were no exception. The ordeal of the Great Hanging came close to ripping the county apart, but the people persevered. Cattle enabled the county to recover economically after the war. Two major cattle trails flanked Cooke County, and the cowboys would roar into Gainesville to visit the saloons, get supplies, gamble, and visit the "soiled doves."

When the last of the major Native American raids occurred in 1868, the county population began to increase, and with the arrival of the "Katy" railroad in 1879, the area prospered. In the 1880s, Gainesville started to resemble a very modern community with electric lights, the telegraph, running water, a streetcar system, and at the end of the decade, a second railroad line, the Santa Fe. Many smaller communities thrived in the county during that time as well. The towns of Muenster and Lindsay, founded by German immigrants in 1891, were settled. Farming became very important to the local economy, and cotton was the major crop produced.

After the turn of the century, automobiles appeared on county roads. The first airplane landed in 1911—not because the pilot wanted to, but because of a navigational mistake on his part. The State Training School for Girls opened. County men marched off to fight in World War I. The discovery of oil at Callisburg in the county was, locally, one of the most significant events of the century. In the same year, the Gainesville Junior College opened, and under the name of North Central Texas College still exists. In 1930, an amazing sight was seen in Gainesville: the first performance of the Gainesville Community Circus. The circus was started by A. Morton Smith, Chowning Moore, and several others. All of the participants were volunteers who built their own props and made their costumes. The circus survived for many years, and brought national attention to Gainesville through newsreels, radio broadcasts, and magazine articles. Many members of the circus were instrumental in starting and supporting the Frank Buck Zoo in Gainesville.

One interruption to the full schedule of circus performances was World War II. The war had an enormous impact on Cooke County. Camp Howze, an army infantry training camp, was established on some of the best farm land in the county. The construction of the camp helped bring Cooke County out of the Great Depression by providing jobs. At the same time, it brought heartbreak to at least three hundred families forced to give up their land so the camp could be established. The county population doubled and the area boomed.

After the war, the circus resumed performing, oil continued to fuel the economy, the airport developed, and new companies moved to the county. Camp Sweeney opened to provide camping facilities for young diabetic patients, and was visited by actor Gregory Peck. In 1950, Gainesville celebrated its centennial with a huge pageant, the Progressorama, and Betty (Yarbrough) Buttolph was chosen queen. Fishing enthusiasts and hunters flocked to the county, drawn by its natural resources, much as the original settlers once did. A major fire in 1954 spelled the beginning of the end for the Community Circus. As the highway system improved and some communities were bypassed, their populations began to dwindle. In time, though, other new communities—Lake Kiowa and Oak Ridge—developed.

In the last several years, tourism has brought renewed prosperity to the area, and the recent return of Amtrak (which makes a stop at the 1902 Santa Fe depot, which had been closed since 1981) has brought Gainesville full-circle, back to one of the original sources of its growth and success.

In 1966, the Cooke County Heritage Society was formed with the mission of gathering, preserving, and displaying the county's history. The first project of the group, led by Mary McCain and generously funded by Granville C. Morton, a native of Gainesville, involved saving the 1884 City Hall/fire station/jail, which they then opened as the Morton Museum of Cooke County in 1968. The focus of the museum continues to be collecting the threads of the county's past before they are irretrievably lost. This book represents one example of that.

One

Life In Downtown

In *Cooke County, Texas—Where the South and the West Meet*, Michael Collins wrote "one newly arrived settler described Gainesville in 1860 as 'a busy metropolis of...four hundred people." While Gainesville grew over the years, the downtown continued to remain the focal point for the community. The same also can be said for the downtown sections in some of the other county towns.

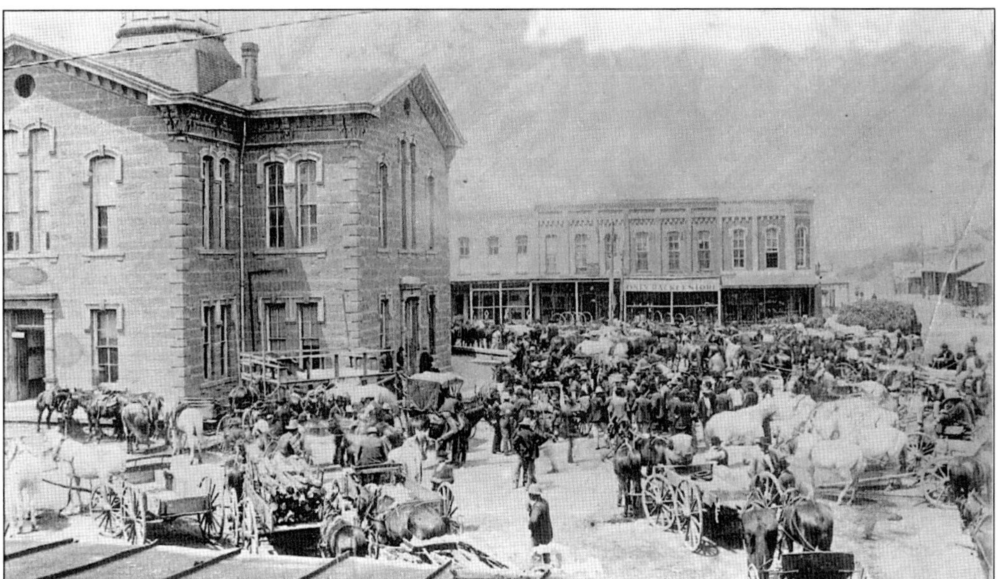

Here is the courthouse square in the mid-1880s. (Morton Museum of Cooke County Collection.)

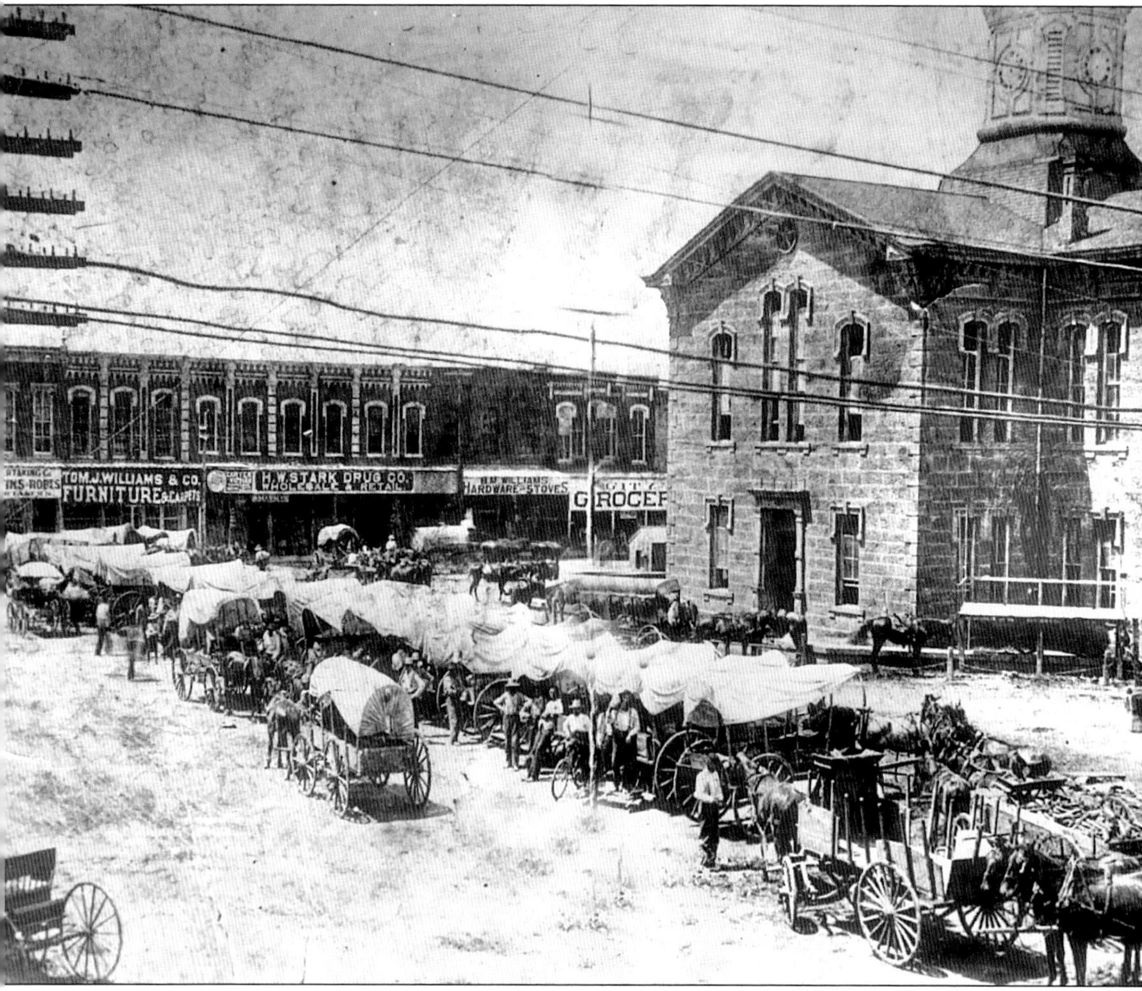

By the 1880s, Gainesville had grown well beyond a population of four hundred, and the downtown was a thriving, vibrant marketplace. (Morton Museum of Cooke County Collection.)

This building housed the city hall in Gainesville from February, 1906 until 1958 when the current city hall was opened. A $20,000 bond issue was passed in 1904 to pay for the city hall. (Morton Museum of Cooke County Collection.)

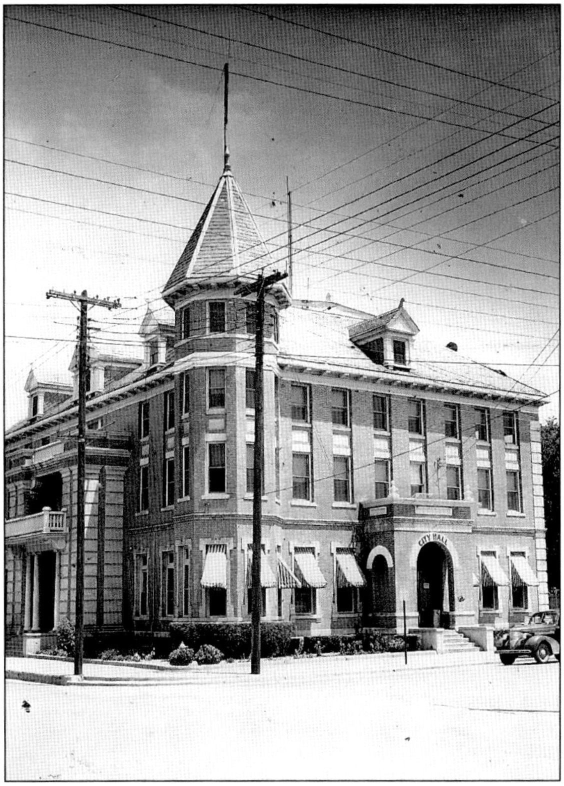

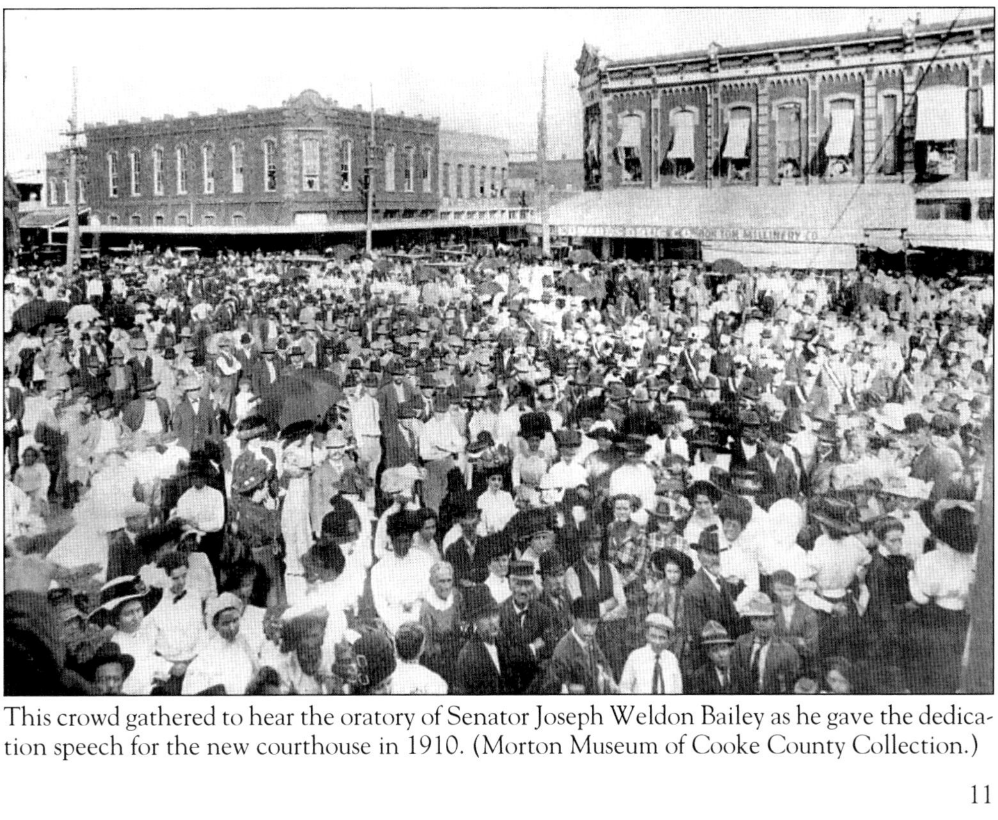

This crowd gathered to hear the oratory of Senator Joseph Weldon Bailey as he gave the dedication speech for the new courthouse in 1910. (Morton Museum of Cooke County Collection.)

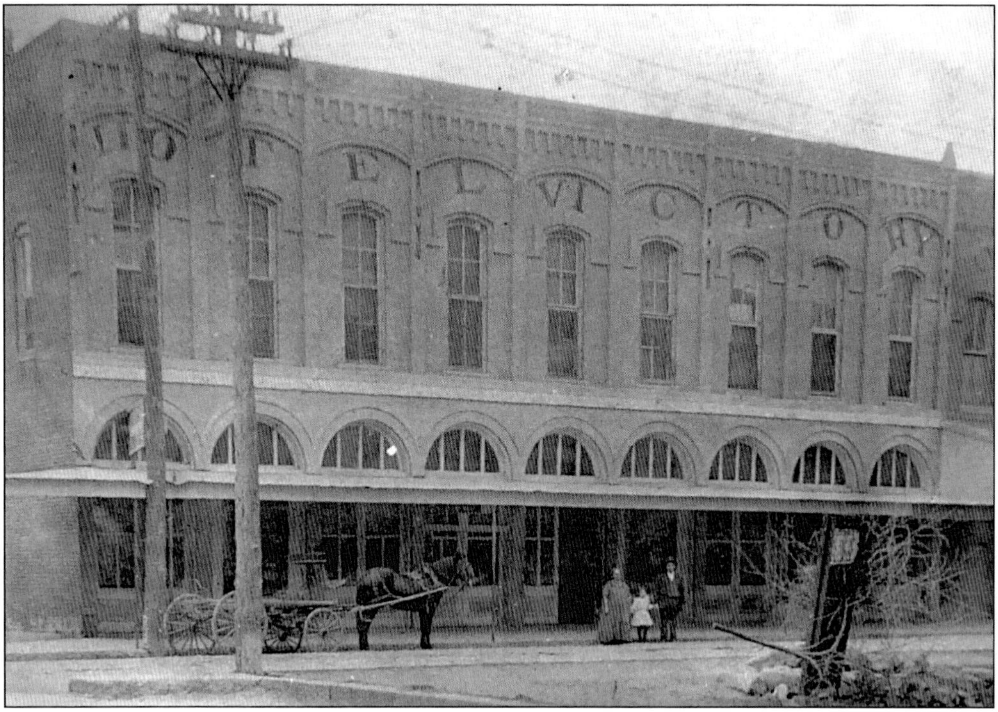

In 1898, this building housed the Hotel Victory, as the letters at the top of the structure indicate. It was located at 114 North Dixon in Gainesville. (Boyd & Breeding Collection, Morton Museum of Cooke County.)

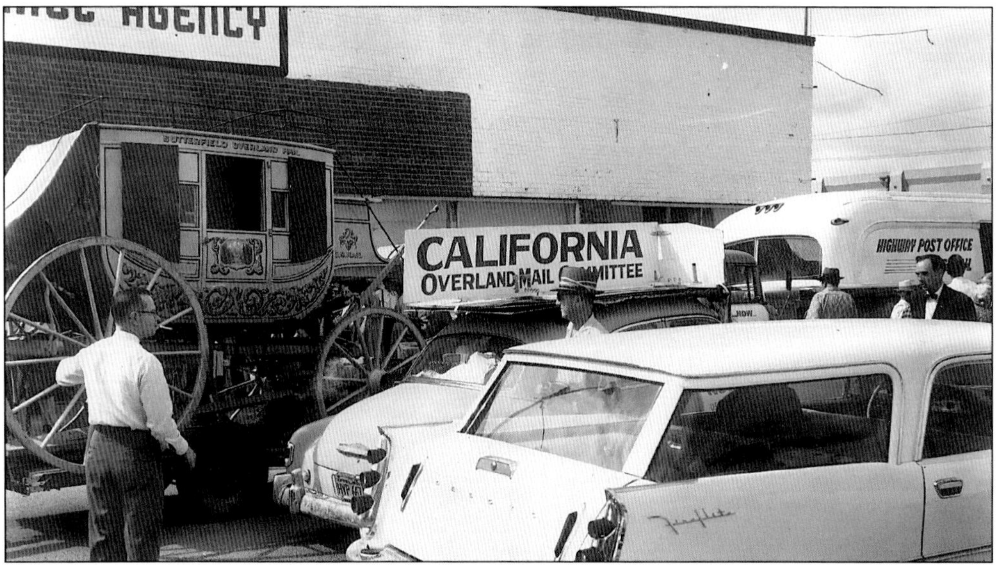

The centennial of the establishment of the Butterfield Overland Stagecoach mail service occurred in September 1958, with ceremonies held in numerous communities along the original route. The Butterfield Stagecoaches came through Gainesville between 1858 and 1861. This photograph shows one being brought into town during the 1958 celebration—a little differently this time, as it sits on a trailer! (Boyd & Breeding Collection, Morton Museum of Cooke County.)

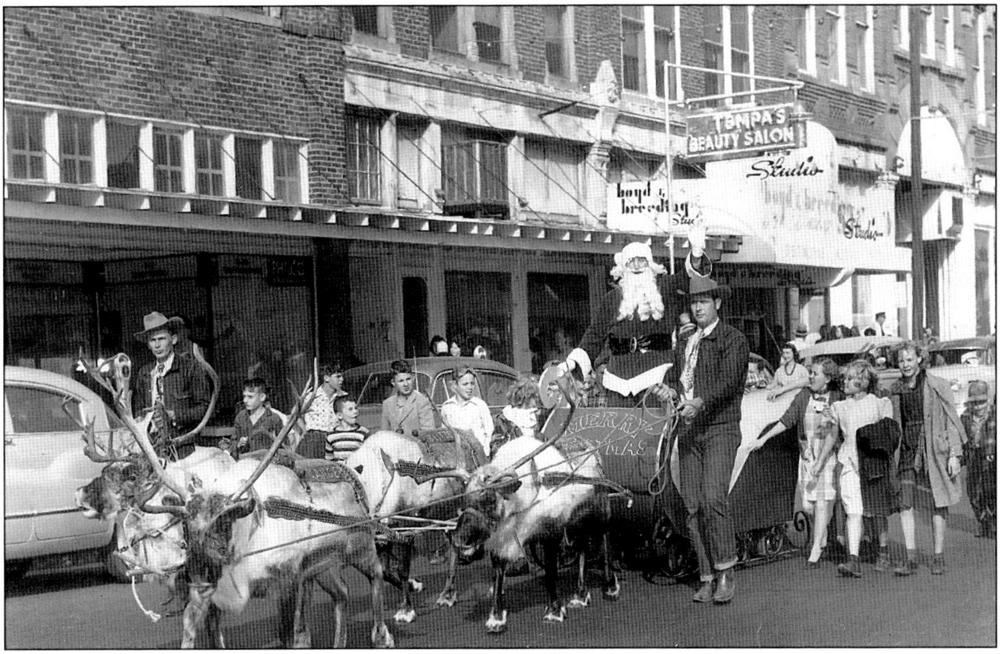

This Christmas parade in 1950 in downtown Gainesville is complete with Santa Claus and live reindeer. The photo was taken by the Boyd & Breeding Photography studio, the store front of which managed to get in the background of this photo. (Boyd & Breeding Collection, Morton Museum of Cooke County.)

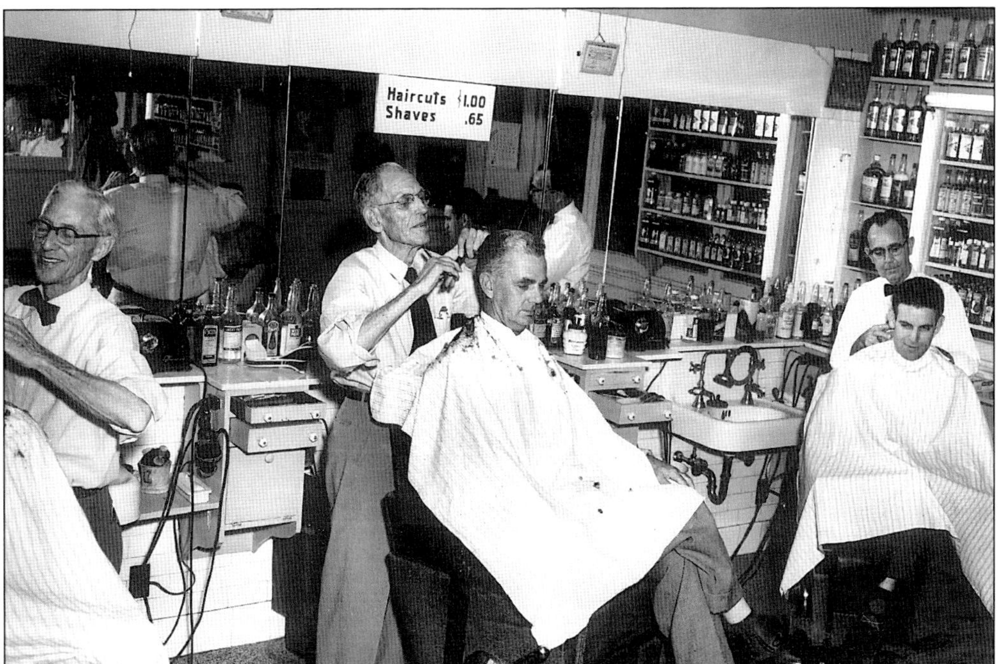

The barber shop at the Turner Hotel was one of many in town. As the sign indicates, a customer could get a haircut for $1 and a shave for 65¢ in 1953. (Boyd & Breeding Collection, Morton Museum of Cooke County.)

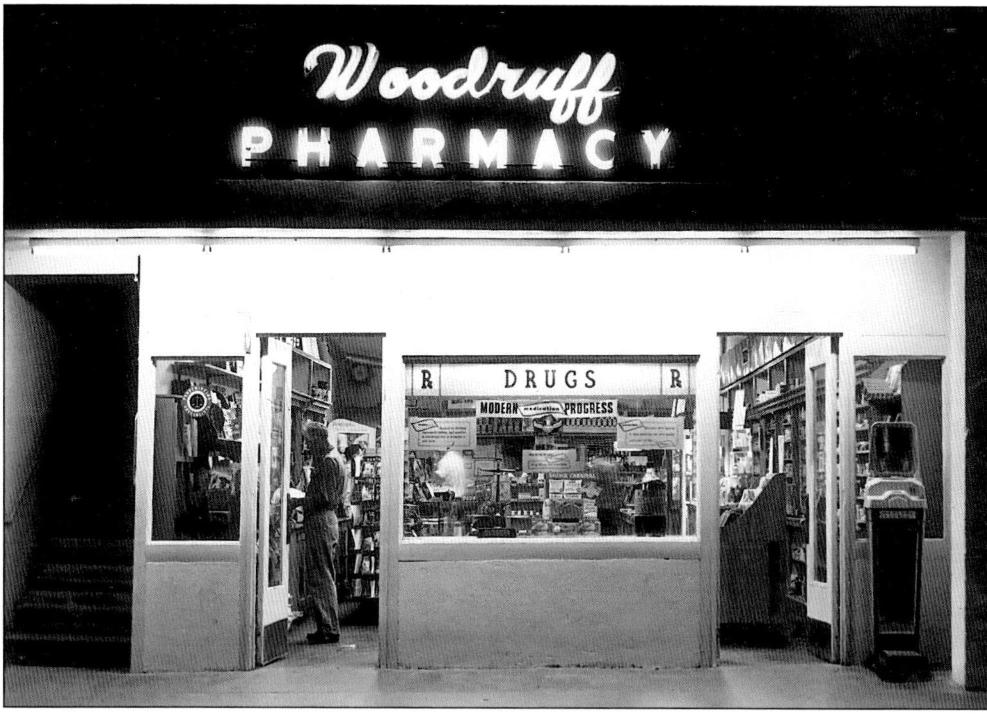

Numerous pharmacies dotted the downtown of Gainesville at one time. Woodruff Pharmacy was one of those. Looking inside the building, note the sign that says "Modern Progress." A weight machine rests on the outside of the building. This photograph was snapped in 1954. (Boyd & Breeding Collection, Morton Museum of Cooke County.)

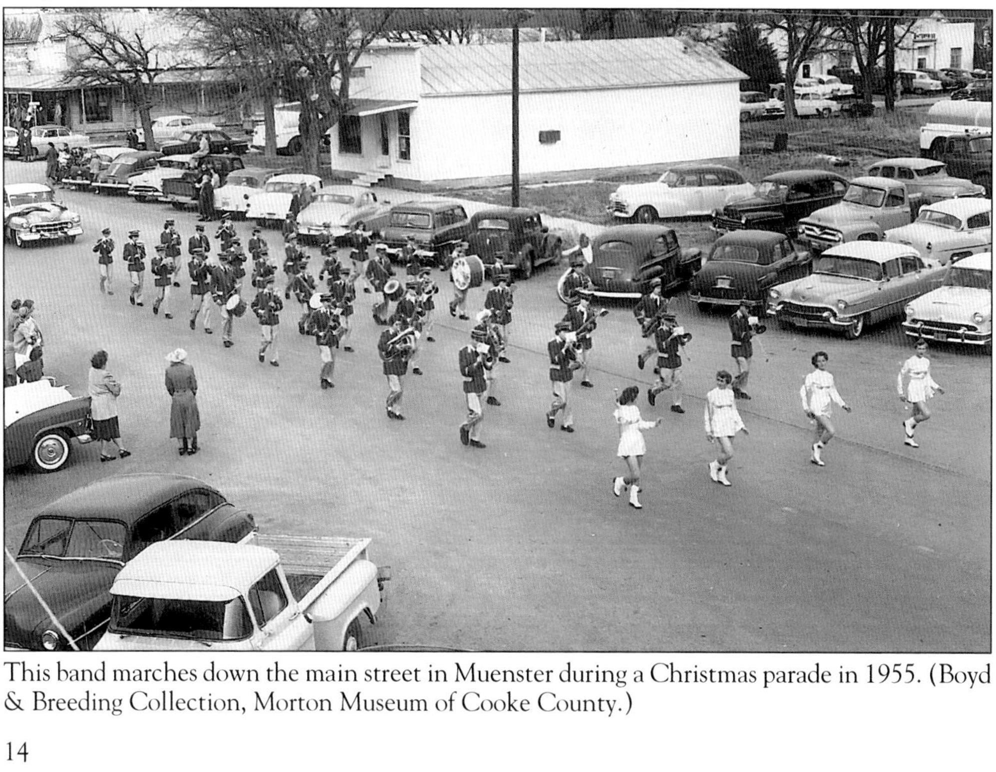

This band marches down the main street in Muenster during a Christmas parade in 1955. (Boyd & Breeding Collection, Morton Museum of Cooke County.)

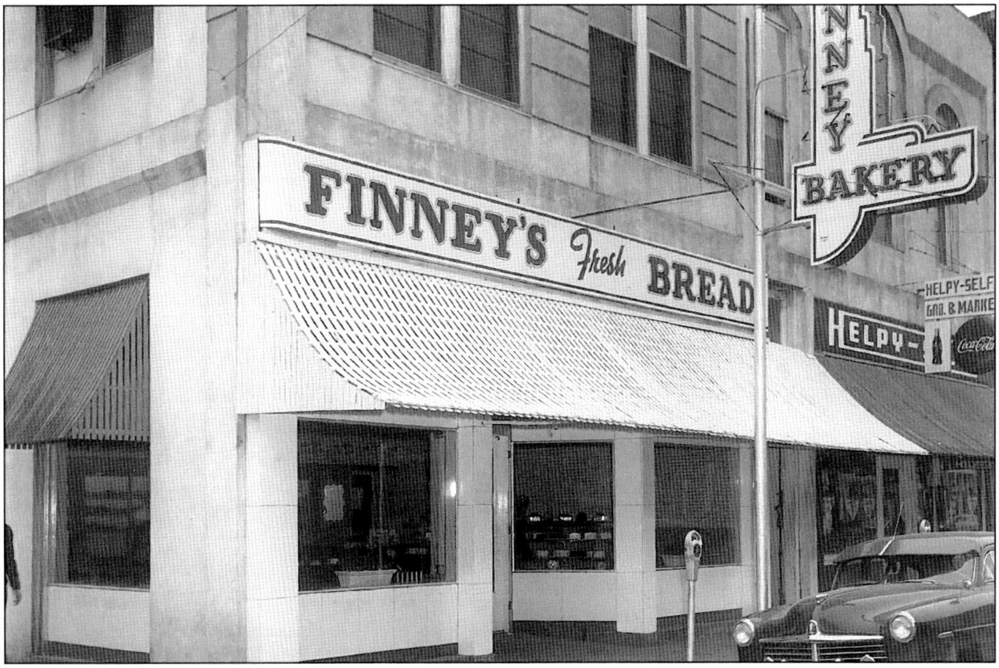

Finney's Bakery opened on California Street in November 1957. Next door to the bakery was the Helpy-Selfy Food Market, owned by Buster Latham, who, at one time, was mayor of Gainesville. (Boyd & Breeding Collection, Morton Museum of Cooke County.)

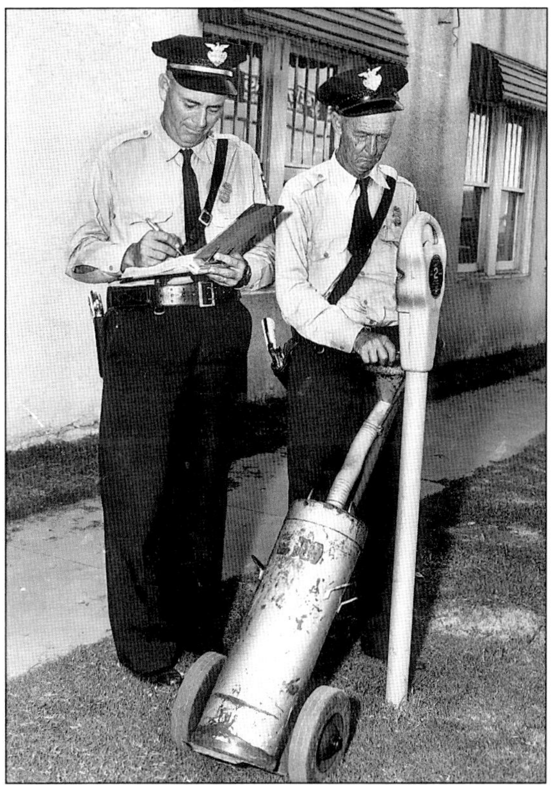

O.S. Potts writes down the register reading from the parking meter, as A.L. Flowers uses the city's special collection cart to carry coins from the meters. The money was removed from the meters on Mondays. In 1955, when these men were emptying the meters, the city projected that the meters would bring in $24,000 for that year. (Boyd & Breeding Collection, Morton Museum of Cooke County.)

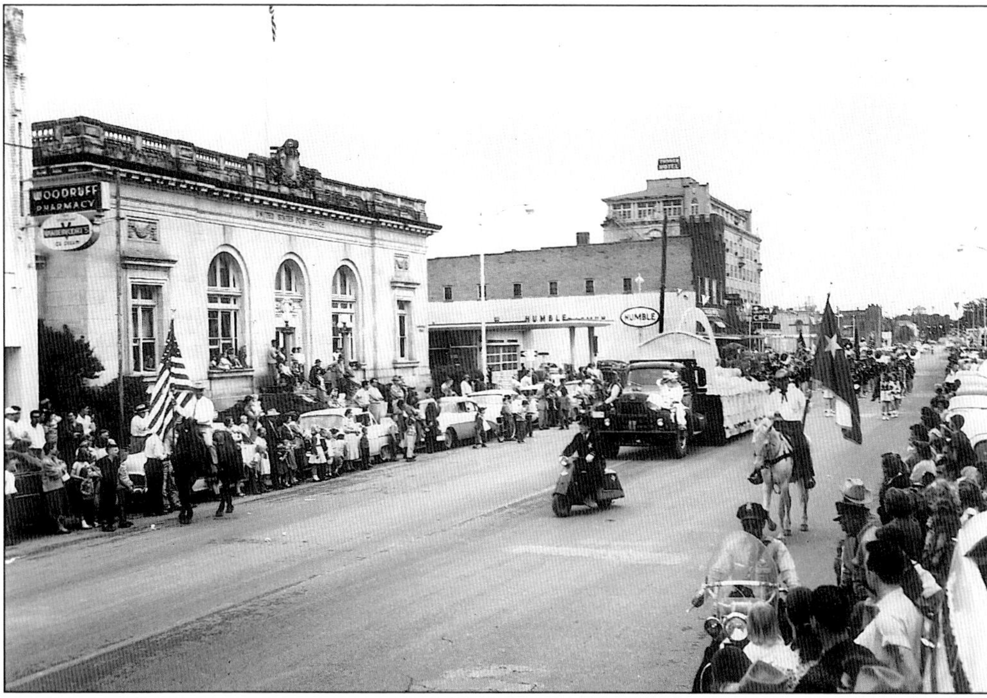

A Gainesville Community Circus parade moved down California street in this 1956 photograph. The old post office, Humble gas station, St. Paul's Episcopal Church, and Turner Hotel line the street as the parade passes by. (Boyd & Breeding Collection, Morton Museum of Cooke County.)

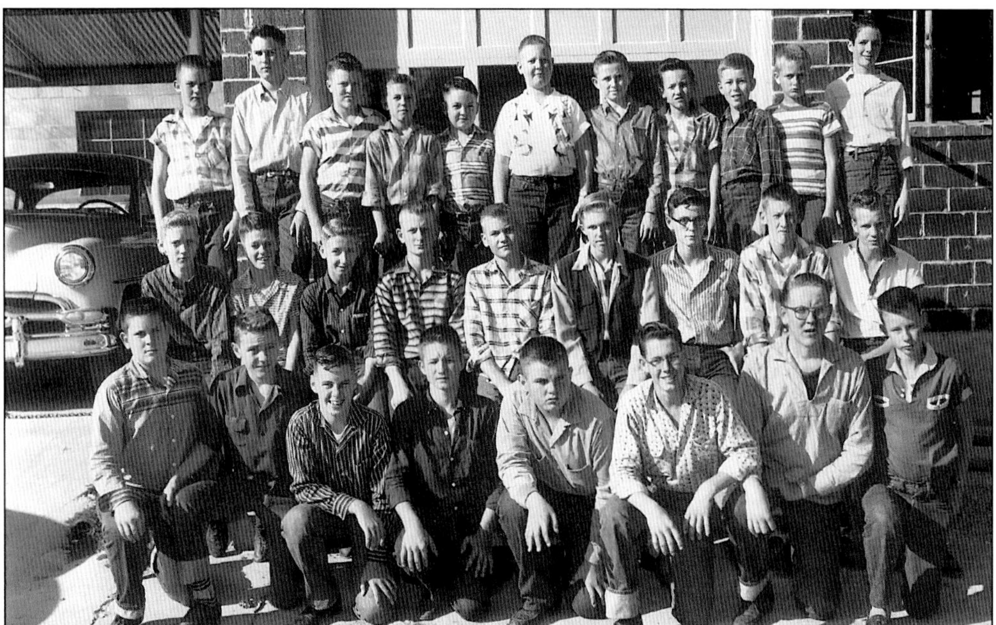

On October 5, 1957, the *Gainesville Daily Register* newsboys (or paper carriers) gathered for this group photograph. Note the absence of any female paper carriers in this picture. (Boyd & Breeding Collection, Morton Museum of Cooke County.)

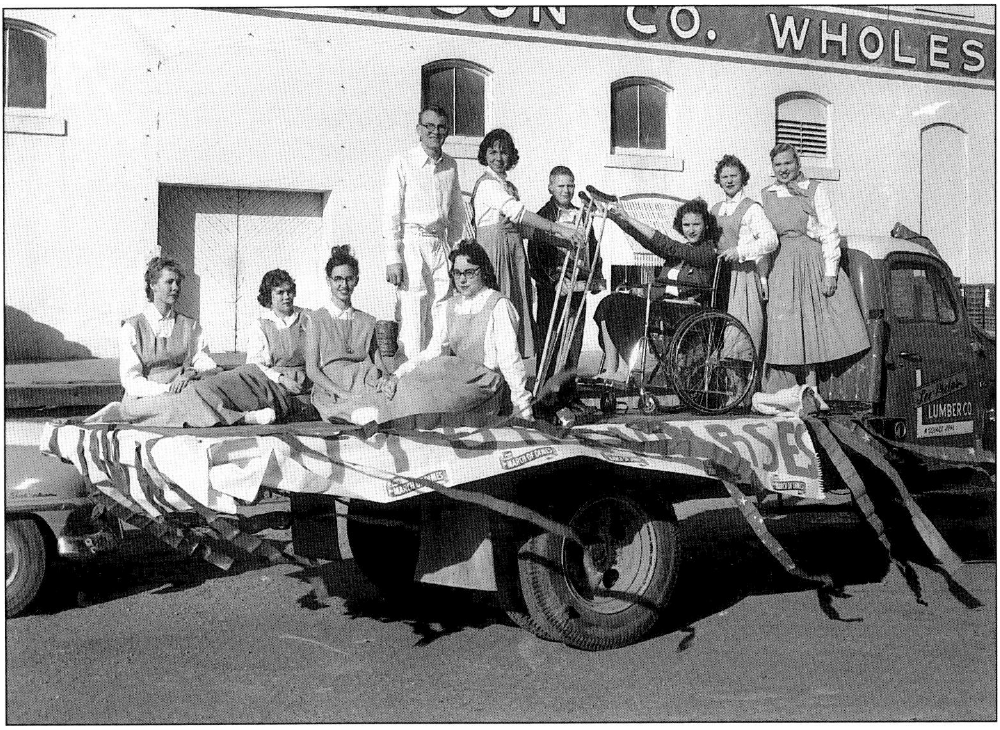

People struggled for decades to find a cure for the serious and often devastating disease of polio. Many individuals raised money for research into and care of the victims of polio. This float, in front of the Tyler & Simpson Building, was part of a polio parade held on January 15, 1957. (Boyd & Breeding Collection, Morton Museum of Cooke County.)

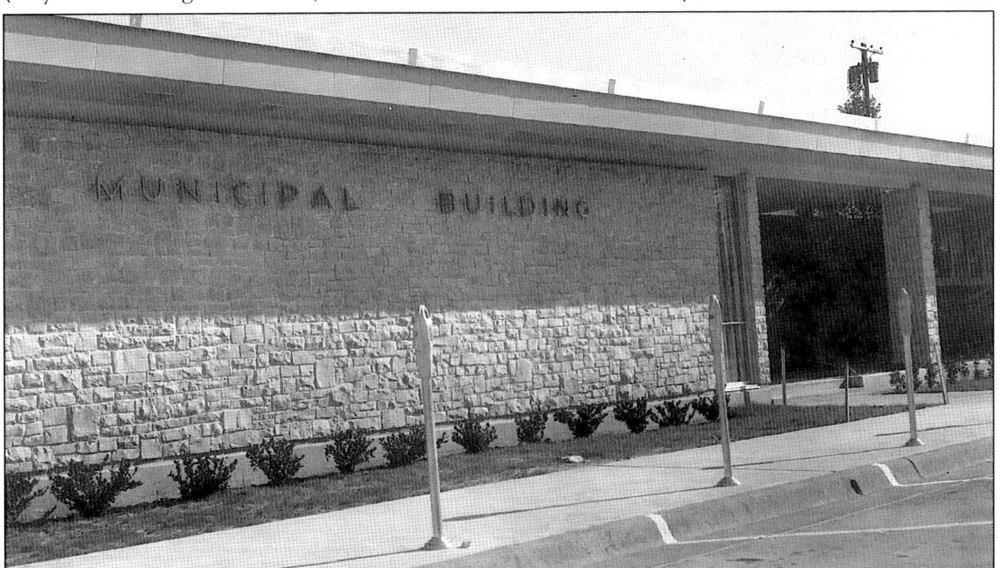

After tearing down the Victorian city hall that existed for several decades, Gainesville erected a new city hall that officially opened in December 1958. This photograph shows the building at its grand opening. Note the parking meters—in order to visit the city hall at that time, people paid for the privilege. (Boyd & Breeding Collection, Morton Museum of Cooke County.)

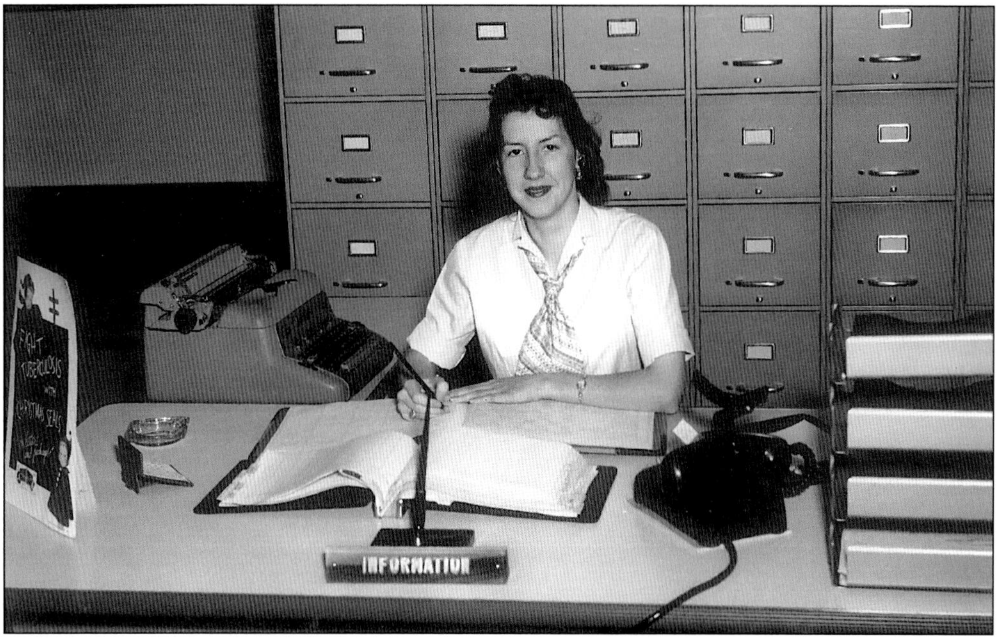

Rita Gray is pictured at her desk inside the new city hall. The sign on her desk says "Fight Tuberculosis with Christmas Seals." Note the manual typewriter—no computers then! (Boyd & Breeding Collection, Morton Museum of Cooke County.)

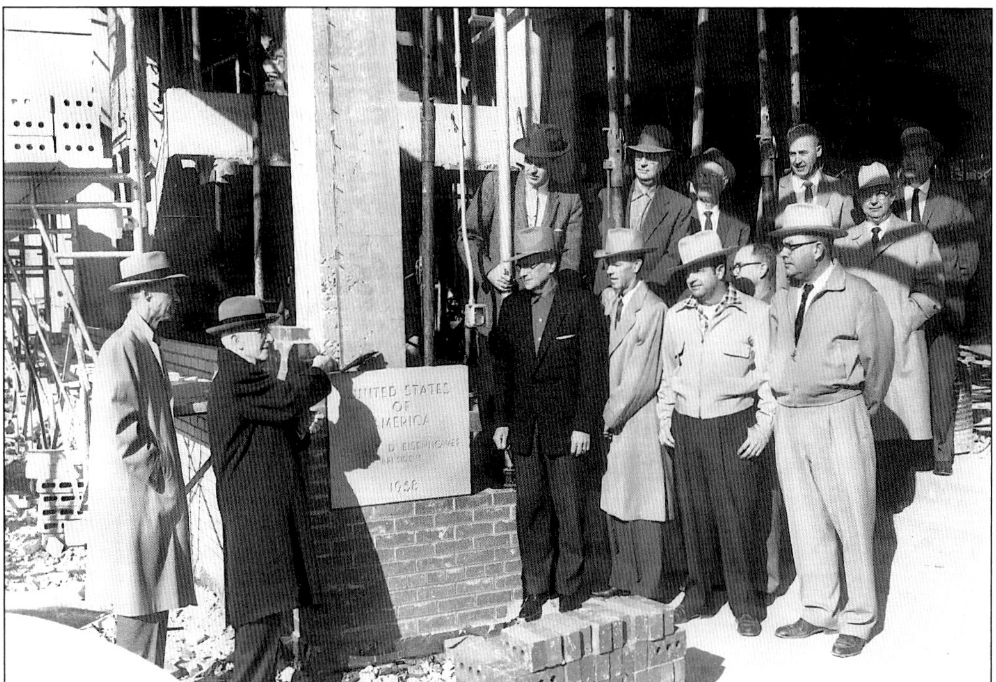

In January 1959, the corner stone for the new post office that was being constructed in Gainesville was laid. Among those present at the ceremony were Postmaster Cecil Tinsley, Mayor Frank Aldridge, Weldon Clack, Leroy Porter, Roy Wilson, Homer Bly, Frank Moore, and Fred Lynn. (Boyd & Breeding Collection, Morton Museum of Cooke County.)

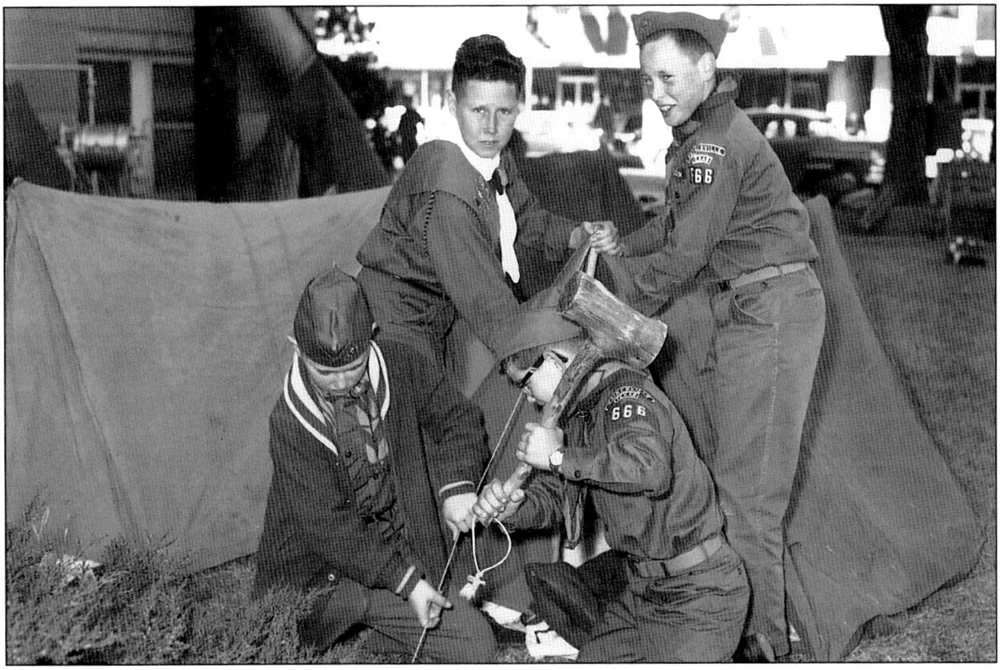

In February 1960, these boy scouts had a very special campground—the courthouse lawn! (Boyd & Breeding Collection, Morton Museum of Cooke County.)

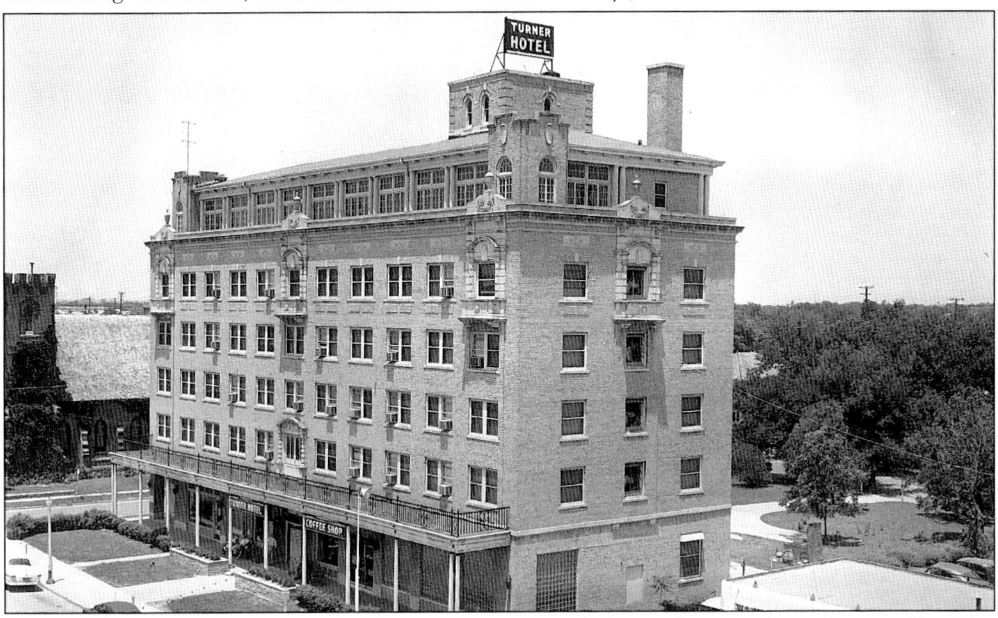

This scene from August 1962 shows the Turner Hotel, long a landmark in Gainesville. The building was constructed in 1927 and dedicated by Senator Joseph Weldon Bailey. Reportedly, it was the first hotel in the state to have a telephone in each room. A frame Turner Hotel was located at this site prior to the erection of this 1927 brick structure. Many famous individuals either stayed at the Turner or ate in the restaurant there. St. Paul's Episcopal Church is visible across the street from the hotel. (Boyd & Breeding Collection, Morton Museum of Cooke County.)

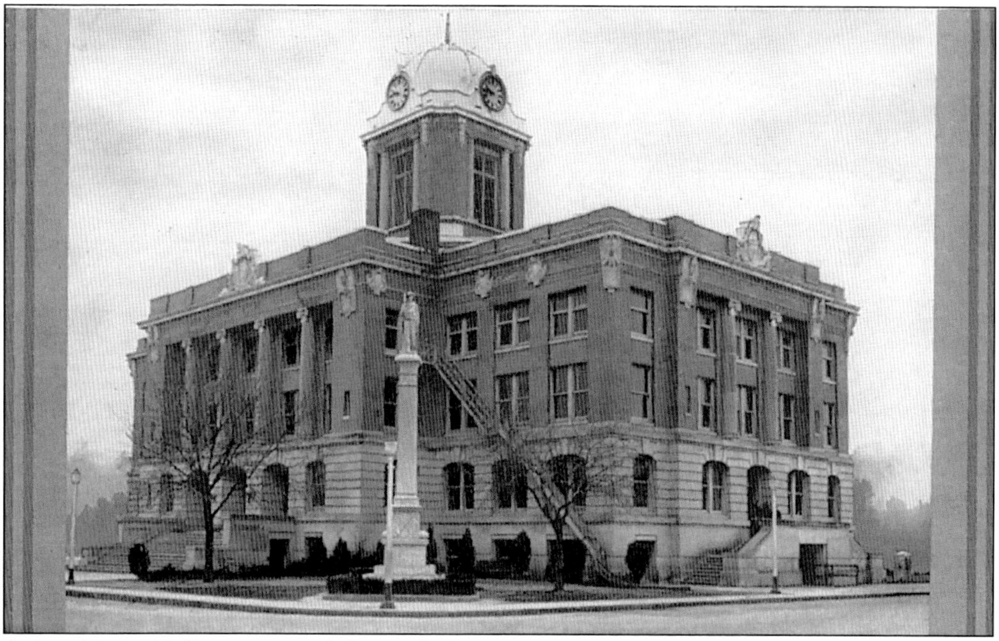

Colonel M.P. Kelley, owner of the "Odorless Sewer Co.," guided the construction of Cooke County's fourth courthouse in 1910. The previous two courthouses burned, and a rampaging bull destroyed the first one. The courthouse appears on the National Register for Historic Places. (Morton Museum of Cooke County Collection.)

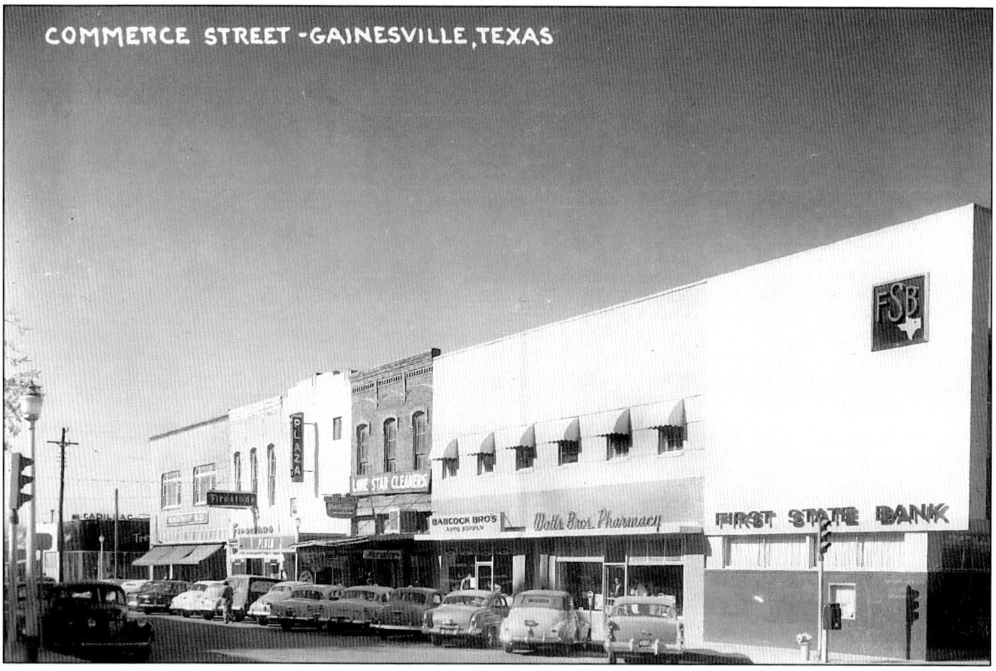

Of the buildings in this panoramic view of Commerce Street in Gainesville, only Watts Bros. remains in that location. The bank moved, and Babcock Bros., Lone Star Cleaners, the Plaza Theater, Firestone, and Montgomery Ward no longer exist in town. (Donated by Mary McCain, Morton Museum of Cooke County Collection.)

Two

BUSINESSES

In 1857, the *Texas Almanac* recorded that Gainesville and the surrounding countryside were "fast filling up with a respectable and industrious people." All types of businesses quickly appeared. Over the years, changing times and other circumstances ended once prosperous enterprises and created new ones. For example, wagon yards gave way to gas stations. The business community continues to evolve and change today.

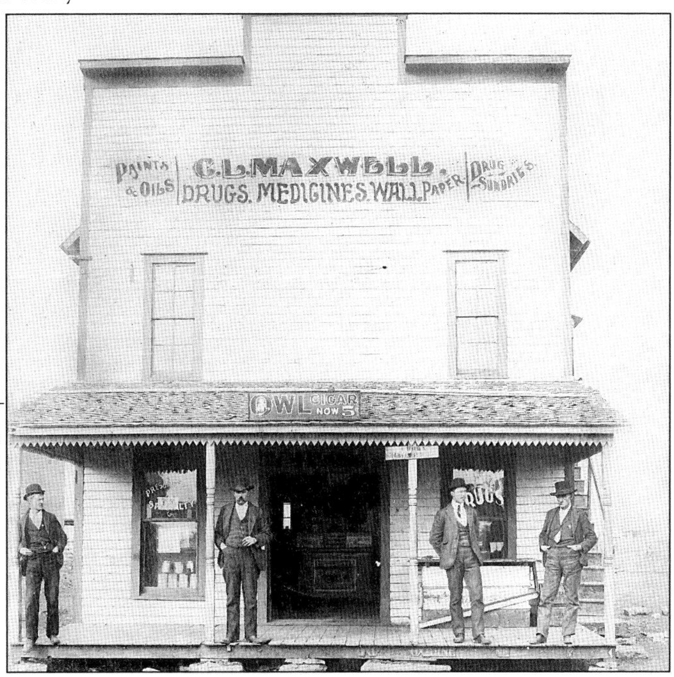

Dr. Corwin L. Maxwell (1869–1936) moved to Myra in 1900, and by 1903 had constructed a large drugstore. An advertisement on this store indicates that if a customer wanted an Owl cigar, 5¢ would do the trick. (Donated by Dr. H.L. Maxwell, Morton Museum of Cooke County Collection.)

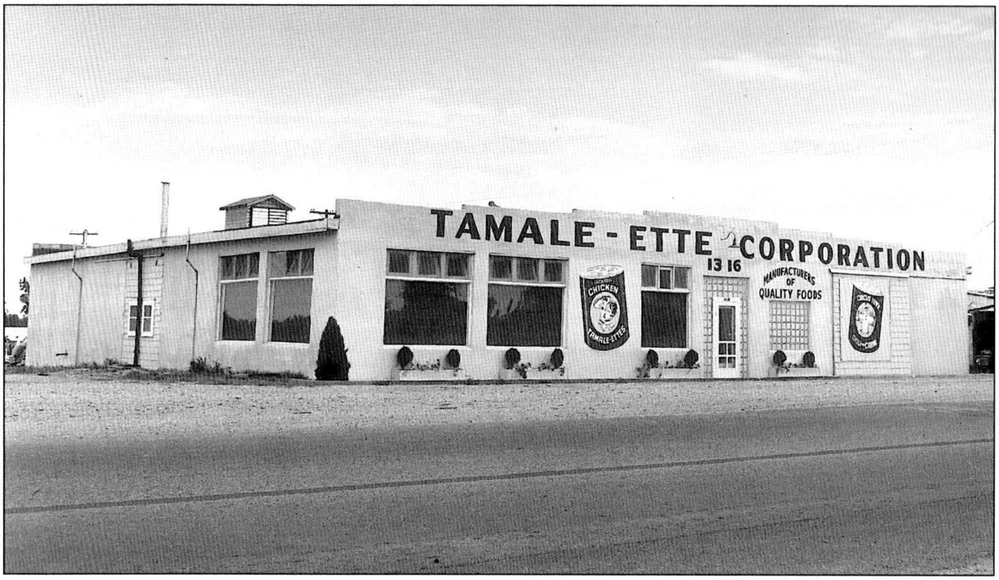

The Tamale-ette Corporation bought out Joanna Hamilton's Home Kitchen Canning Company in 1950. Mrs. Hamilton started the company in the 1930s, out of her own kitchen, to raise funds for the First Methodist Church. The customer base quickly grew to attract both national and international markets. In March 1939, the *Gainesville Daily Register* reported "Guy Lombardo, the noted orchestra leader, appreciates good food. On one of his visits to the Southwest with his band, he ate some tamales, which struck him as being extraordinarily good. He learned they were made by Mrs. Hamilton of Gainesville and she recently received an order from him for three dozen cans." She remained in charge of production in the Tamale-ette Corporation. Mrs. Hamilton's cocktail tamales were known as tamalettes. (Boyd & Breeding Collection, Morton Museum of Cooke County.)

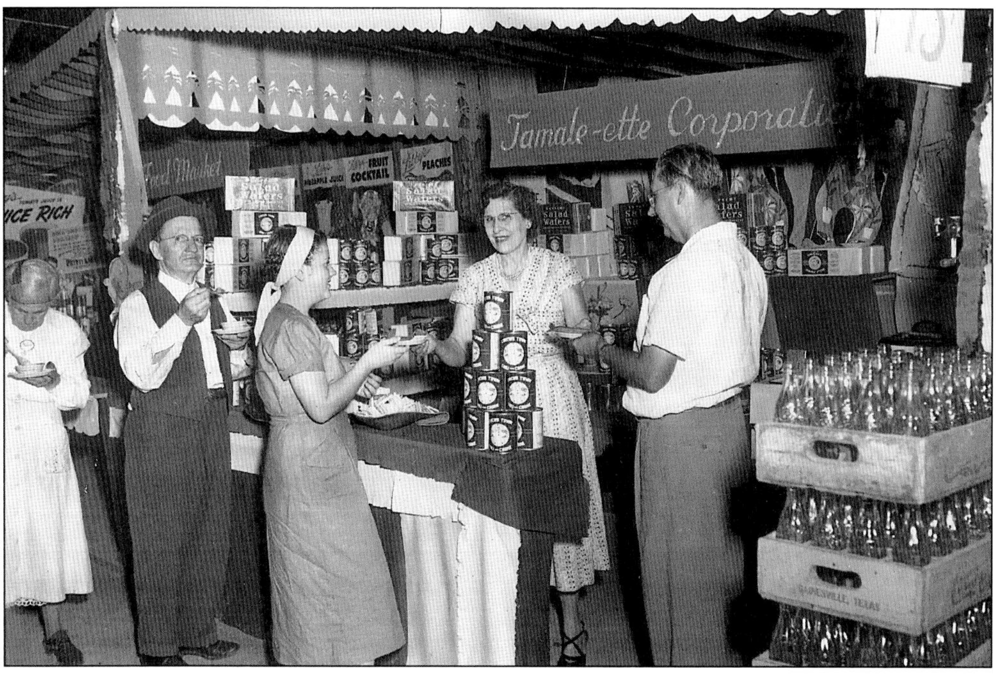

This photograph shows a box of some of the products that people could purchase at the Tamale-ette Corporation. Note the Circus Town logo on the products in honor of Gainesville's nickname, "Circus Town, U.S.A." (Boyd & Breeding Collection, Morton Museum of Cooke County.)

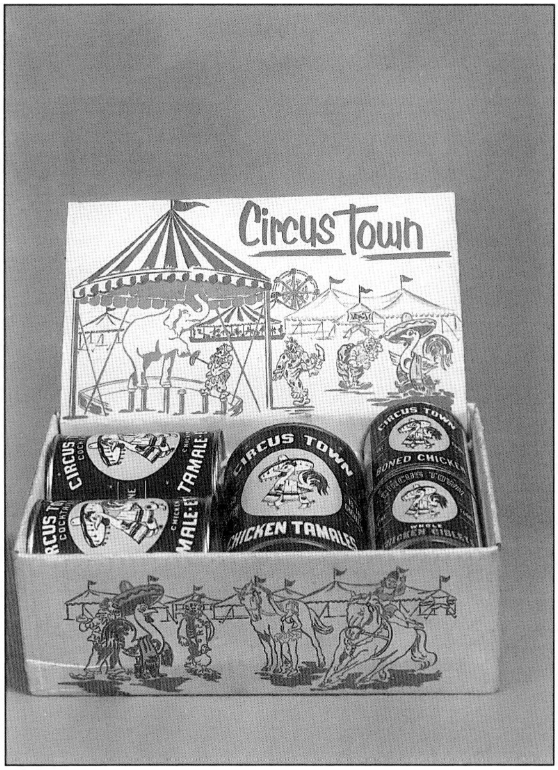

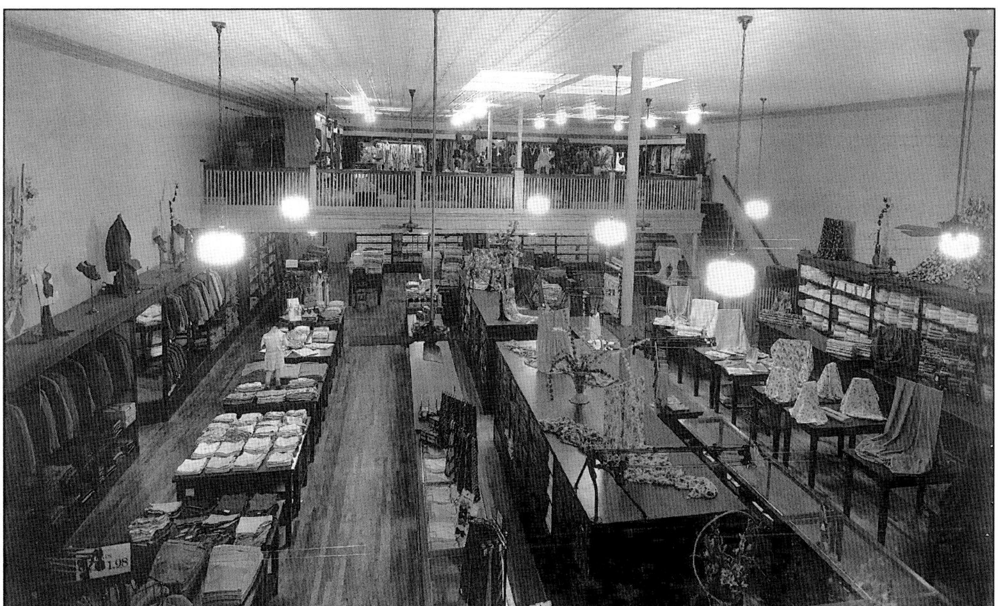

Here is an interior shot of the JC Penney store on California Street in Gainesville shortly after the store opened. (Donated by Glenda Alexander, Morton Museum of Cooke County Collection.)

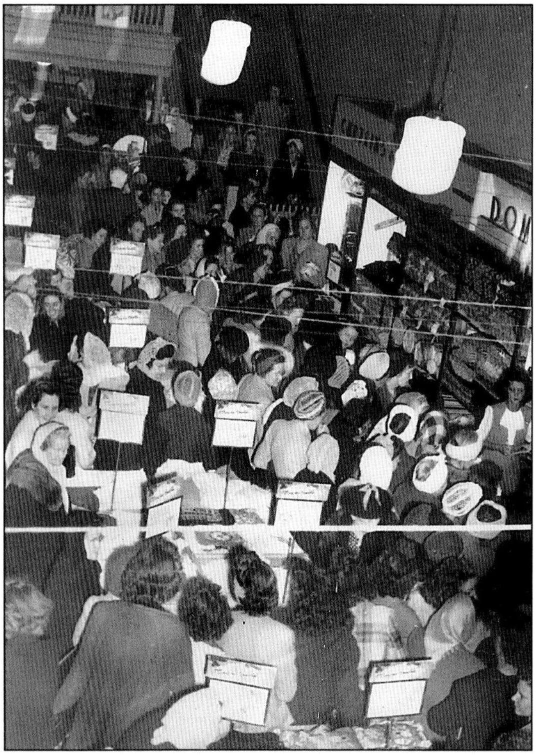

In contrast to the earlier shot of the interior of the JC Penney store, this photo is filled with shoppers who have come to take advantage of a rare sale during World War II. (Donated by Glenda Alexander, Morton Museum of Cooke County Collection.)

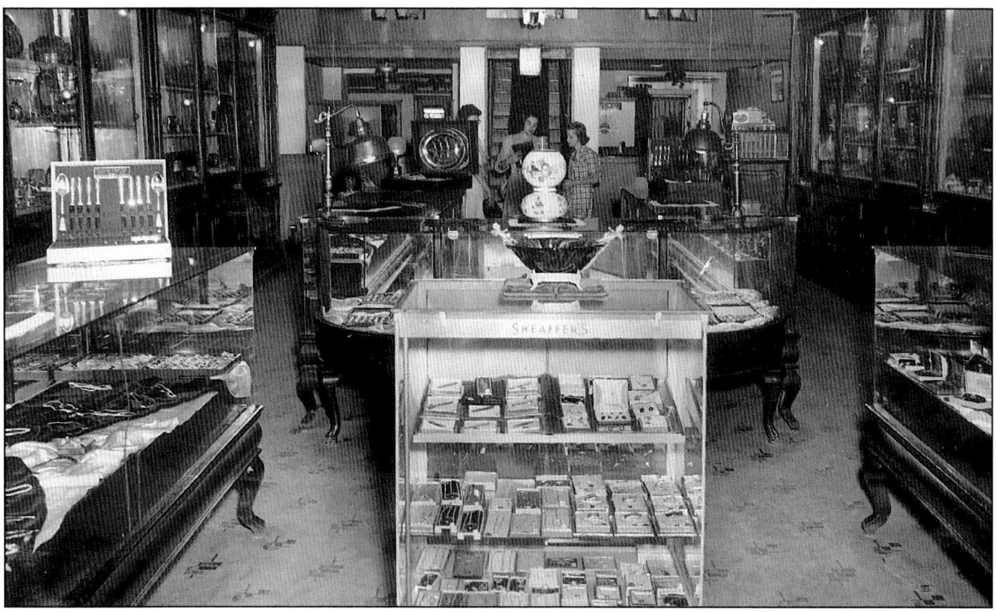

This is an interior scene of Kinne's Jewelers taken in June 1948. Many of the store's features remain the same. On November 28, 1889, "W.B. Kinne opened his first jewelry store in Gainesville on North Dixon Street. In 1913, Mr. Kinne purchased the present location on California Street, a two-storied brick building owned by Senator Joseph Bailey." The store has since been located there. The store celebrated its centennial in 1989. (Boyd & Breeding Collection, Morton Museum of Cooke County.)

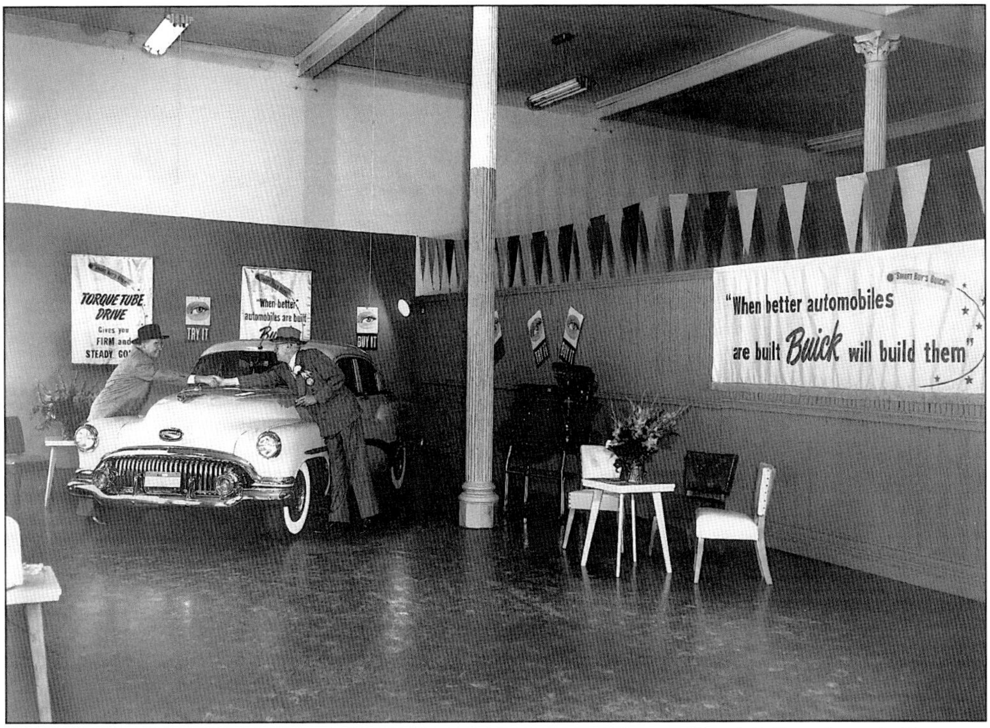

The interior of the Buick sales room in Gainesville is pictured here. (Boyd & Breeding Collection, Morton Museum of Cooke County.)

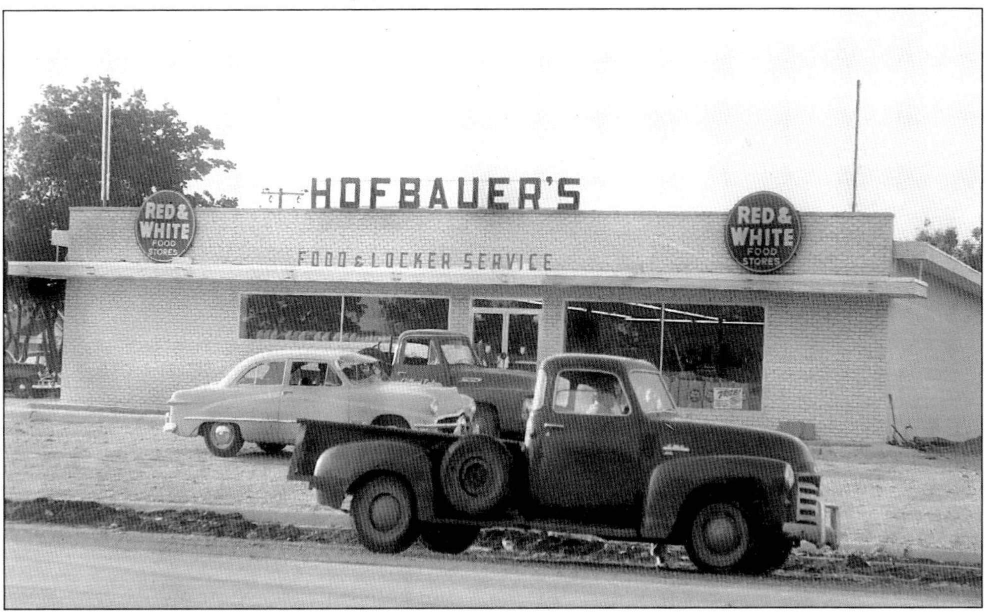

Hofbauer's Food & Locker grocery store in Muenster originally was owned by the Farmers Marketing Association. It was managed by Andrew Hofbauer. After buying the store in 1954, Mr. Hofbauer moved to a new location in 1956. The store has been known "from the beginning for marketing authentic German sausage." (Boyd & Breeding Collection, Morton Museum of Cooke County.)

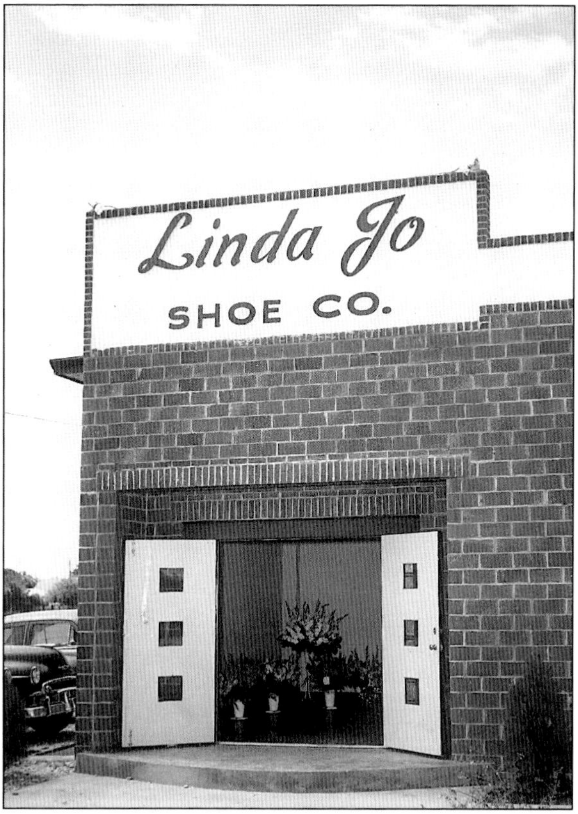

In 1952, the Linda Jo Shoe Company, shown in these two photographs, had its grand opening in Gainesville. (Boyd & Breeding Collection, Morton Museum of Cooke County.)

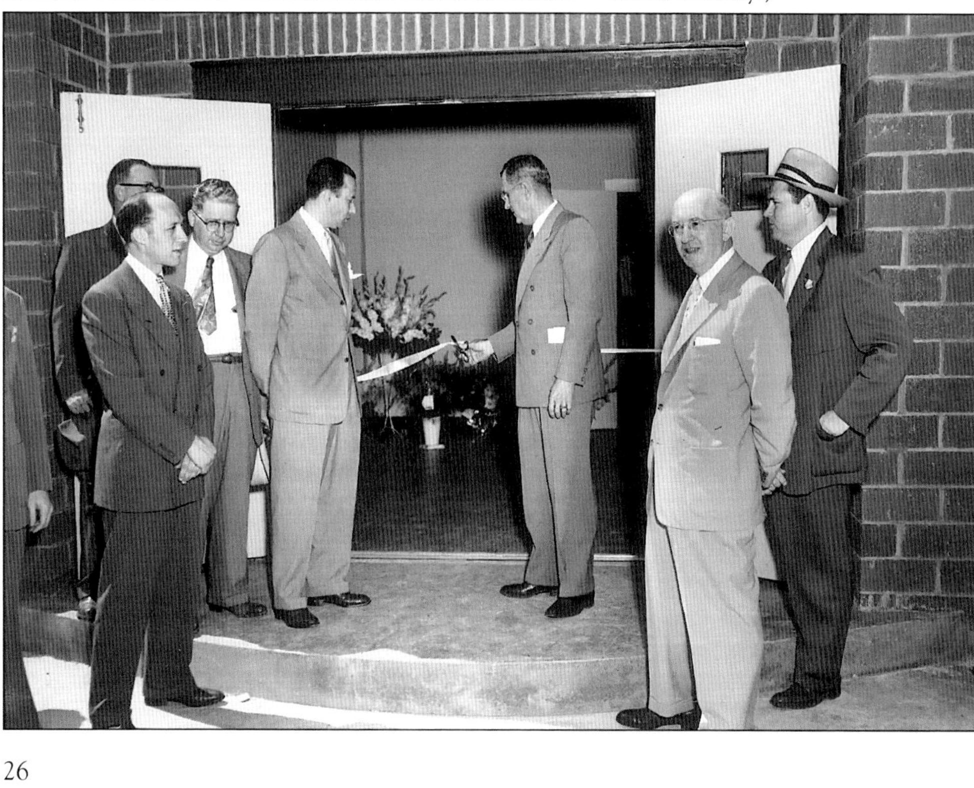

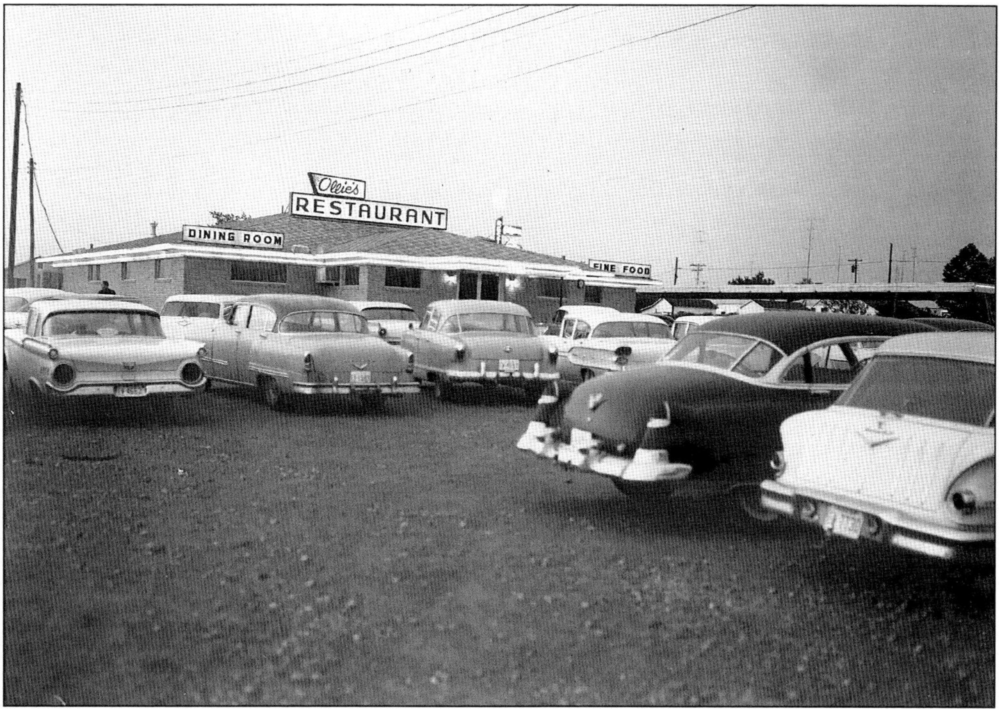

Ollie Patterson operated Ollie's Restaurant in 1959. It was located at the "Y" on Grand Avenue. By that time, Mr. Patterson had acquired a great deal of experience in running a restaurant. In 1954, he owned another restaurant shown below called the Two-Way Café. (Boyd & Breeding Collection, Morton Museum of Cooke County.)

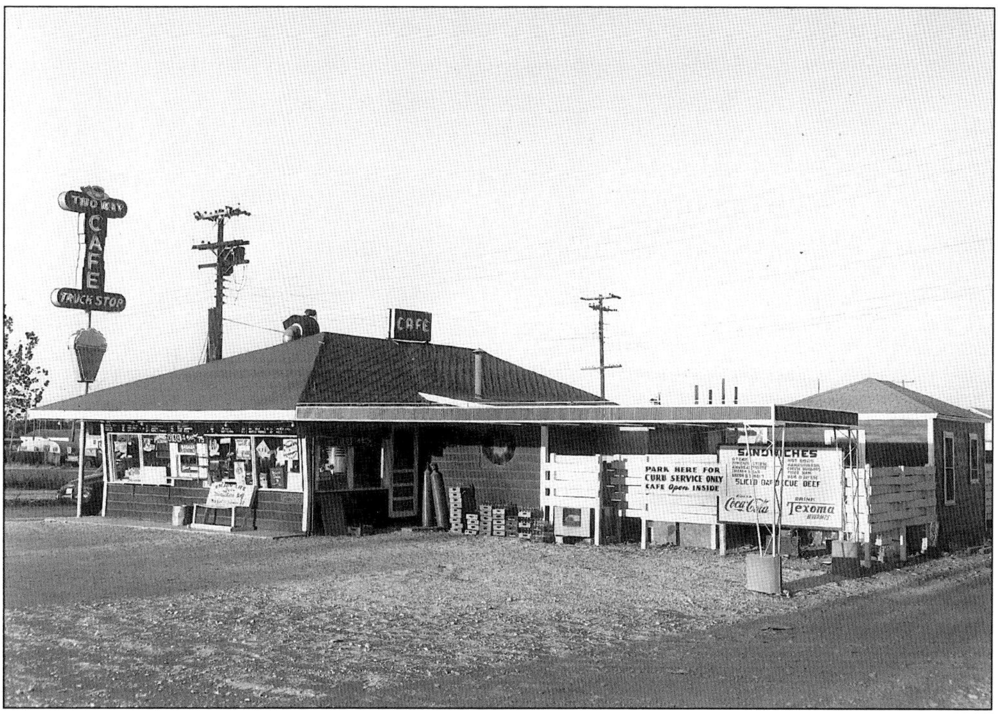

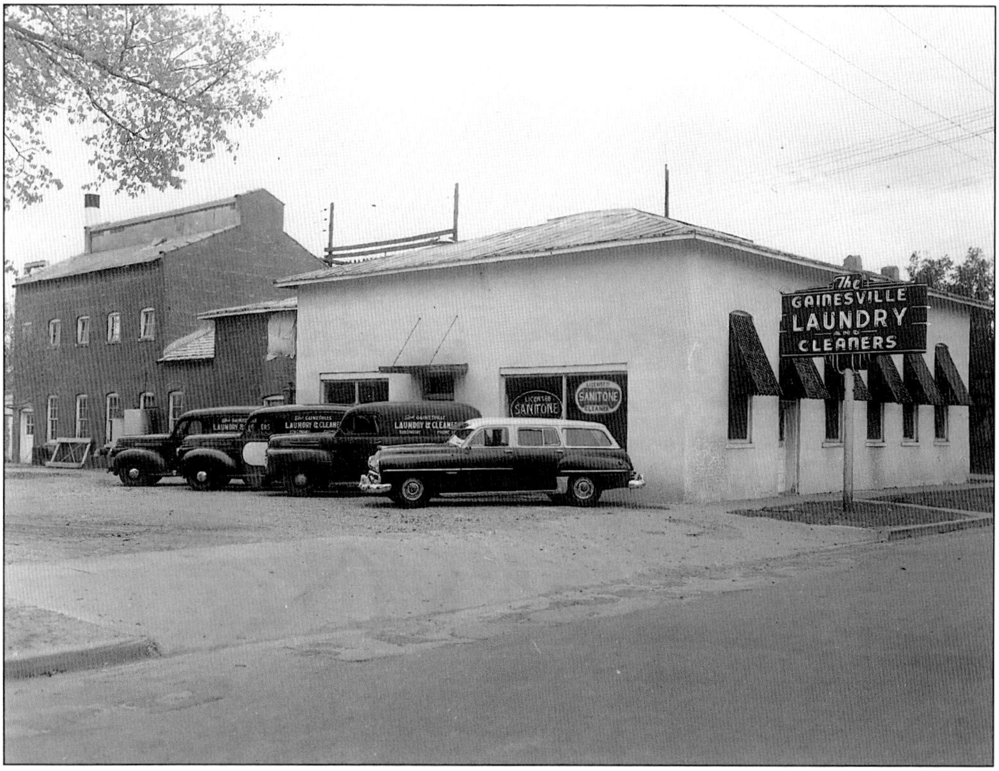

The top photograph shows the Gainesville Laundry & Cleaners and the bottom photograph shows the Robran Laundry. (Boyd & Breeding Collection, Morton Museum of Cooke County.)

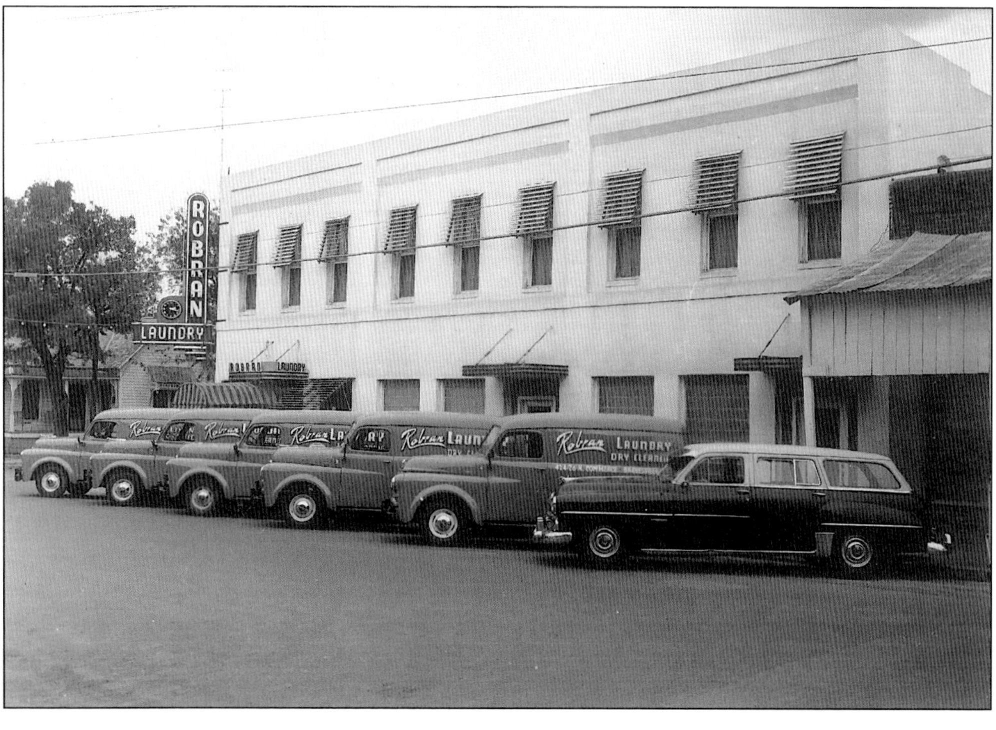

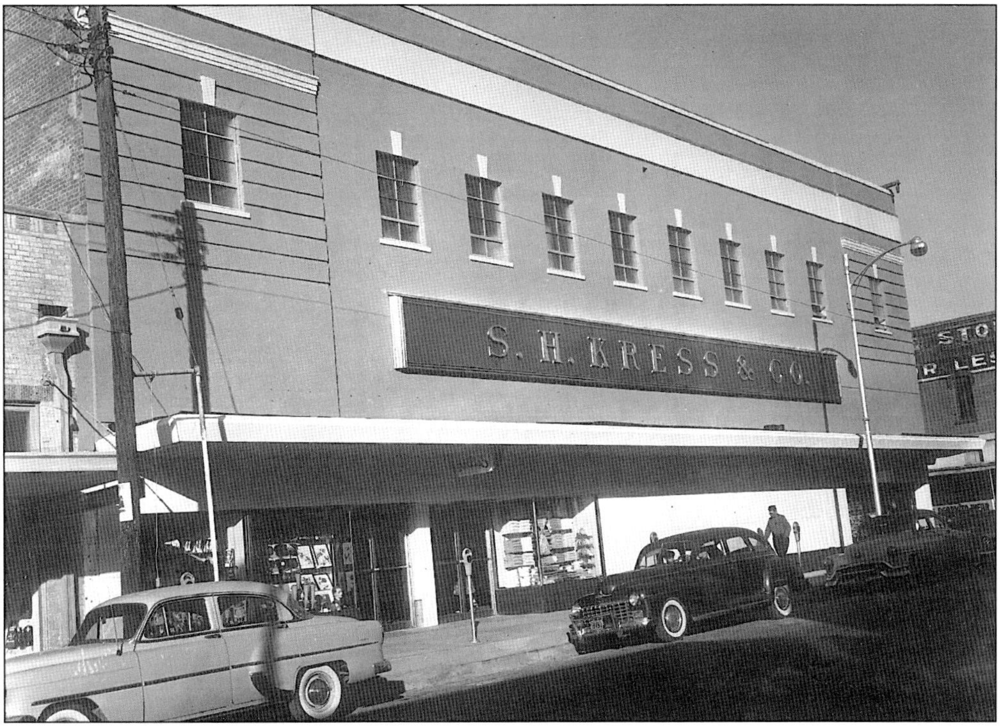

The new Kress Building at the corner of California and Commerce Streets in November 1955 appears in this scene. (Boyd & Breeding Collection, Morton Museum of Cooke County.)

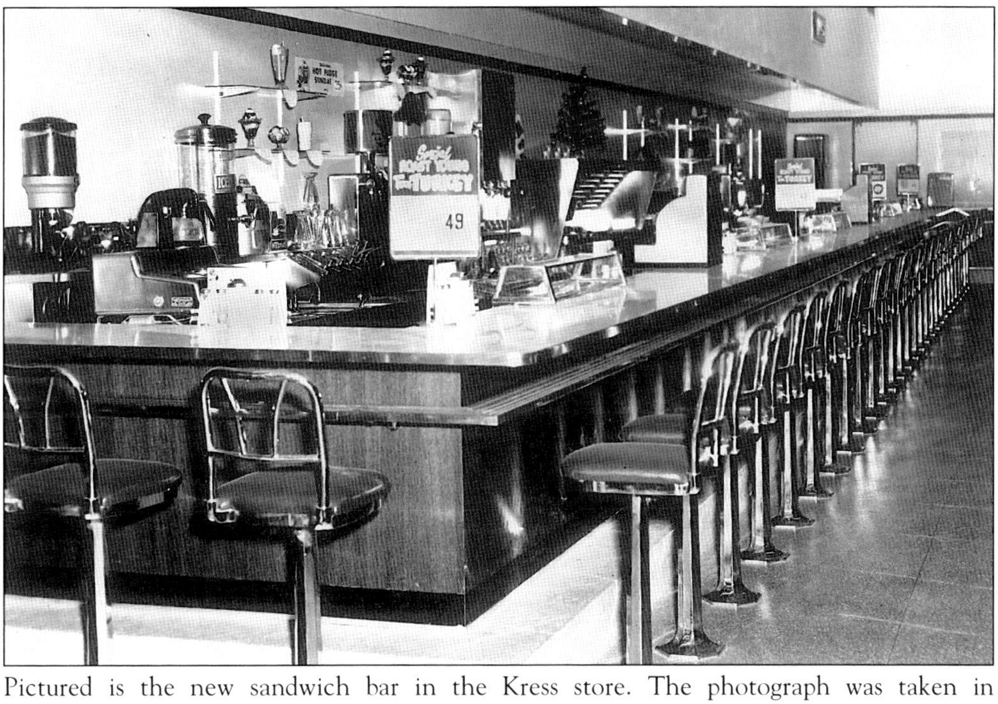

Pictured is the new sandwich bar in the Kress store. The photograph was taken in November 1955 when the store opened. (Boyd & Breeding Collection, Morton Museum of Cooke County.)

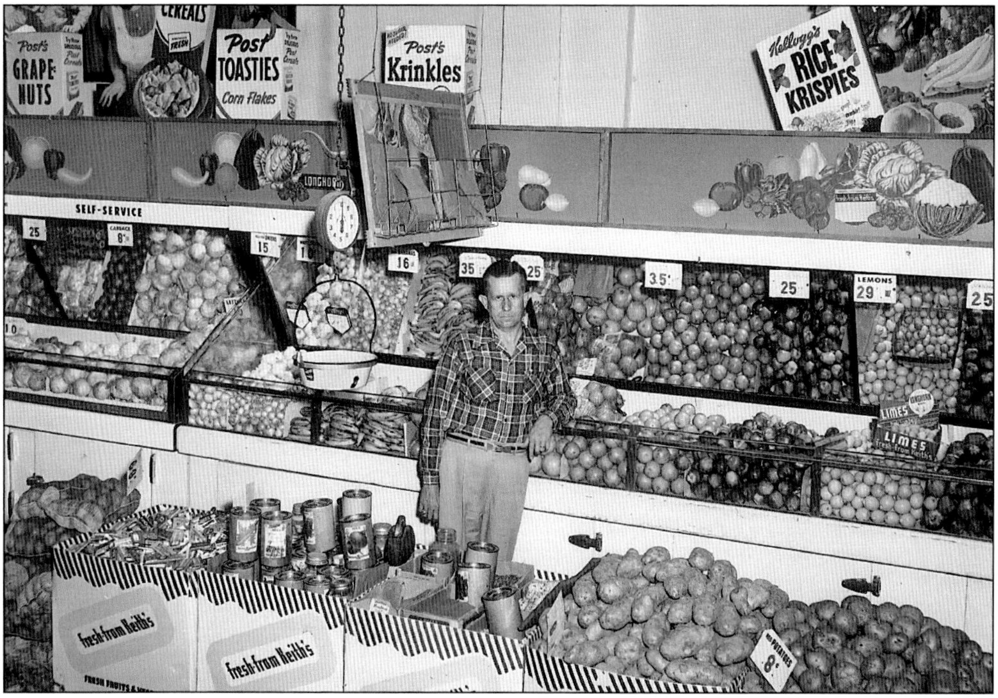

In 1952, the Temple Cash Grocery advertised its produce department in this scene. Note the advertisements for Post's Krinkles and Post Toasties. The prices on the vegetables are also worth noting. (Boyd & Breeding Collection, Morton Museum of Cooke County.)

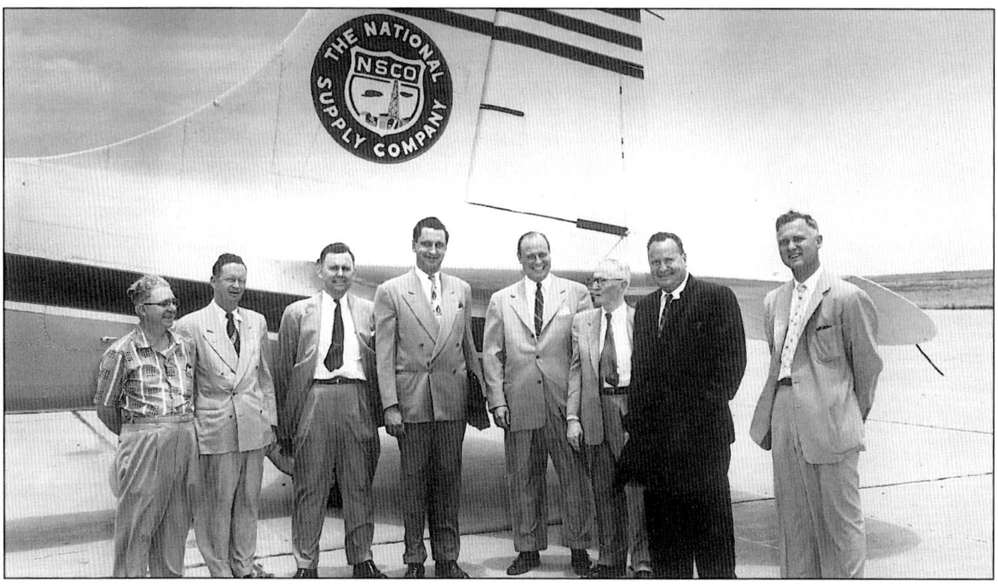

As the rotary method of drilling for oil and gas developed during the 20th century, the National Supply Company "emerged as the world's largest independent manufacturer of the equipment and tools needed to drill for and produce oil and gas from wells of ever increasing depth." In 1954, the company opened a plant in Gainesville. National Supply was "a significant contributor to the local economy for over 35 years." (Boyd & Breeding Collection, Morton Museum of Cooke County.)

On June 5, 1933, the First National Bank of Gainesville was reorganized with a new name—the Gainesville National Bank. The history of the bank is more complicated than that, though, involving other banking institutions dating back to 1882. Currently, the bank operates under a different name—the Guaranty National Bank. (Boyd & Breeding Collection, Morton Museum of Cooke County.)

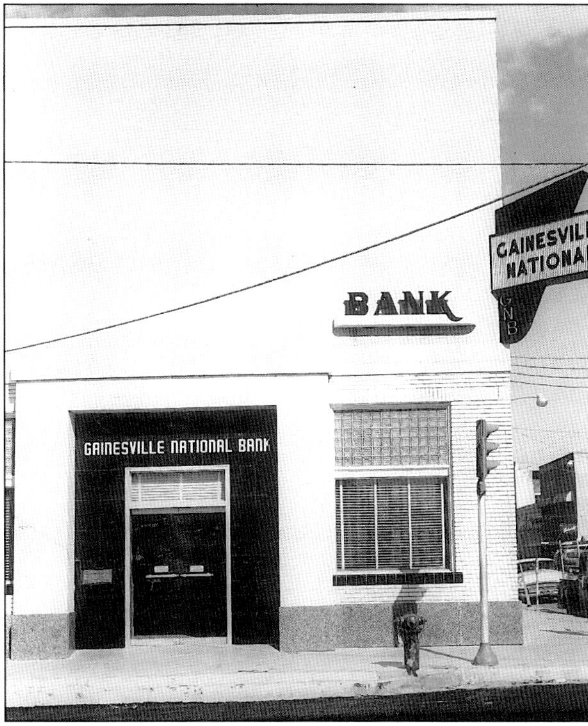

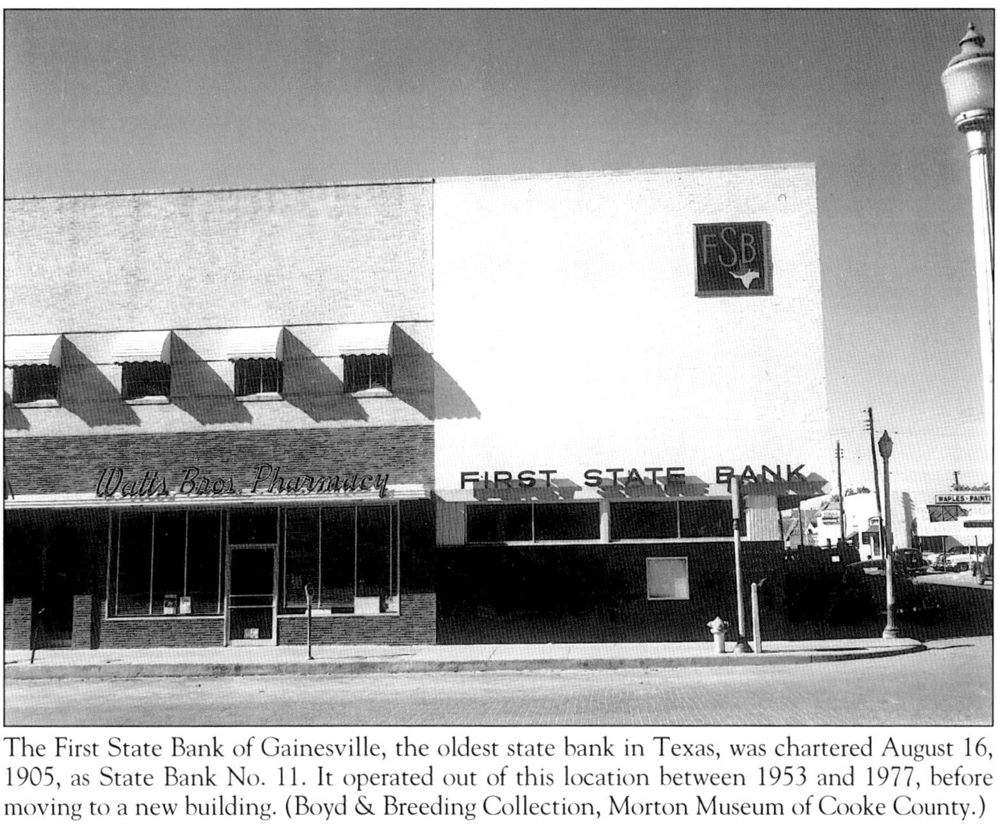

The First State Bank of Gainesville, the oldest state bank in Texas, was chartered August 16, 1905, as State Bank No. 11. It operated out of this location between 1953 and 1977, before moving to a new building. (Boyd & Breeding Collection, Morton Museum of Cooke County.)

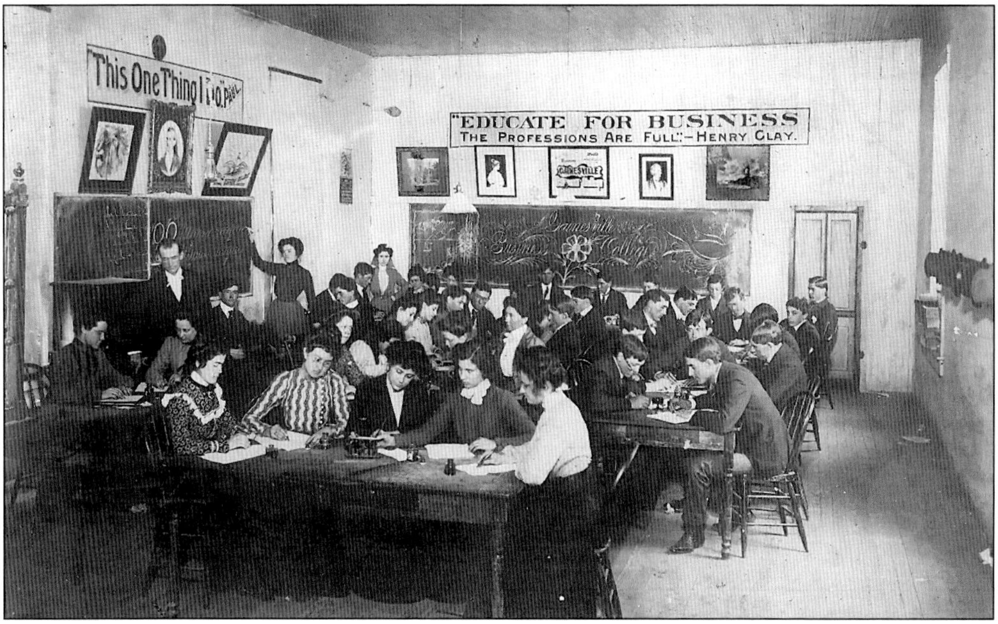

Pictured is the interior of one of the classrooms in the Gainesville Business College. This school was located on Broadway Street in Gainesville in the early 20th century. (Morton Museum of Cooke County Collection.)

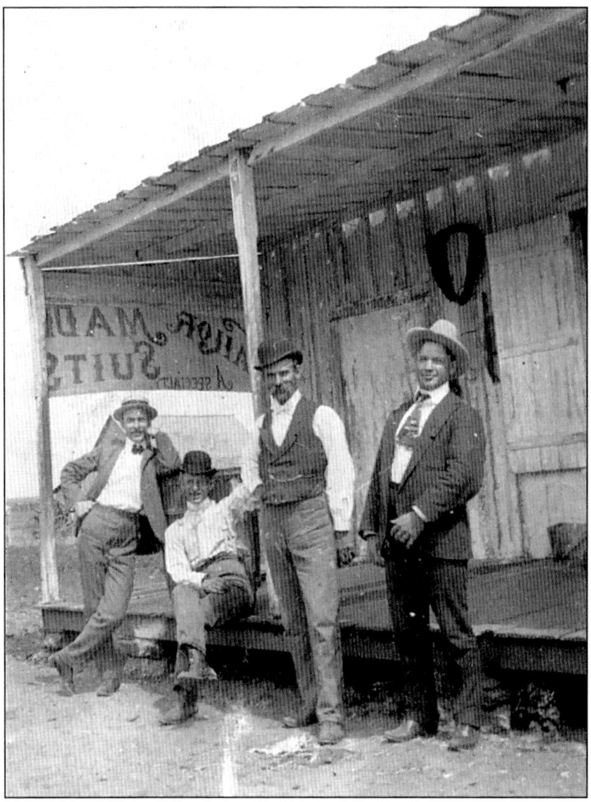

In 1901, these men enjoyed lounging on the front porch of Dr. S.A. Greever's store in Sivells Bend. Pictured, from left to right, are as follows: unknown, Bert Greever, Dr. Snead A. Greever, and Garret Greever. (Donated by Lena J. Greever, Morton Museum of Cooke County Collection.)

Three

PERSONALITIES

Over the years, residents from all walks of life strove to enrich not only their own lives but the "life" of the county as a whole. Many fascinating characters also have called Cooke County home. Some of their stories follow.

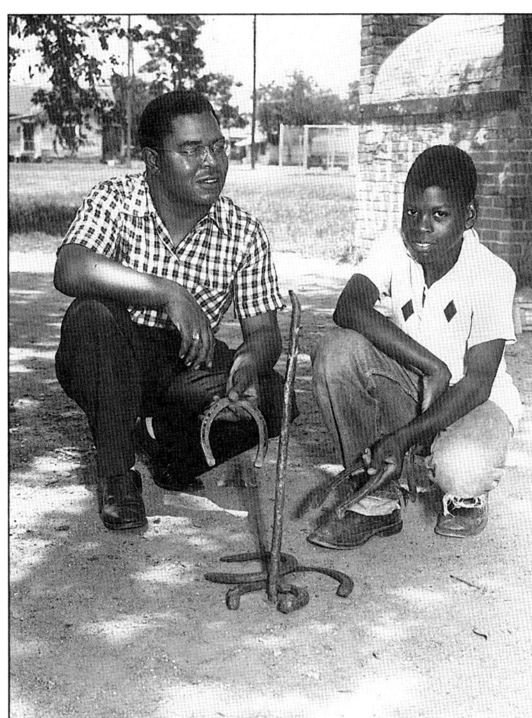

On the left is B.P. Douglas, principal of Booker T. Washington School, and on the right is William Charles Behon. The photo was taken on June 22, 1955. (Boyd & Breeding Collection, Morton Museum of Cooke County.)

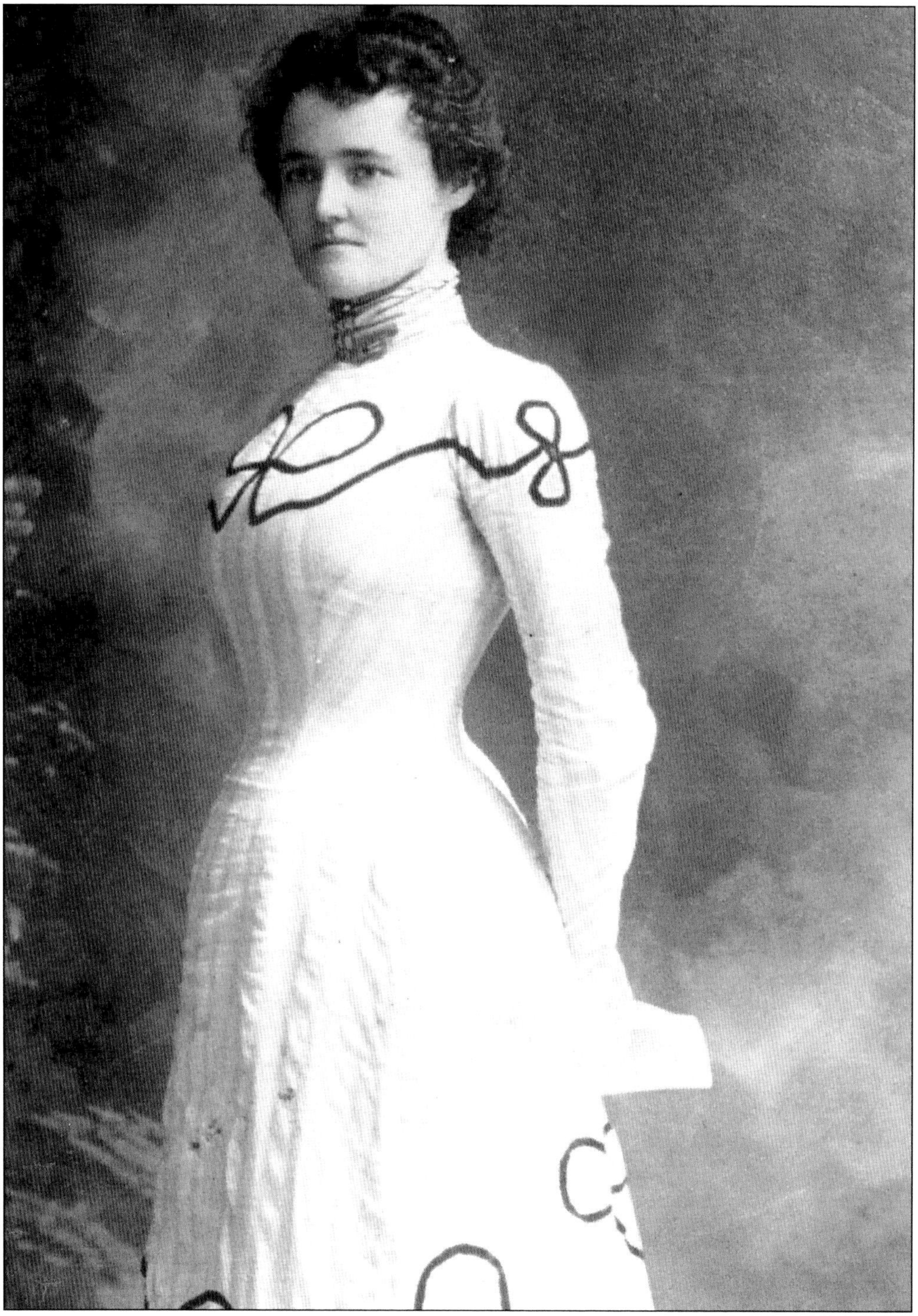

Lillian Gunter was born in Sivells Bend in 1870, and after moving to Gainesville became involved in the XLI Club, the first women's group in the city. She was instrumental in Gainesville's acquisition of a Carnegie Library, and also the passage of the County Public Library Law at the state level. (Courtesy of Bettie Gunter Cheaney.)

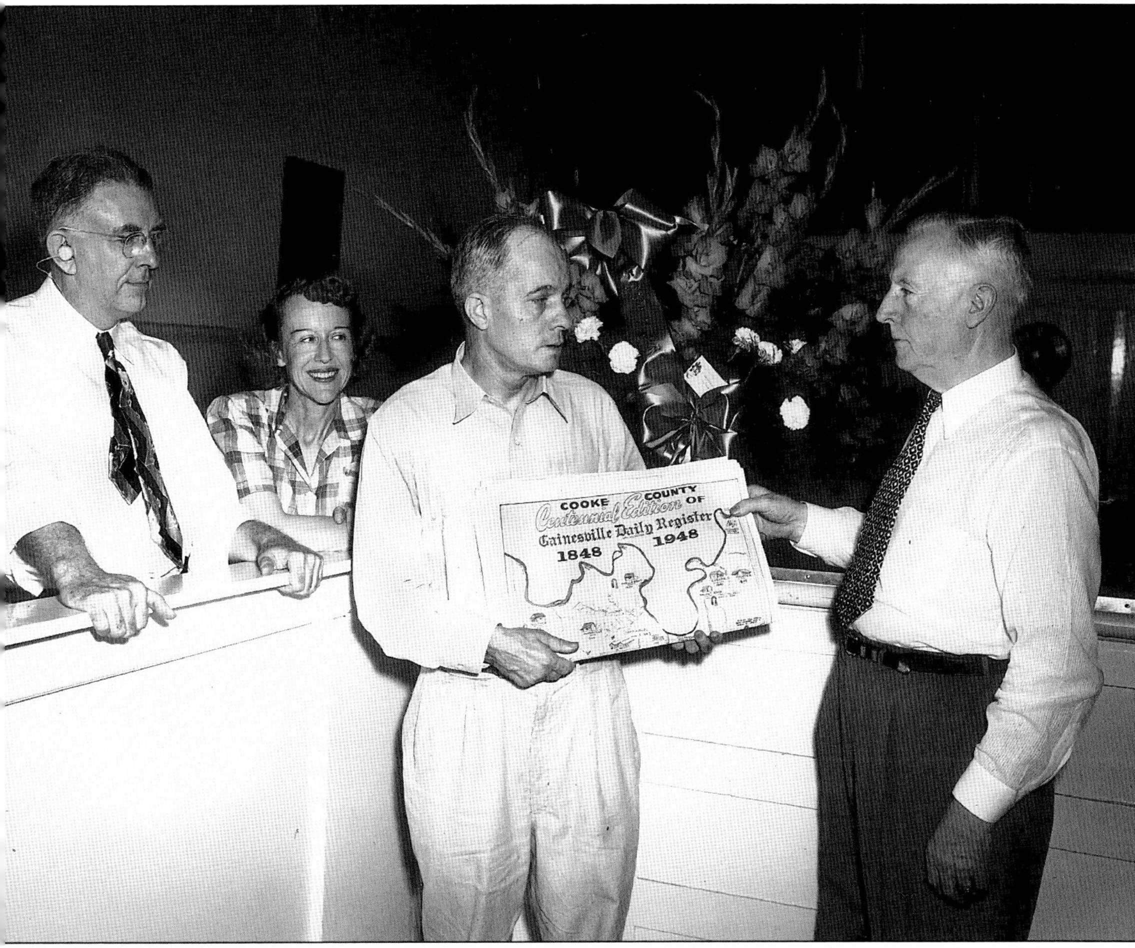

In 1948, Cooke County celebrated its centennial. A special edition of the *Gainesville Daily Register* was produced in honor of the festivities. Pictured, from left to right, are as follow: A. Morton Smith, editor of the newspaper and founder of the Gainesville Community Circus; Gerry Murrell, member of the circus and the person for whom Gerry the Elephant was named; Dr. S.M. Yarbrough, also a member of the circus (who is receiving the first copy of the newspaper); and Clarence Leonard, son of the original founder of the newspaper (John T. Leonard, and the man for whom Leonard Park is named). (Boyd & Breeding Collection, Morton Museum of Cooke County.)

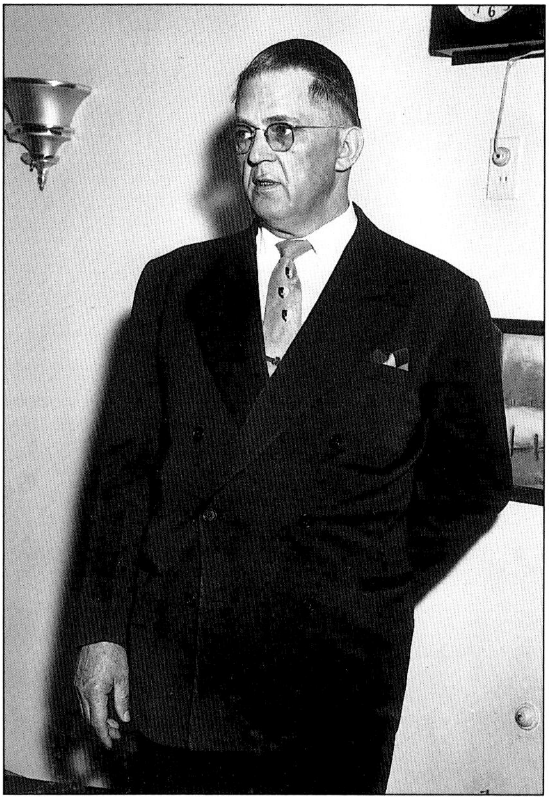

Dr. William Herbert Locke (May 20, 1895–October 6, 1971) practiced medicine in Gainesville for many years and also served on the city council. In March 1954, he was the director of the Gainesville Owls baseball organization. Locke Field was named for him. (Boyd & Breeding Collection, Morton Museum of Cooke County.)

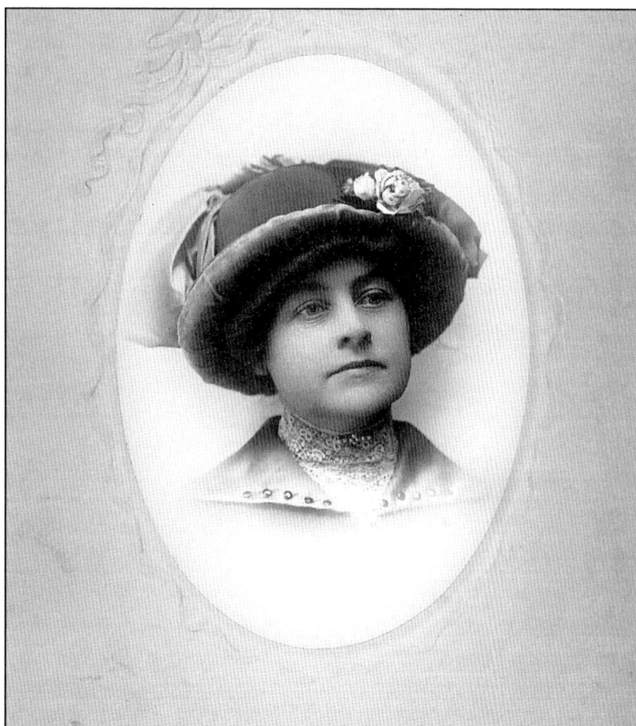

Grace Hickson (August 9, 1873–January 13, 1963) was the assistant postmaster of the Gainesville Post Office in the early 1920s, when air mail service was first established. Altogether, she worked for the post office for 31 years. She retired in 1934, after having been the assistant postmaster for several years. Her brother J.L. Hickson served as postmaster on two different occasions and owned a bookstore in town. (Morton Museum of Cooke County Collection.)

Hubert Moss was born in Woodbine but grew up in Valley View. After he graduated from officers' training school, he went to France during WWI, sharing in the leadership of an all-black company. Moss later taught chemistry at the junior college and served as treasurer. In the summer of 1946 Moss ran for county school superintendent and was elected. He served in that capacity until his death in 1952. He was concerned about Gainesville's future need for water, and so promoted the creation of a lake on Fish Creek. When Moss Lake was later created, it was named in his honor. (Morton Museum of Cooke County Collection.)

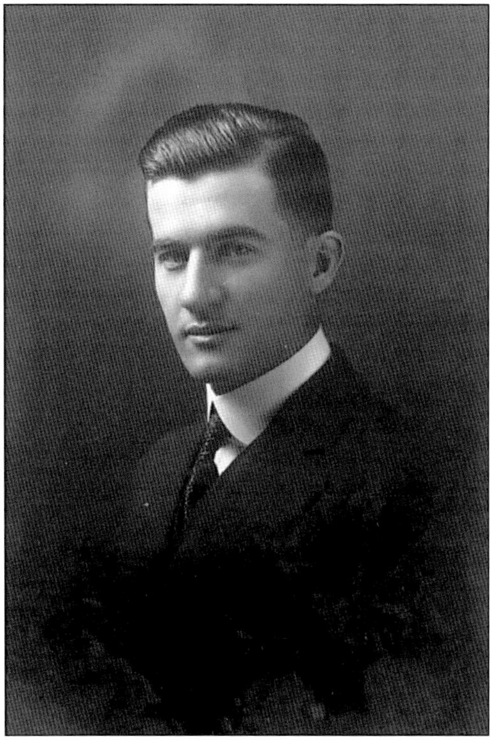

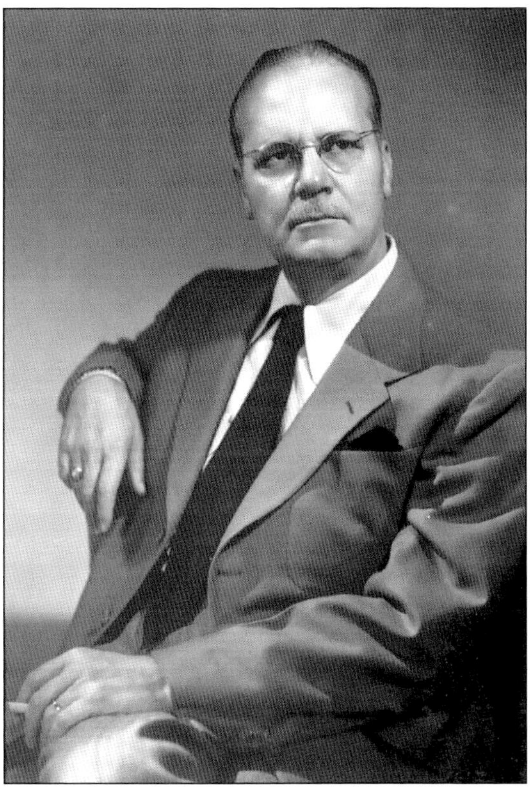

In the 1940s, Dr. J. Shirley Sweeney, a prominent Dallas physician who had grown up and attended school in Gainesville, wanted to establish a summer camp at which young diabetic patients could experience the outdoor life and learn more about their illness. Sweeney contacted influential leaders in Gainesville and they agreed to help. "In December 1947, the Sweeney Diabetic Foundation was established. By 1949, the Foundation had raised enough money to purchase over 400 acres of land. The first camping season opened in 1950 with 73 diabetic boys and girls in attendance. Today, Camp Sweeney continues to thrive and help young patients as Dr. Sweeney envisioned." (Boyd & Breeding Collection, Morton Museum of Cooke County.)

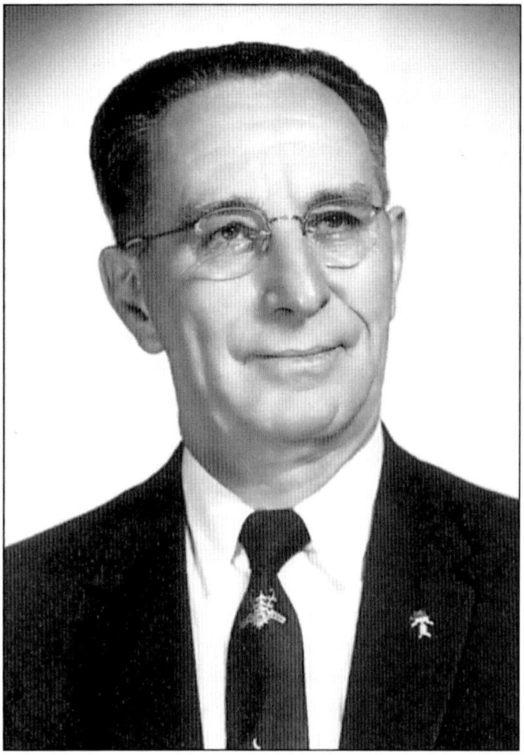

Joseph Michael Weinzapfel moved to Muenster with his family in 1923, "in order to help organize the Muenster State Bank. During the next 50 years, Mr. Weinzapfel served as cashier, vice-president, president, and chairman of the board. He also was very involved in the creation of the Cooke County Electric Cooperative." (Boyd & Breeding Collection, Morton Museum of Cooke County.)

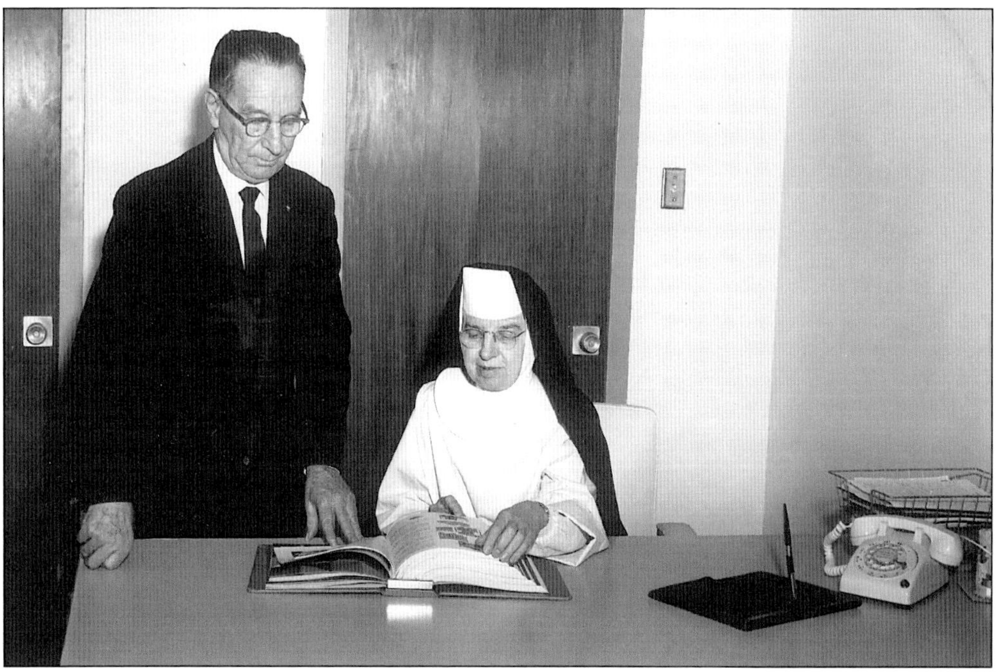

The Muenster Memorial Hospital opened on February 3, 1964. J.M. Weinzapfel was the driving force behind the establishment of the hospital. Mr. Weinzapfel is pictured in this photograph taken at the opening of the hospital. Sister Mildred Felderhoff, administrator of the hospital, is also pictured. (Boyd & Breeding Collection, Morton Museum of Cooke County.)

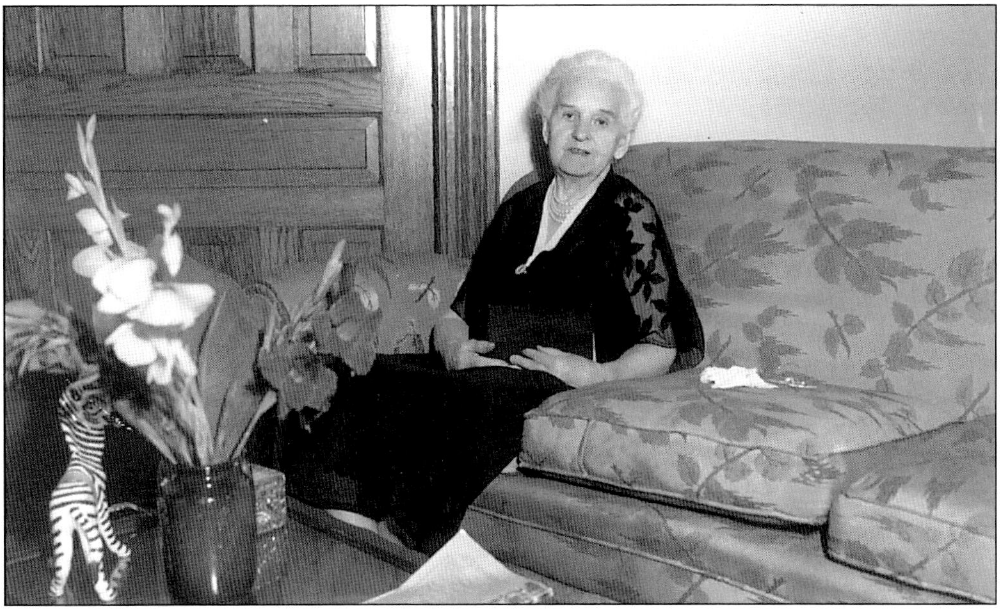

Nora Hudson Rose (1879–1953), daughter of General William Hudson and wife of cotton buyer Robert Rose, established the first chapter of the American Red Cross in Cooke County, belonged to the XLI Club, and worked for the rights of African Americans in Gainesville. (Boyd & Breeding Collection, Morton Museum of Cooke County.)

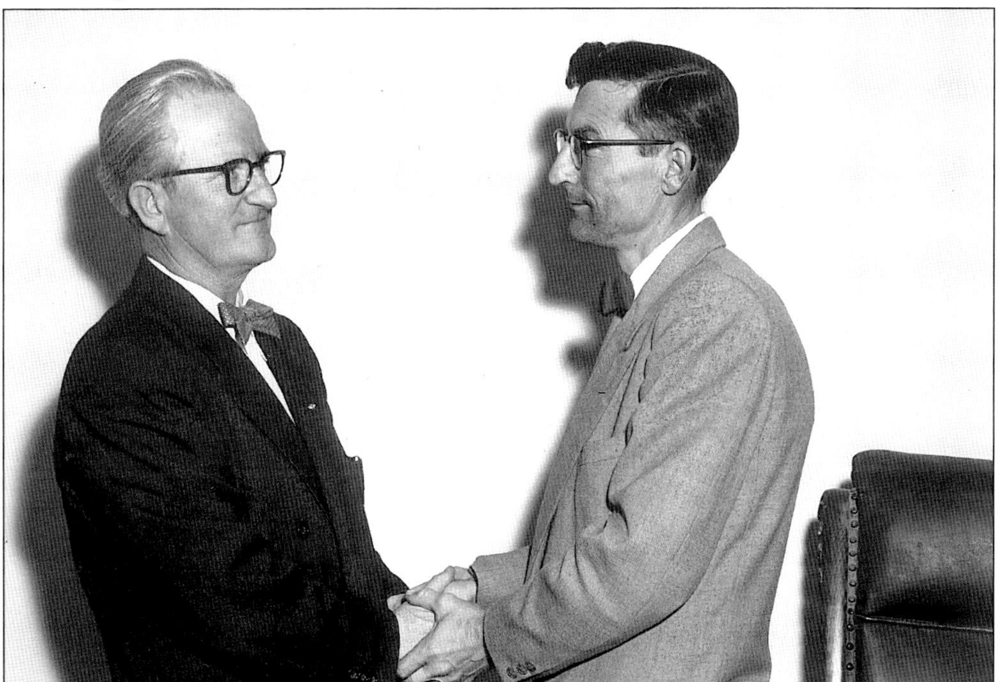

Among other achievements, Carroll Sullivant (1902–1978) served in the Texas Legislature in 1931 and 1933, as the Chief Enforcement Officer of the Railroad Commission, and as County Judge and County Attorney for Cooke County. Carroll Sullivant is pictured on the left shaking hands with L.V. Henry. (Boyd & Breeding Collection, Morton Museum of Cooke County.)

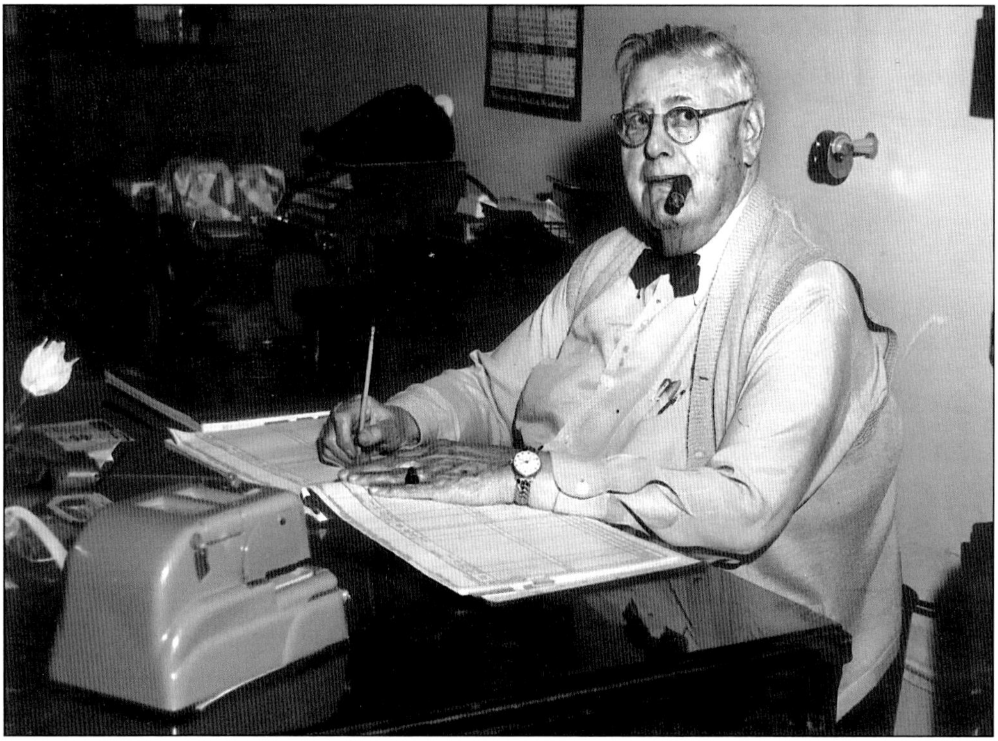

Sol Zacharias (1882–1955), a mathematical whiz, worked as the bookkeeper for the Gainesville Owls baseball club. It was a difficult job, as the club always hovered on the brink of bankruptcy. (Boyd & Breeding Collection, Morton Museum of Cooke County.)

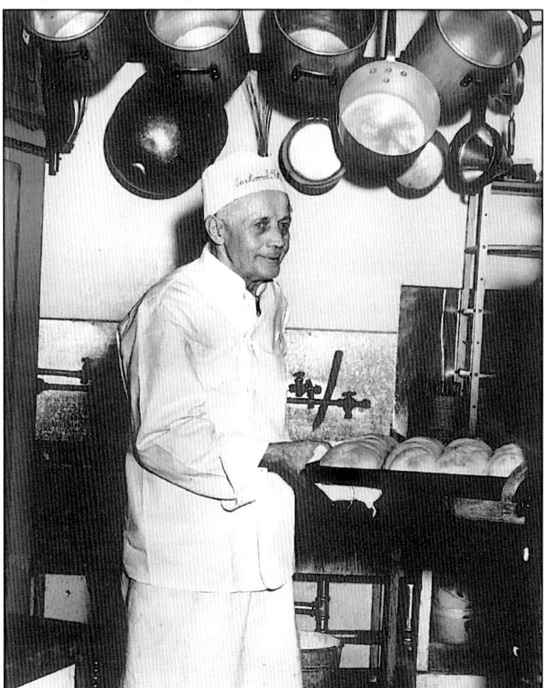

Emil Schurig, known for his delicious French bread, was the chef in the Harvey House Restaurant inside the Gainesville Santa Fe depot. He also worked as a chef on some of the dining cars on the railroad. Later, Mr. Schurig worked for Emmett Curtis as a chef in his restaurant in Gainesville. (Boyd & Breeding Collection, Morton Museum of Cooke County.)

Mr. and Mrs. Chin Goon posed for this portrait in their wedding finery. Chin Goon owned a restaurant in Gainesville. He later operated several other business enterprises in Oklahoma. His wife eventually filed for divorce, accusing him of trying to poison her and holding her hostage. The divorce was granted. (Morton Museum of Cooke County.)

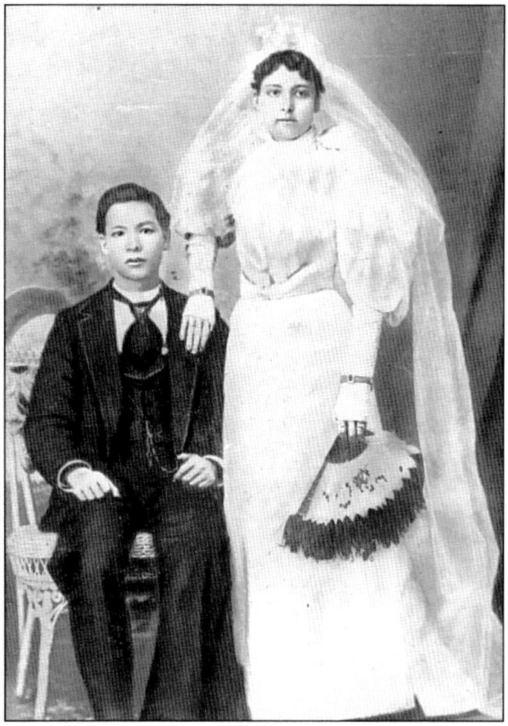

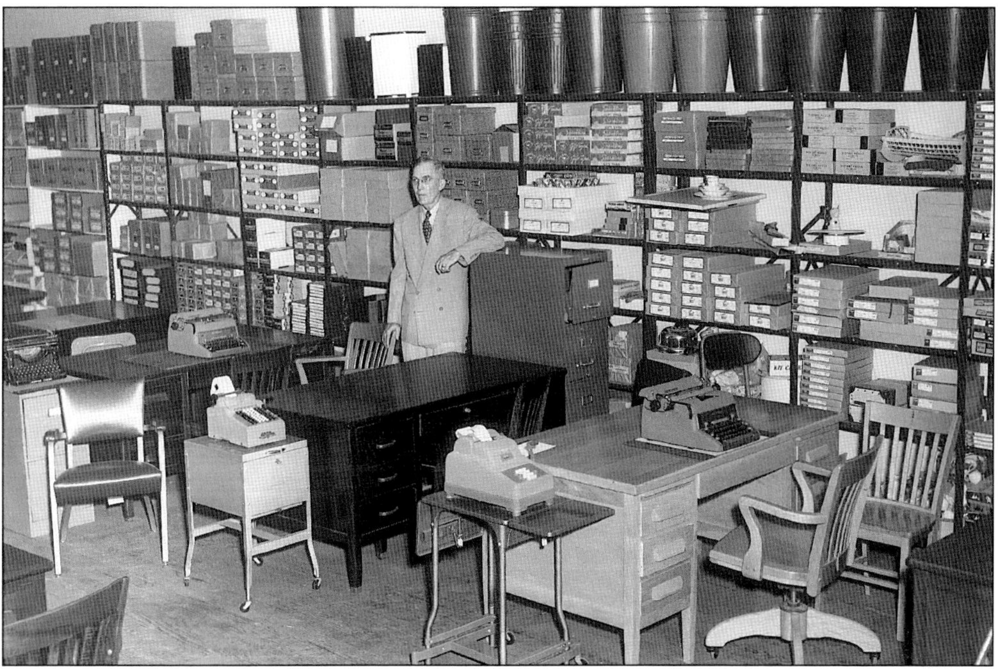

Frank Dustin (1890–1962) was born east of Gainesville at "Oak Valley, attended Gainesville schools, served in WWI, and published a weekly newspaper in Marietta, Oklahoma, until 1932. In that year, he and his wife Elvis returned to Gainesville and opened Frank Dustin Office and School Supplies." The store still exists today. In 1952, Mr. Dustin stood among some of the items in the store. (Boyd & Breeding Collection, Morton Museum of Cooke County.)

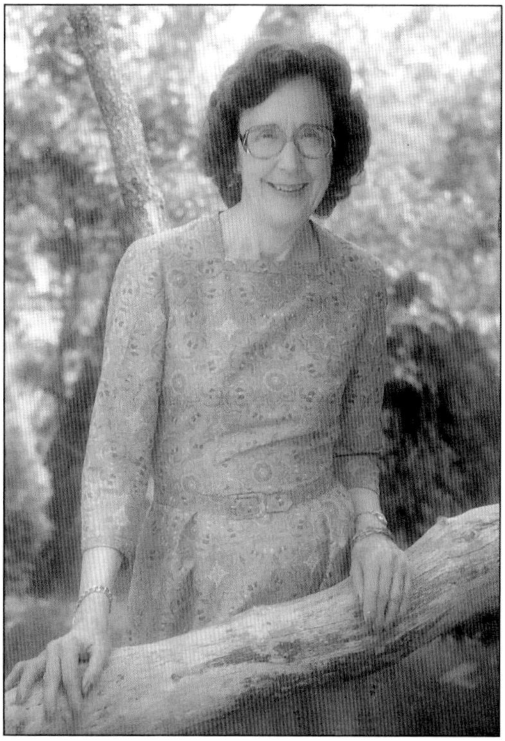

Margaret Hays has led an interesting life. From 1931 until 1942, she worked at what is now the University of North Texas—two years of that period was spent as the registrar of the Demonstration School, and the rest as secretary to the dean of the university. She served in the Foreign Service from 1942 until 1964. In August 1966, she returned to Gainesville and became involved in establishing the Morton Museum of Cooke County. Miss Hays was the director of the Mental Health Clinic from 1972 until 1978, and in 1981 became mayor of Gainesville—the first woman to hold that office. Miss Hays helped to form the Community Preservation Foundation and has been instrumental in helping to save the 1902 Santa Fe Depot in Gainesville. (Courtesy of Margaret Hays.)

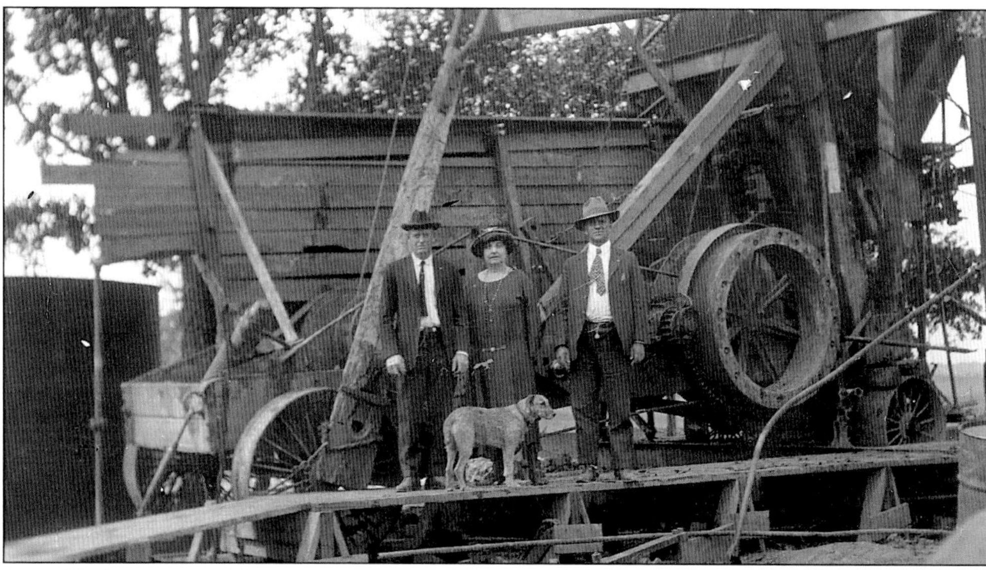

Irene Hathaway stands between two men at the site of the Big Indian Oil Well in Callisburg—the first oil well in Cooke County. Hathaway was a single, traveling encyclopedia saleslady interested in oil. Traveling from Kansas to Cooke County on her regular sales route, she listened to oil men talk of the possibility of oil just waiting to be found in Cooke County. Back in Kansas, Hathway convinced the Big Indian Oil Company to come to Cooke County and drill. They did and after two years with no oil in sight, company officials decided to leave. Hathaway persuaded them to stay and shortly afterwards, the oil well came in. (Donated by F.W. Blagg, Morton Museum of Cooke County Collection.)

Four

Famous Folks

Several sons and daughters of the county—Gene Autry, Rose Franken, General Lew Allen, Bishop Augustine Danglmayr, Marvin Jones, and Charles Paddock, among others—found success and fame in a variety of professions. Other famous or soon-to-be famous individuals often visited the area, particularly after the arrival of the railroad. People as diverse as Al Jolson, Amelia Earhart, Frances Perkins (the first woman to serve in a U.S. president's Cabinet), and Gregory Peck have all passed through.

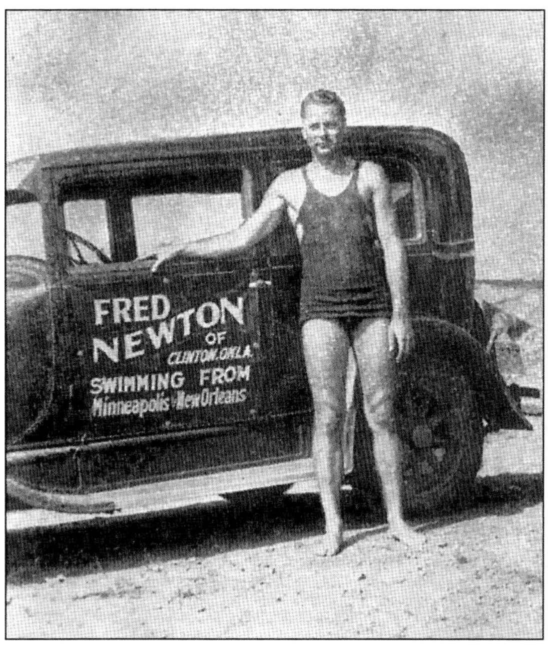

This postcard advertises Fred Newton, who was attempting to swim the Mississippi River from Minneapolis to New Orleans in 1930. Mr. Newton later moved to Gainesville and opened his own business. (Morton Museum of Cooke County Collection.)

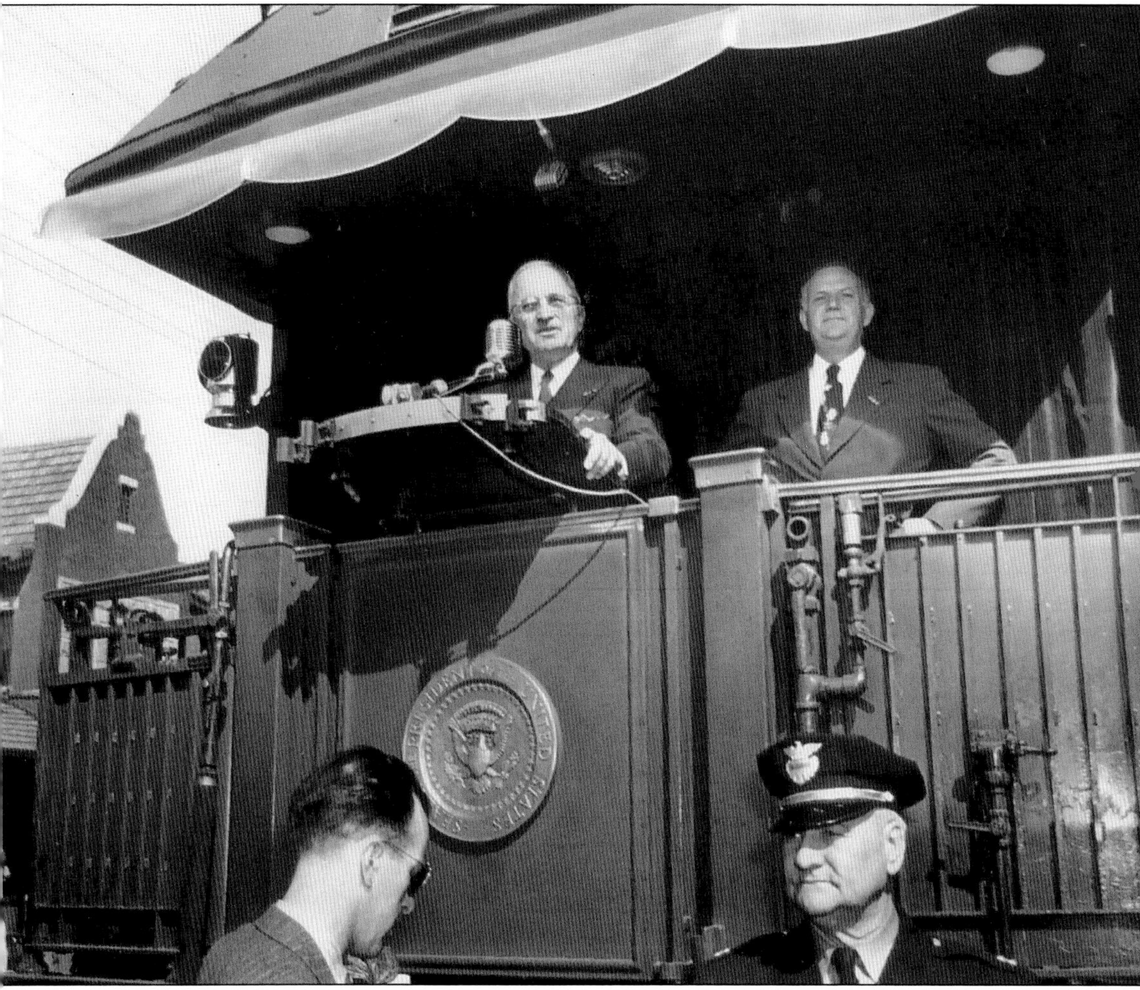

Few people imagined that President Harry Truman would win the 1948 presidential election. Only Truman felt that the people would support him if he appealed to them directly, and with that idea the "whistle-stop" campaign was born. Truman traveled the country by train, giving speeches in both large cities and small towns. On September 28, 1948, Harry Truman visited Gainesville, speaking to a crowd of ten thousand. The man with the glasses standing in front of the train was Dr. J.R. Reuther. The 1902 Santa Fe depot can be seen in the background. The negative for this photograph was discovered by accident 50 years later. (Boyd & Breeding Collection, Morton Museum of Cooke County.)

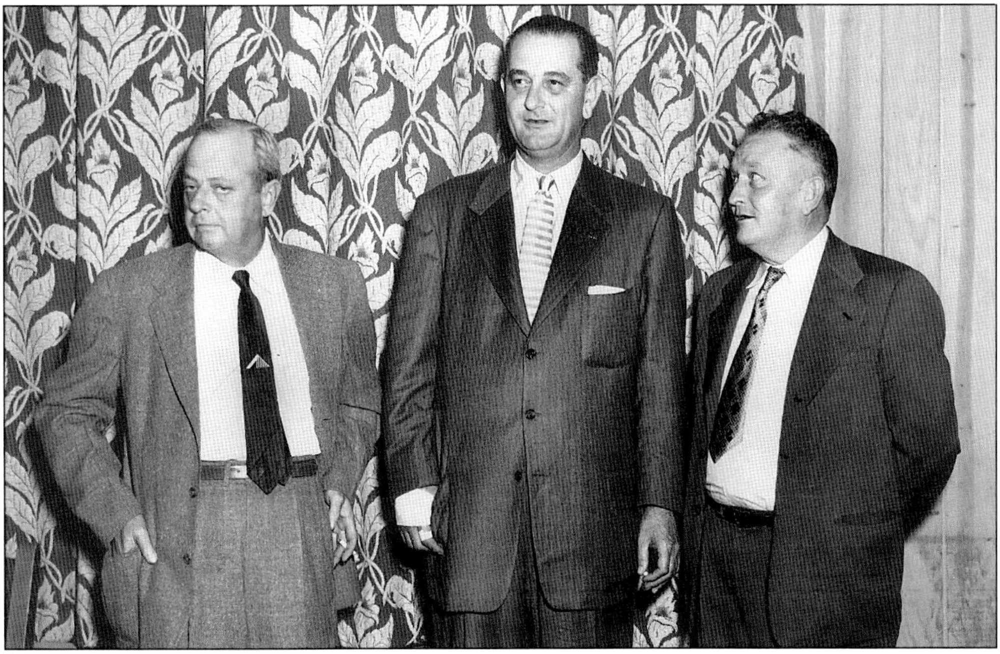

On Wednesday, November 18, 1953, Senator Lyndon Johnson was honored with a reception at the Community Center building in Gainesville. Johnson gave a brief address "taking pot shots at Republican farm, domestic, foreign, and defense policies while carefully avoiding direct criticism of President Dwight D. Eisenhower." Pictured at the reception are, from left to right: Cecil Murphy, Lyndon Johnson, and Dock Monroe. (Boyd & Breeding Collection, Morton Museum of Cooke County.)

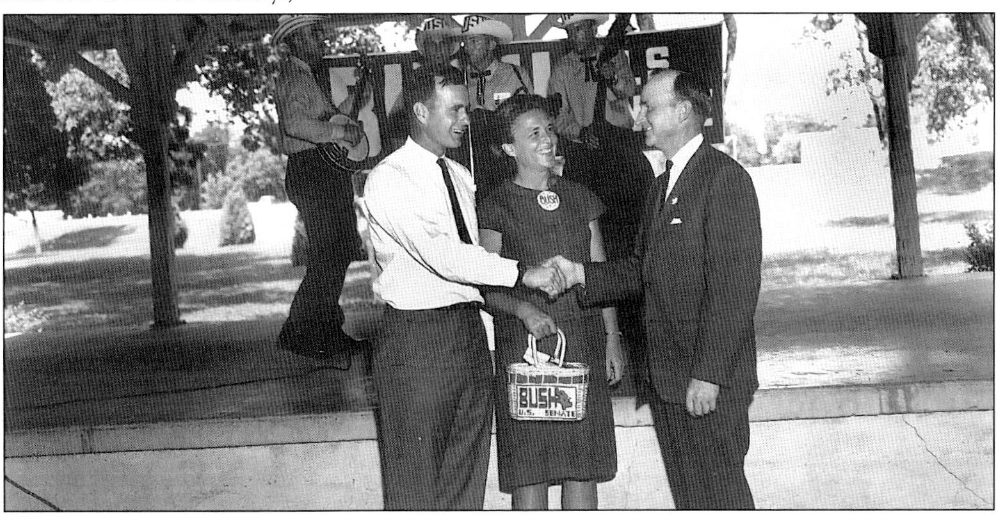

George and Barbara Bush greet a supporter at the pavilion in Leonard Park on September 8, 1964. It was reported that "George Bush, Republican candidate for the U.S. Senate…met an enthusiastic crowd of listeners in Leonard Park. In Muenster, Bush paid a visit to Sacred Heart Catholic Church, where a carnival was being conducted to raise funds for a Catholic college. Gainesville was the only stopping place where Bush actually presented a formal speech. George Jr. also accompanied his parents on this trip." (Boyd & Breeding Collection, Morton Museum of Cooke County.)

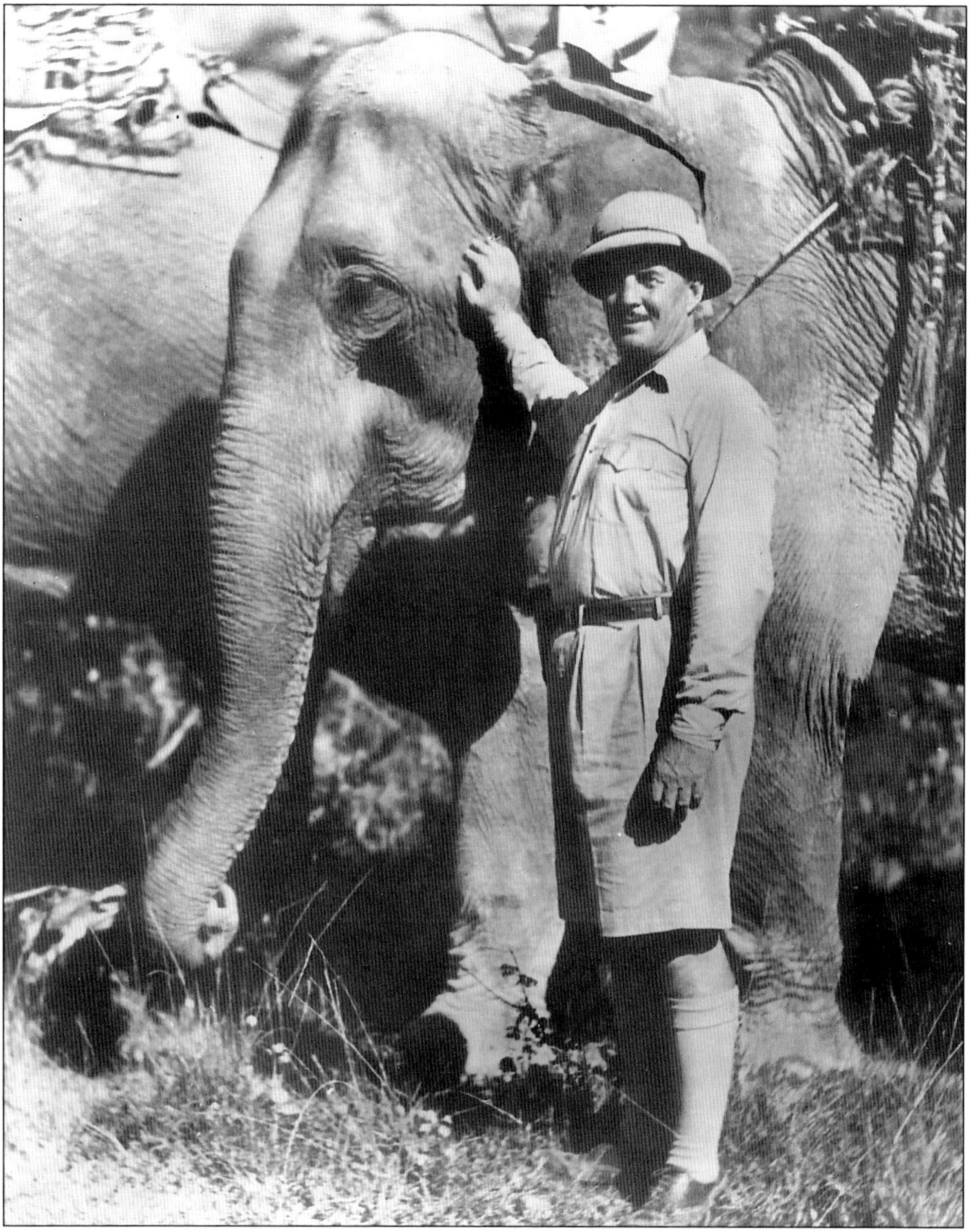

Frank Buck was born in a wagon yard in Gainesville in 1883. At the height of his career as a wild animal hunter, he was known as "Bring 'Em Back Alive" Frank Buck, as he brought animals back from overseas to sell to numerous zoos. His exploits were mirrored in motion pictures and written about in books, magazines, and newspapers for many years. Buck returned to Gainesville in 1936. A special luncheon was held in his honor on the roof garden of the Turner Hotel, where Buck entertained the audience with stories of capturing wild animals in the jungles. In 1948, Buck served as honorary ringmaster for the opening of the Gainesville Community Circus. Frank Buck died in 1950. The zoo in Gainesville was named in his honor. (Donated by Jerry Bayless, Morton Museum of Cooke County Collection.)

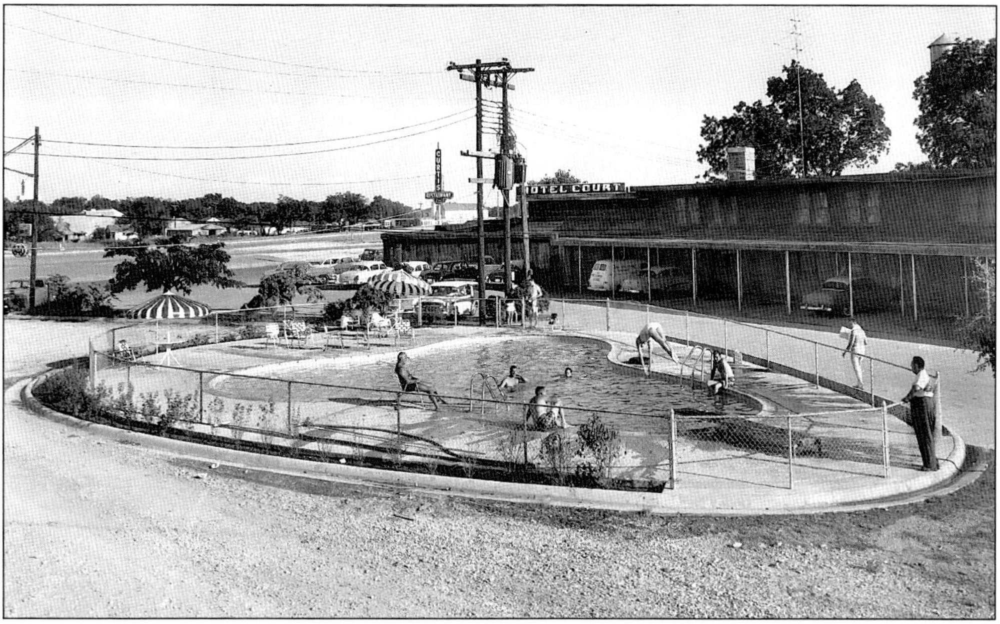

On April 14, 1955, Elvis Presley performed in Gainesville, and though adult tickets were $1 and tickets for children 50¢, he bombed, not even bringing in $300. He was brought to town by Joe Leonard Jr. Pictured is the Curtwood Motel where Presley stayed during his visit to town. (Boyd & Breeding Collection, Morton Museum of Cooke County.)

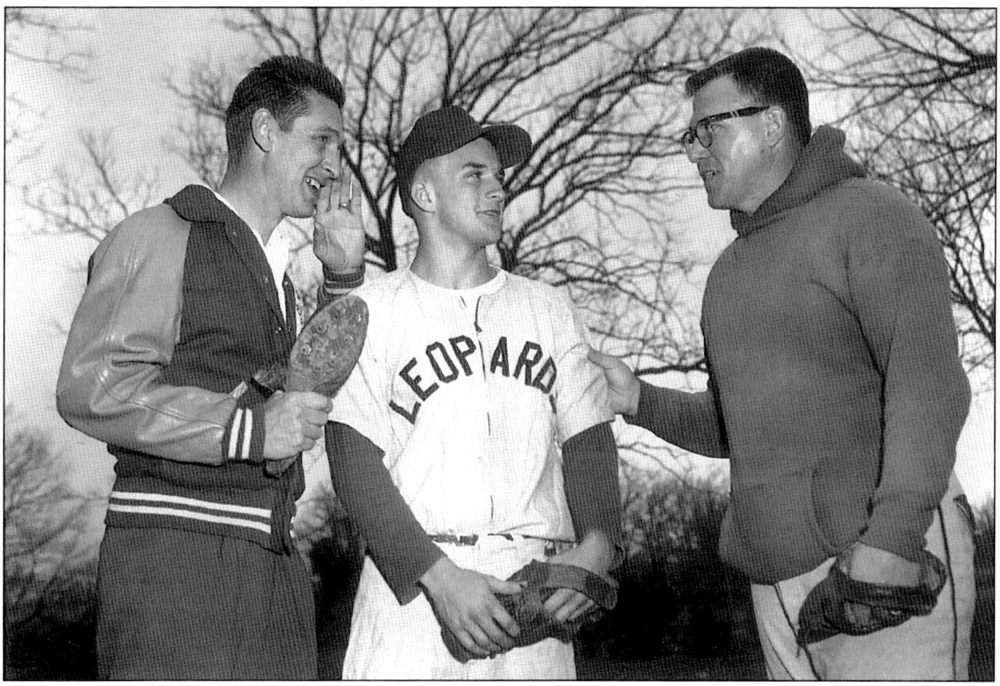

This photograph was taken in March 1958 and shows the Gainesville High School baseball and football coaches seemingly fighting over a prospective player. The football coach shown on the right was Buddy Ryan, who later went on to coach pro football in Philadelphia. (Boyd & Breeding Collection, Morton Museum of Cooke County.)

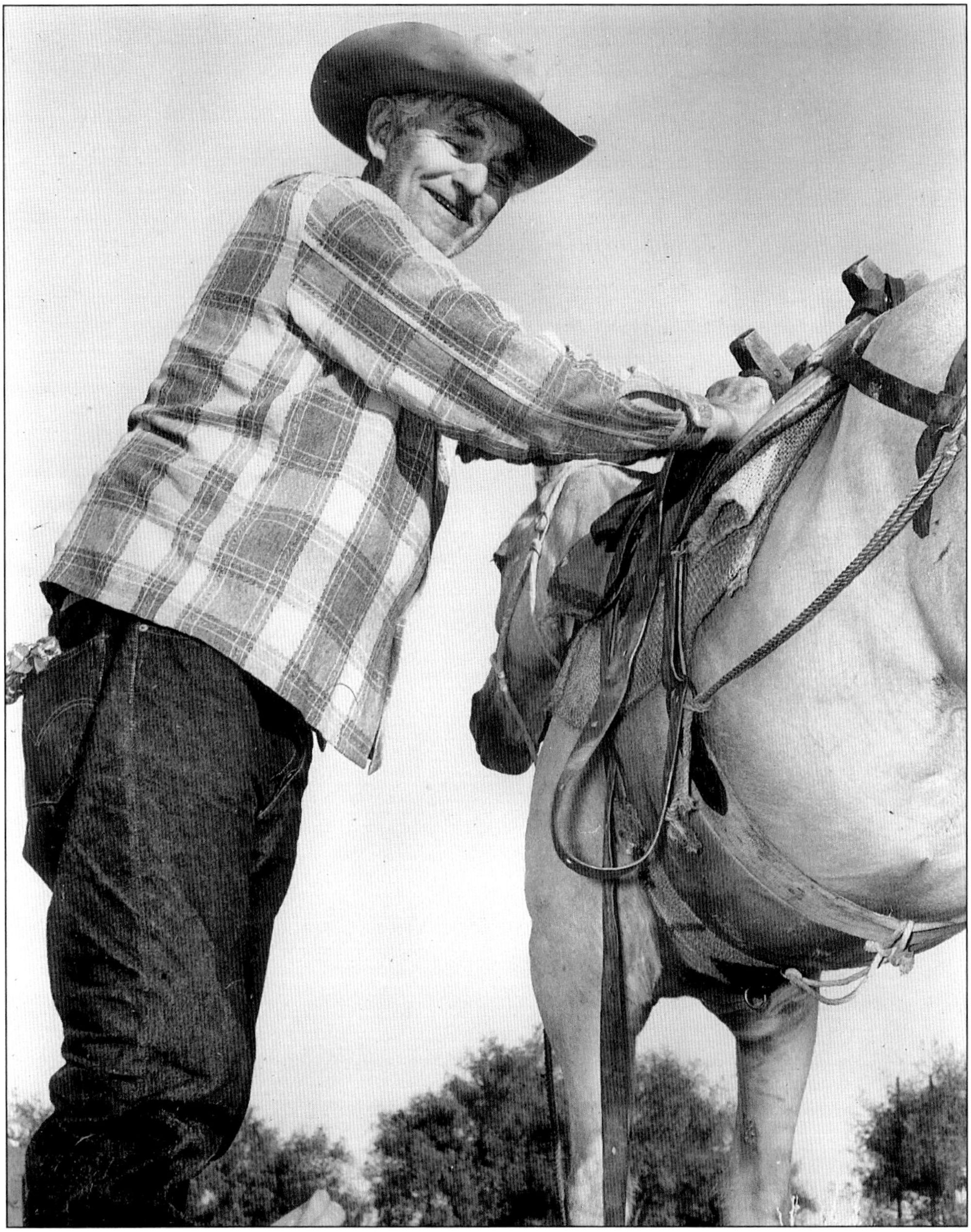

Thomas Rufus Hickman was born February 21, 1886, in Cooke County. He "became a Cooke County deputy sheriff in 1912 and joined the Texas Rangers in 1919. Mr. Hickman remained with the Rangers for 17 years. He died on January 19, 1962." (Donated by Peggy Johns, Morton Museum of Cooke County Collection.)

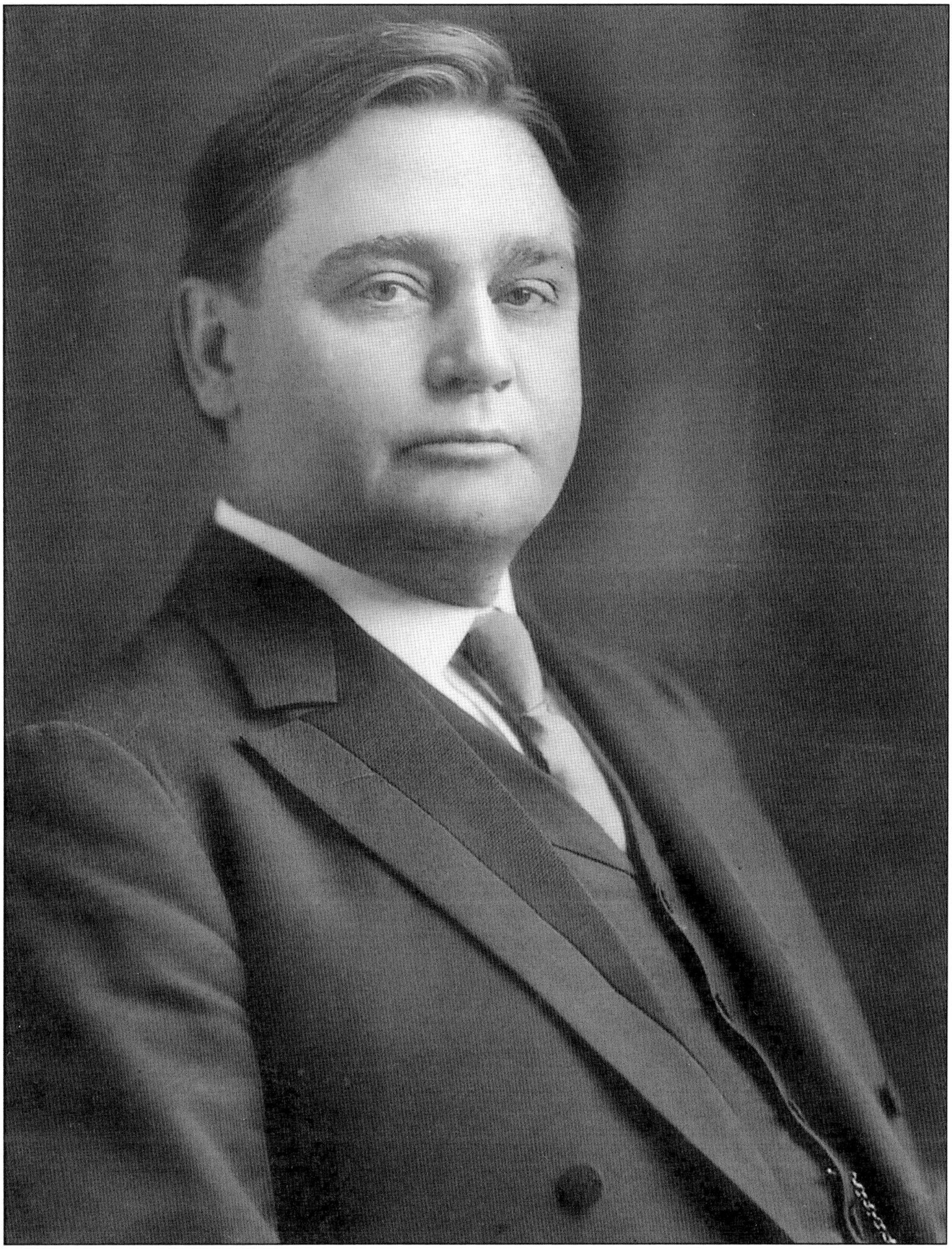

Senator Joseph Weldon Bailey came to Gainesville as a young man and opened a law practice. He served in the House of Representatives and then moved to the Senate. Bailey was known for his oratory skills. He ran unsuccessfully for governor of Texas in 1920 against Pat Neff of Waco, and another native son of Cooke County, Ewing Thomason. He died in Sherman while arguing a court case. His body was brought to Gainesville on the train and the entire town was shut down to allow everyone to attend the funeral. Planes flew over the funeral procession and the pilots dropped flowers out over the mourners as they accompanied the body to Fairview cemetery. (Morton Museum of Cooke County collection.)

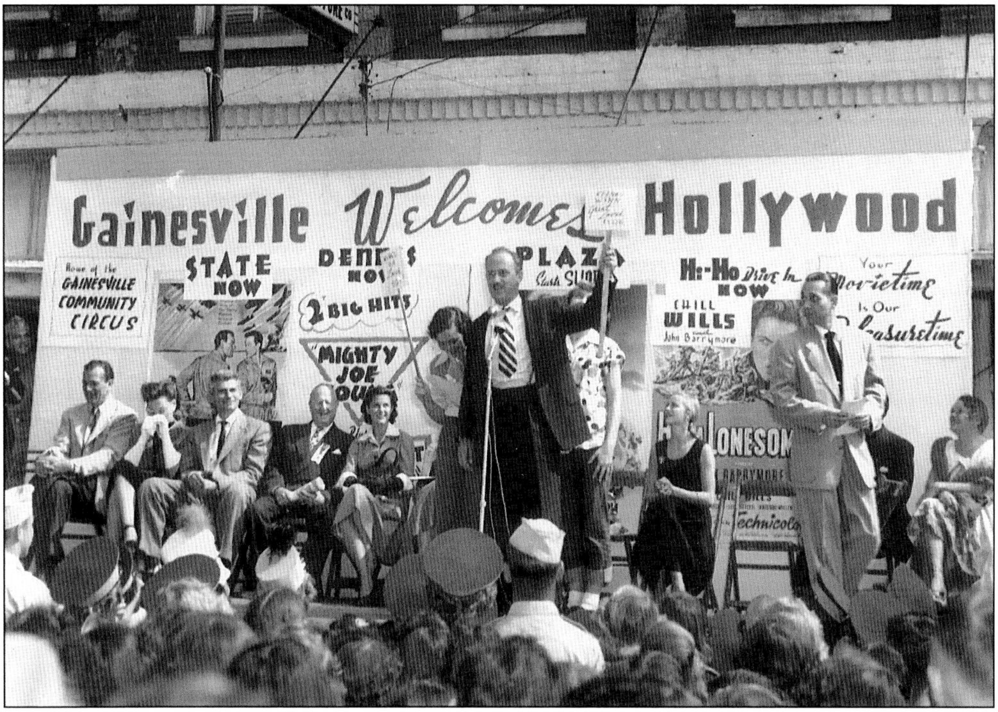

In the top photograph ("Gainesville Welcomes Hollywood"), several stars including John Wayne, Keenan Wynn, and Jeff Chandler are pictured. The group had come to town to promote the movie industry. It turned out that Jeff Chandler had been stationed at Camp Howze during World War II. In the bottom photograph, the crowd even hangs out the courthouse windows to get a glimpse of their favorite star. (Boyd & Breeding Collection, Morton Museum of Cooke County.)

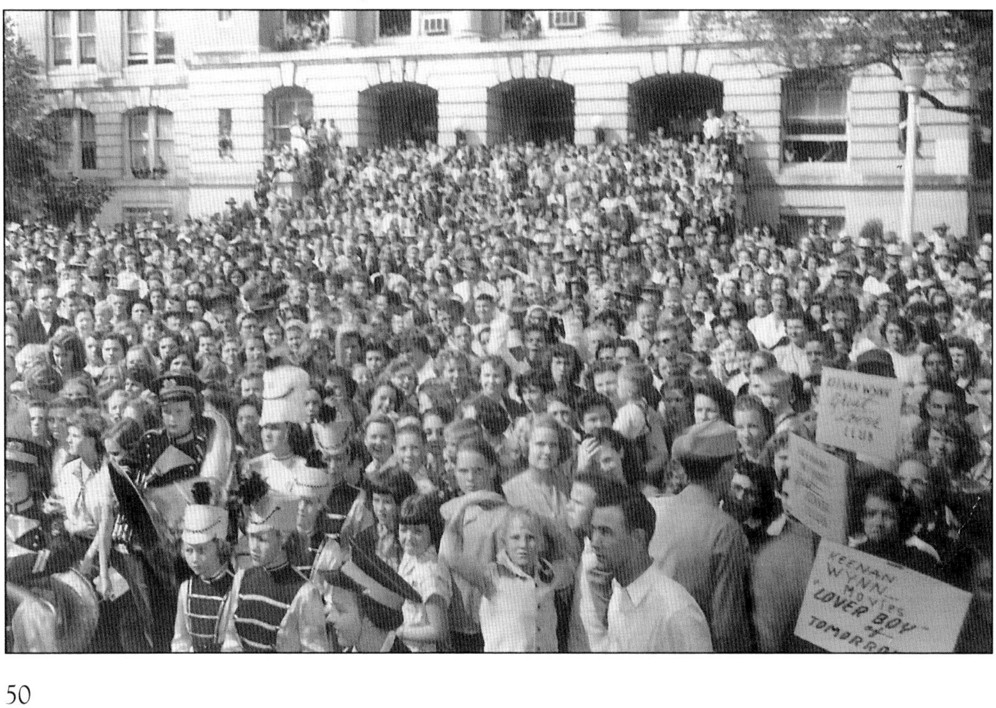

Five

Those Who Served

County residents struggled on the home front and valiantly fought in every war, from the Civil War to Desert Storm, and many continue to serve in the Armed Forces today.

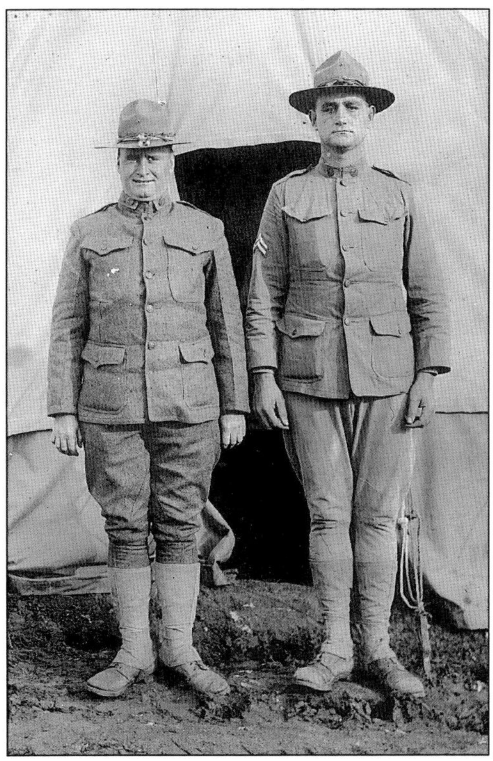

In 1917 the United States entered World War I, and two companies of men from Cooke County were recruited to go and fight. Here, from left to right, are two of those "doughboys": Carl Thurman and Albert Greer. (Donated by Mrs. Lonnie Thurman, Morton Museum of Cooke County Collection.)

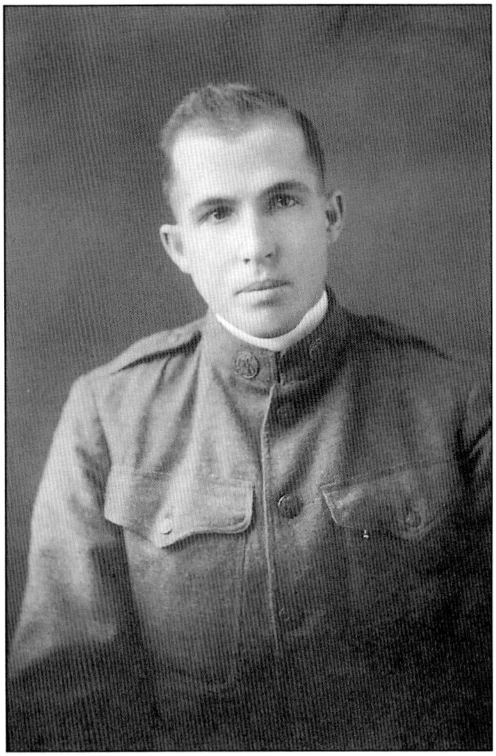

Twenty-seven-year old Clyde Lemaster of Callisburg, a stenographer in civilian life, was assigned to a medical unit in the military during WWI and rose to the rank of sergeant. (Morton Museum of Cooke County Collection.)

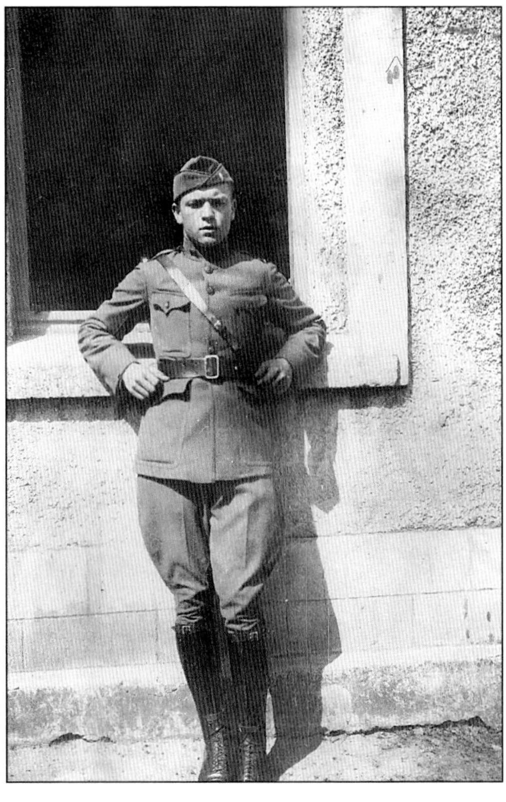

Single student Thomas Mitchell of Gainesville posed for this photograph during World War I. (Morton Museum of Cooke County Collection.)

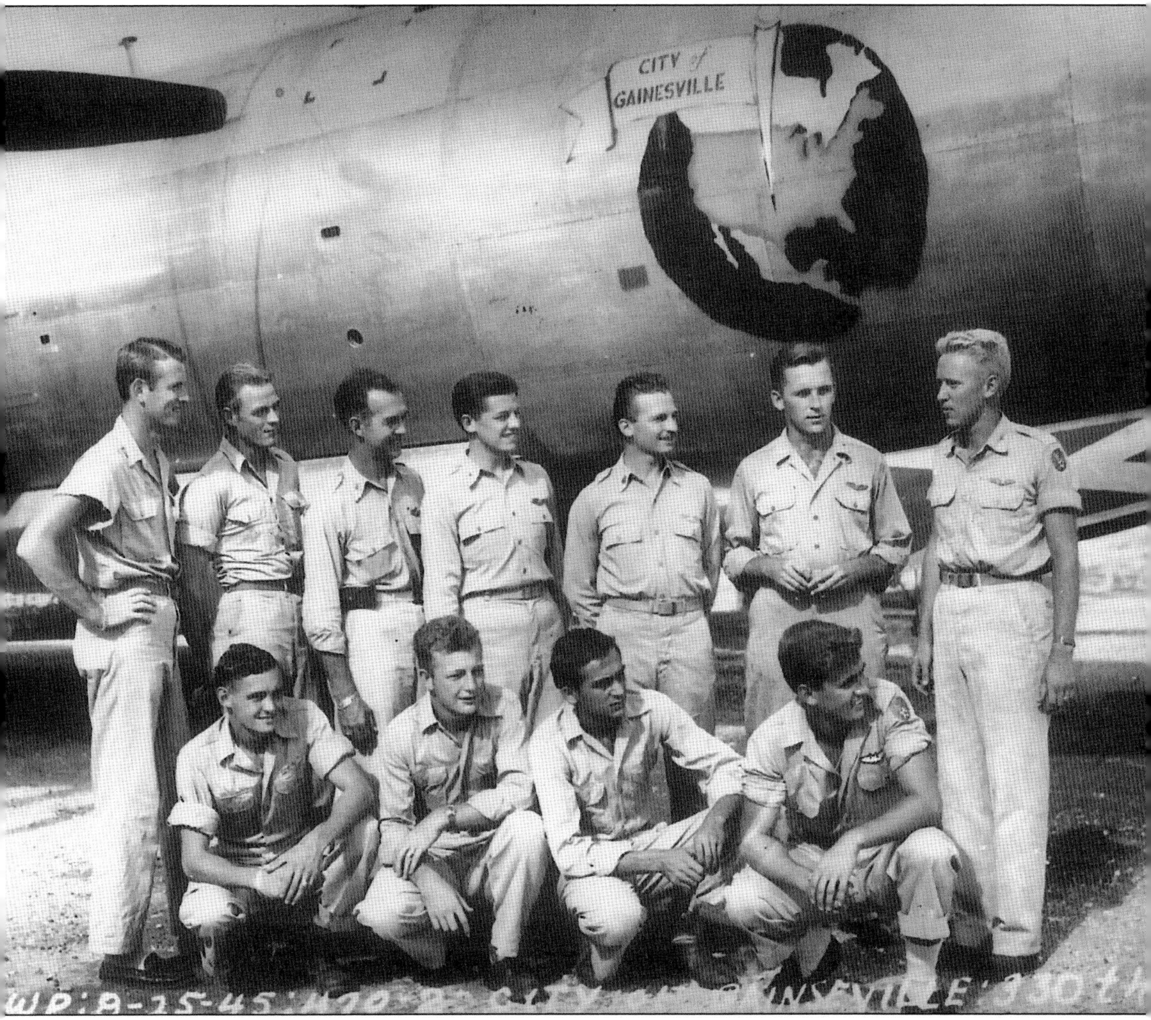

Gainesville native Travis Budlong flew this B-29 Superfortress during WWII in numerous missions over Japan from its base in Guam in the last months of the war. "All combat crews like to have a special name for their airplane," related Budlong's commander in a letter. "The crew usually gets together," he continued, "and votes, so to speak, on a name for their Superfortress. In this particular case, airplane commander First Lt. Budlong convinced the boys that the 'City of Gainesville' would be a good name to carry into the war." Pictured kneeling, from left to right, are as follows: Donald Bush, Lewis Wilhelm, Nick Munas, and Robert Flick. Standing, from left to right, are: James Parrish, Orval Haugan, Garrett Stephenson, Edward Hyde, Thomas Spencer, James McGuire, and Travis Budlong. Note the misspelling of Gainesville at the bottom of the photograph. (Donated by Travis Budlong, Morton Museum of Cooke County Collection.)

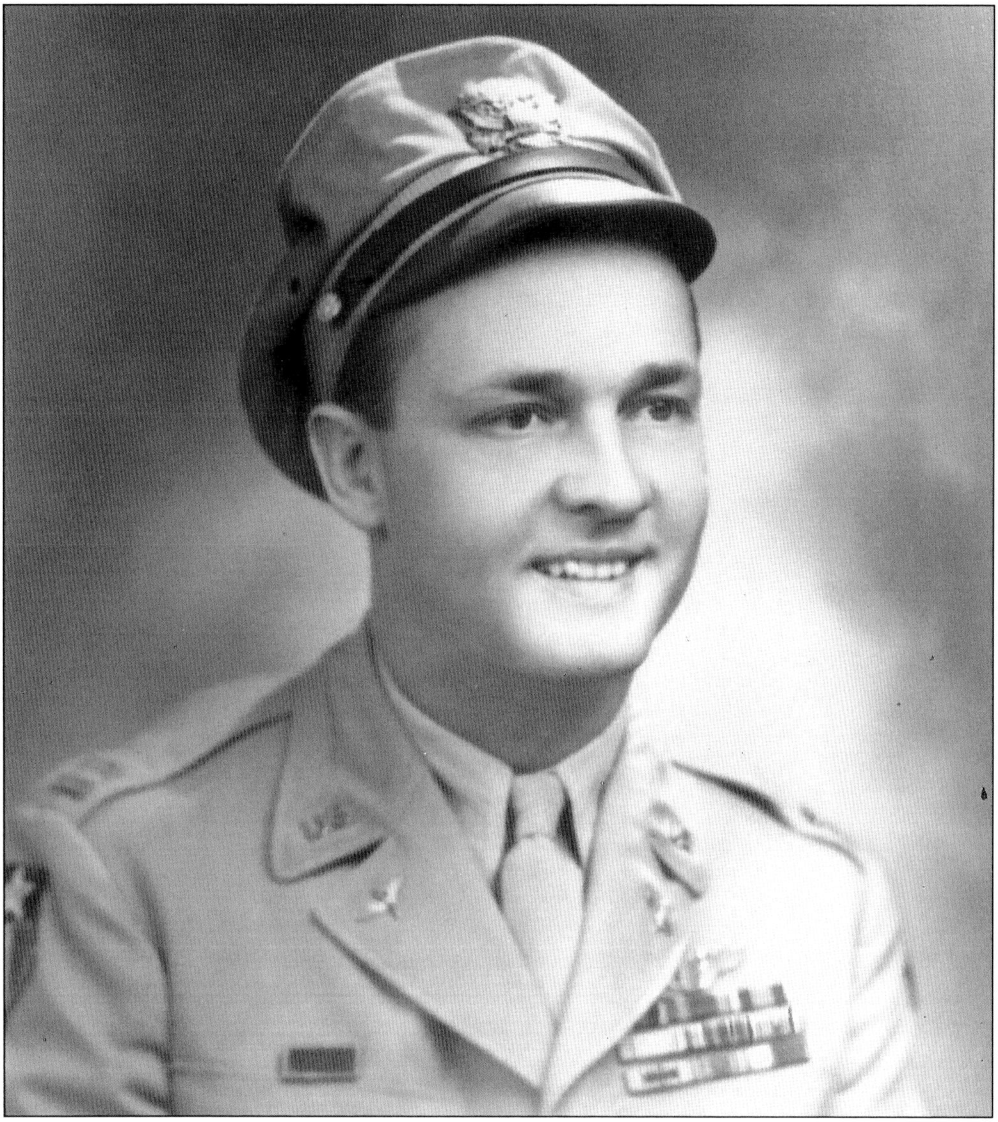

Thadd Blanton grew up in Gainesville and graduated from the high school. After attending college, he went to flight school and joined the military. After the U.S. entered WWII, he volunteered for a special mission in 1942—the Doolittle bombing raid over Tokyo. (Courtesy of Cassandra Blanton.)

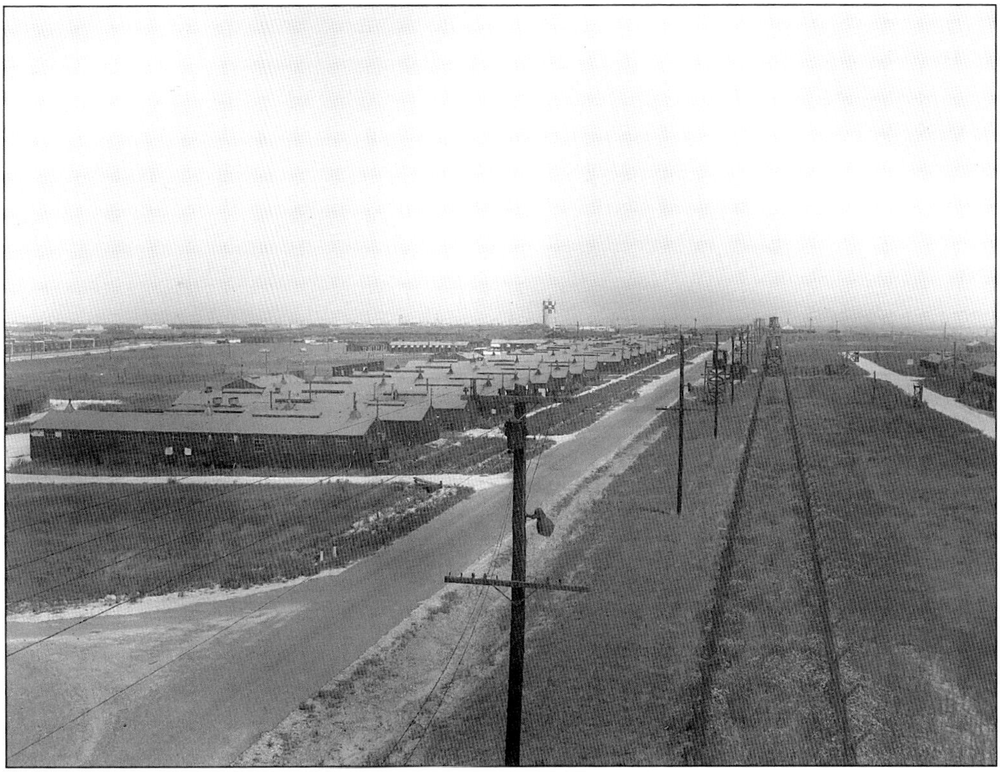

Construction of Camp Howze, an army infantry training camp, commenced in April 1942. Activation of the camp occurred in August. Erected on nearly 59,000 acres of some of the best farm land in Cooke County, three major divisions trained there. It also housed a German P.O.W. camp. A small section of the camp appears here with more buildings fading into the distance. (Boyd & Breeding Collection, Morton Museum of Cooke County.)

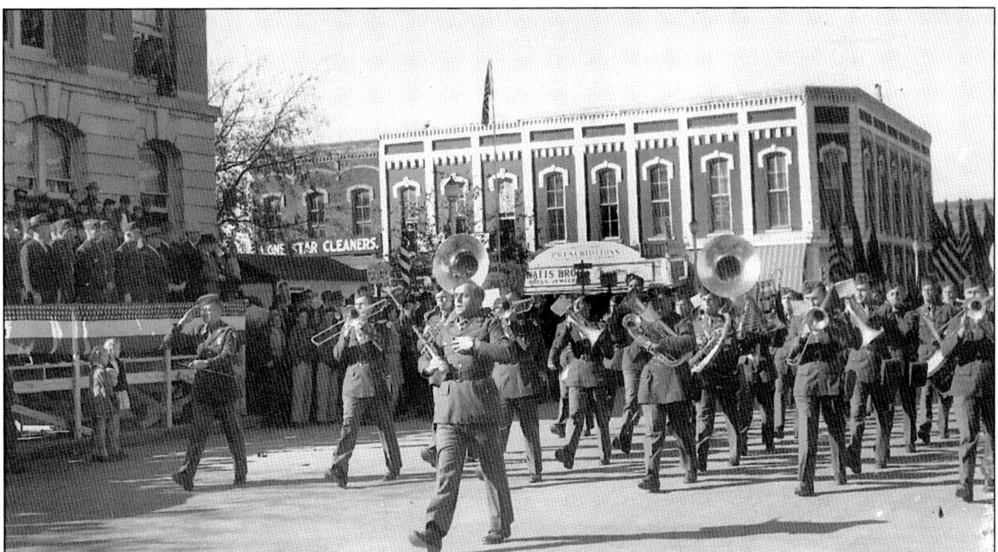

A band from Camp Howze is pictured here marching in a parade on California Street in the early 1940s. (Morton Museum of Cooke County Collection.)

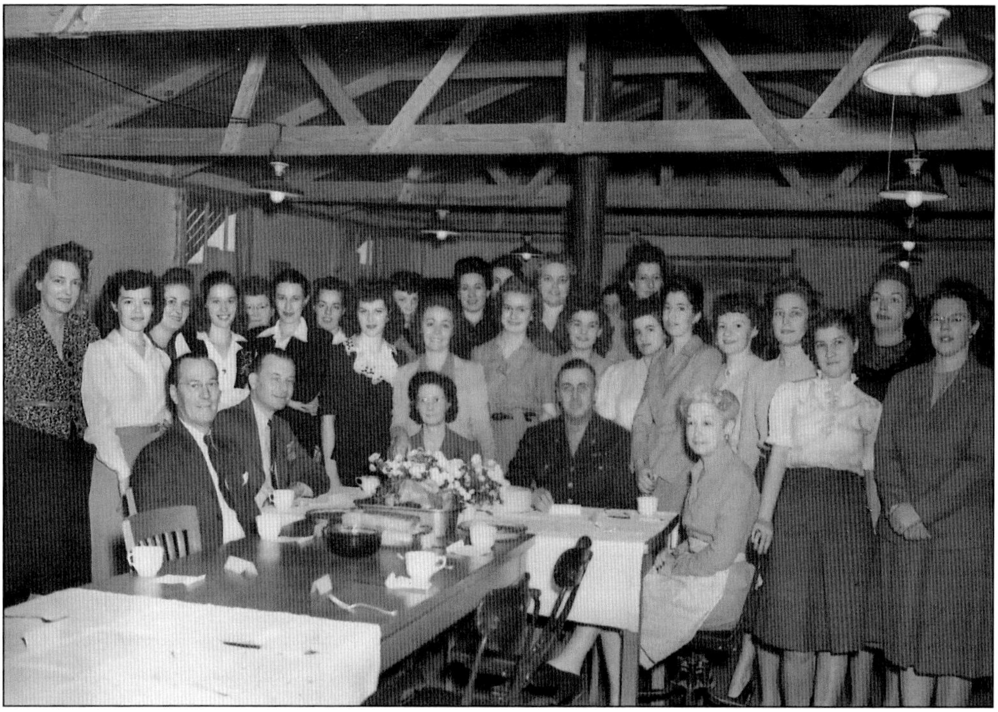

Pictured are the personnel of the civilian personnel office at Camp Howze. (Donated by Louise Blake Kline, Morton Museum of Cooke County Collection.)

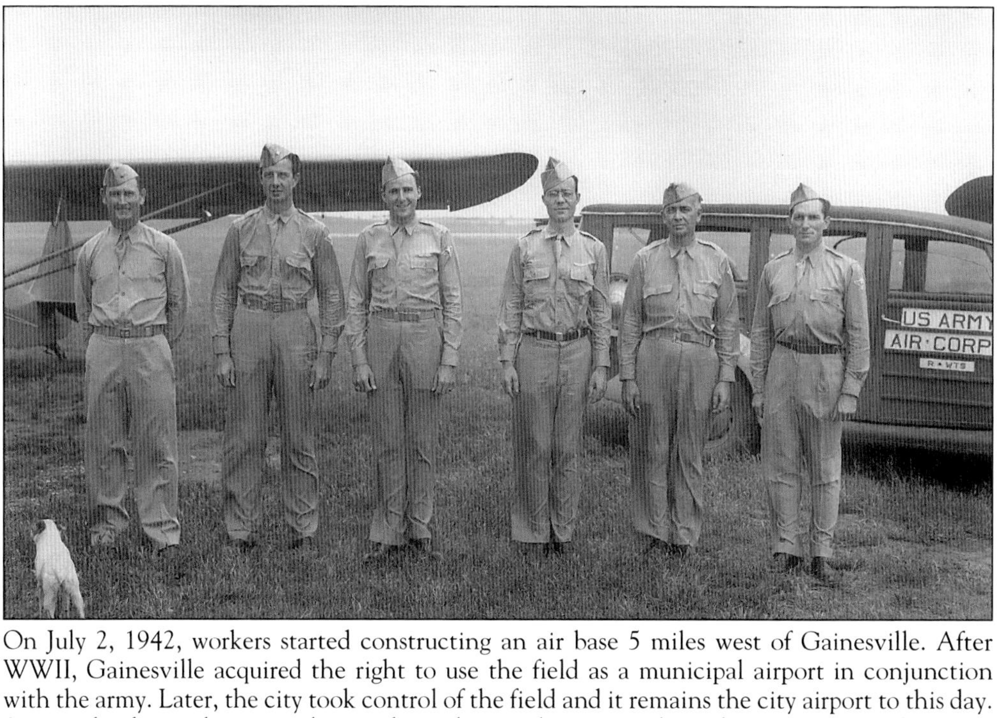

On July 2, 1942, workers started constructing an air base 5 miles west of Gainesville. After WWII, Gainesville acquired the right to use the field as a municipal airport in conjunction with the army. Later, the city took control of the field and it remains the city airport to this day. Seemingly, these pilots were about to have their ranks increased as a dog tries to get in line with them. (Boyd & Breeding Collection, Morton Museum of Cooke County.)

Jack Merrick of Gainesville stands with his bicycle in this May 1944 photograph taken in Wiltshire County, England. Mr. Merrick was a glider pilot, assigned to the 84th TC Squadron of the 437 Troop Carrier Group. He participated in the D-Day invasion of Allied Forces landing in France in WW II on June 6, 1944. (Courtesy of Jack Merrick.)

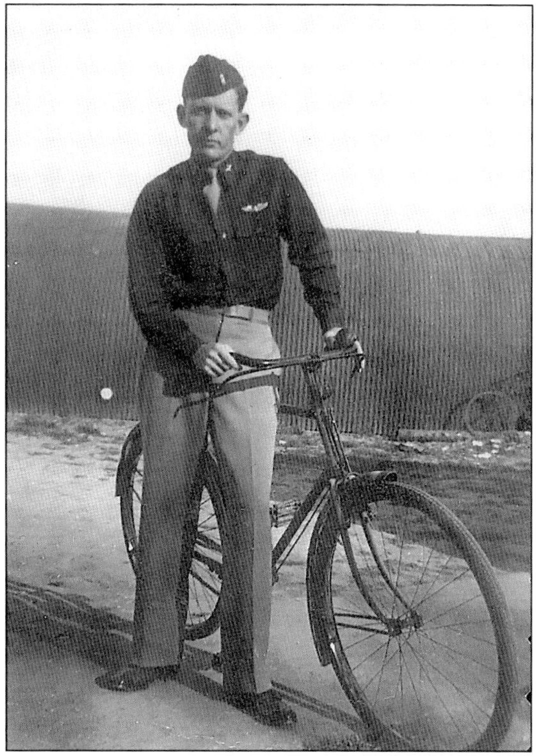

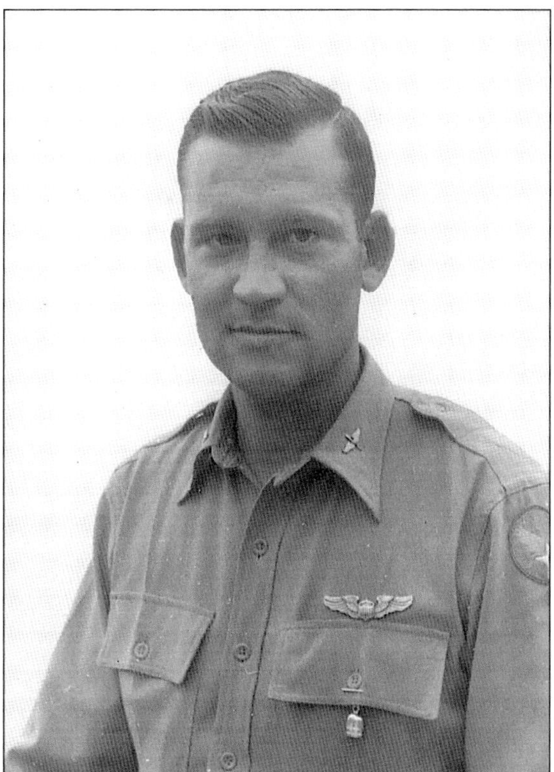

Paul Schad is pictured here on rest leave on the Isle of Capri. After flying 25 missions, crews were given a week's leave. Serving as first pilot on a B-24 Liberator, he was based in Italy and flew missions against Vienna and other targets in Germany. Mr. Schad was a First Lieutenant, ending the war as a Lt. Colonel. (Courtesy of Paul Schad.)

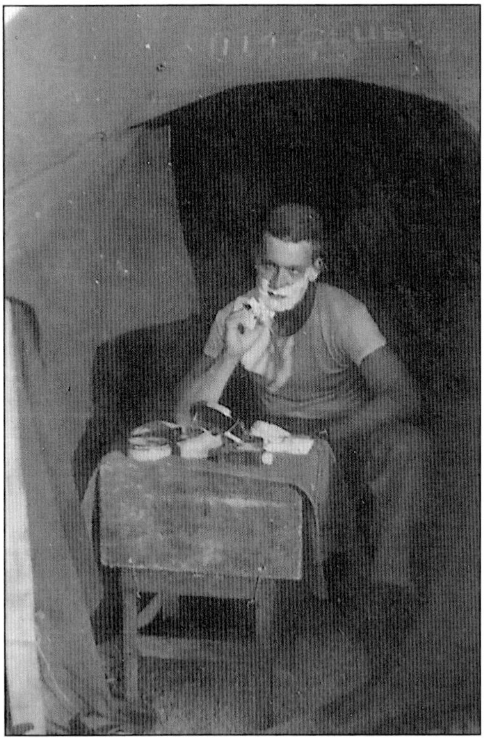

Paul Schad shaves in a tent at Pantanella, Italy, during a break from his flying duties in 1944. Mr. Schad wrote that the tent "was named the 114 Club after the Cocktail lounge in Casper, Wyoming. Cold shaving water in helmet on ground not shown in picture. The table was made from an Ammunition box mounted on a metal bomb Fin Cover which made a dandy stool. It protected the bomb fins during shipment and handling." (Courtesy of Paul Schad.)

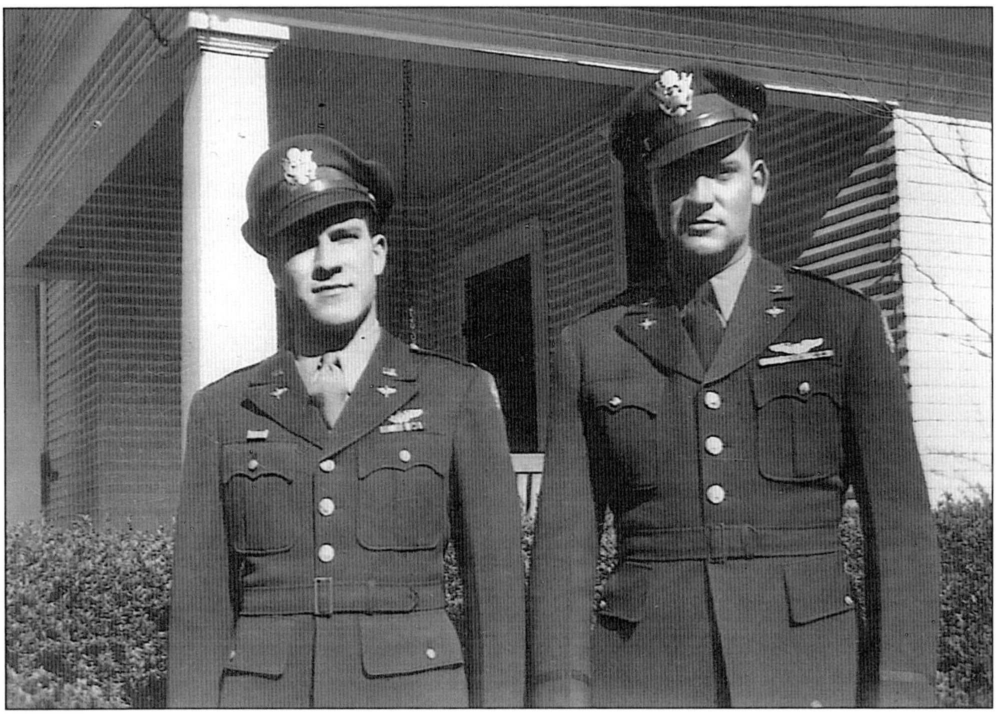

Richard and Paul Schad stand outside their home after returning from duty in World War II. Richard Schad was a bombardier on a B-24 Liberator. He was stationed in England. (Courtesy of Paul Schad.)

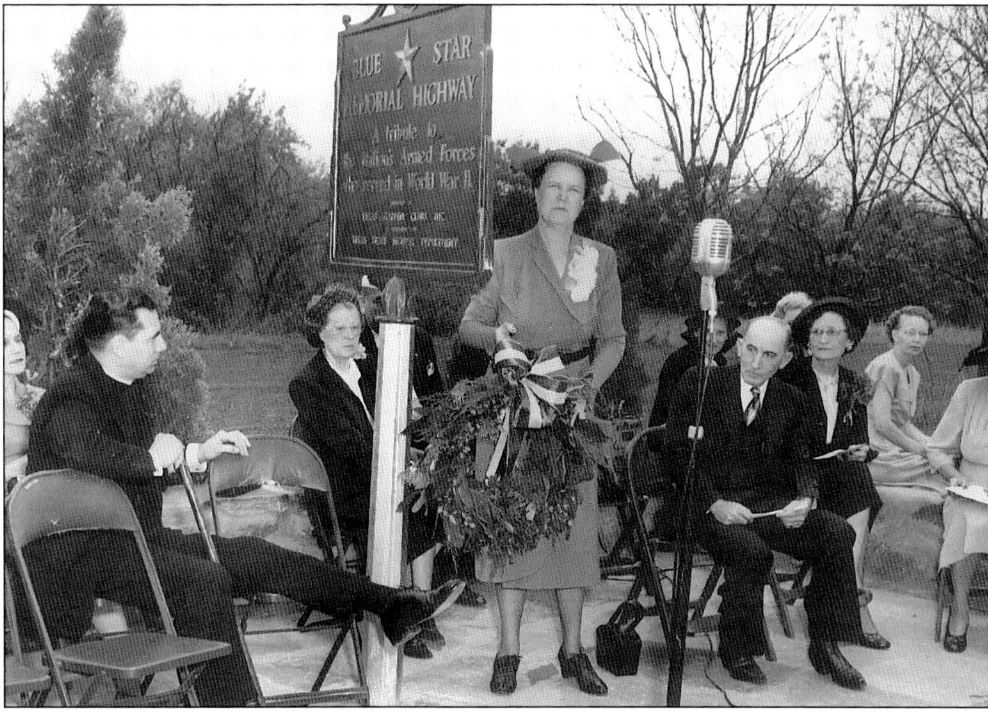

The individuals in this photograph were attending the dedication ceremony for the Blue Star Memorial Highway on April 22, 1949. The highway was a tribute to the nation's Armed Forces of World War II. (Boyd & Breeding Collection, Morton Museum of Cooke County.)

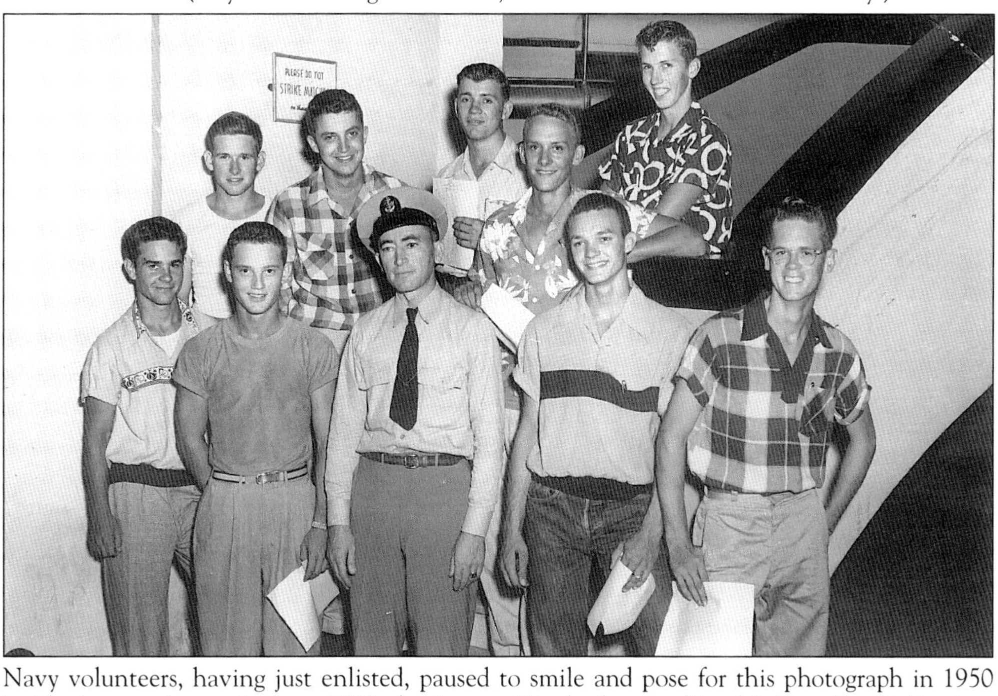

Navy volunteers, having just enlisted, paused to smile and pose for this photograph in 1950 inside the courthouse. In June 1950, the Korean War broke out. (Boyd & Breeding Collection, Morton Museum of Cooke County.)

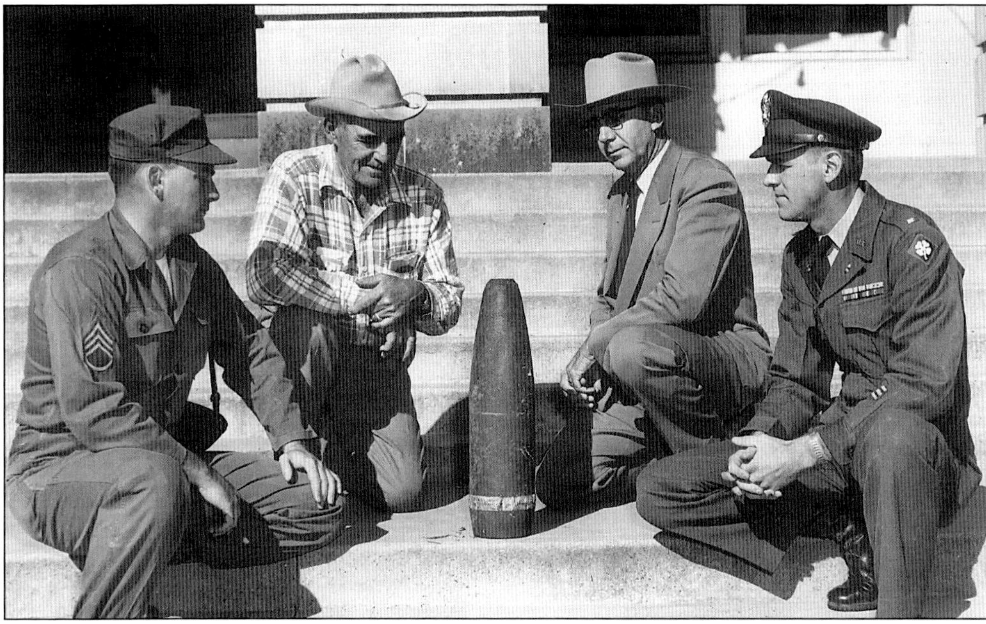

At the end of WWII, the military moved out of Camp Howze and dismantled it. Farmers then returned to the area. Shells and other types of ammunition often appeared as the farmers began to plow up the land. Concern over whether they contained live rounds or were duds filled many conversations and newspaper columns. Over 50 years after the closing of the camp, concerns over pieces of ammunition that still remain in the area continue. Here, men sit on the courthouse steps in 1953 contemplating a "dud" shell from the camp. (Boyd & Breeding Collection, Morton Museum of Cooke County.)

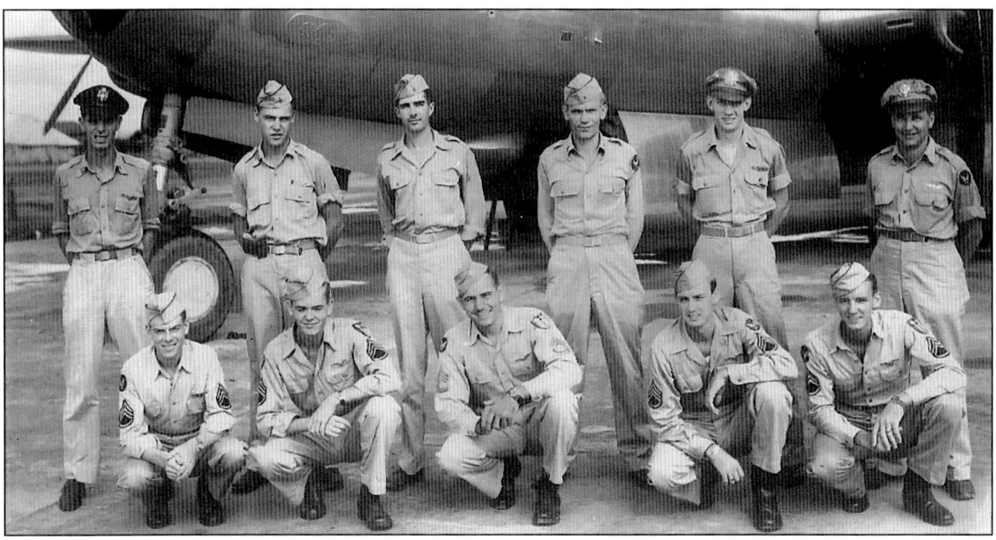

Born in Lindsay, F.A. Wiese was inducted into the Army Air Corps on February 3, 1943. After being trained in Aircraft Armament and Central Fire Control Gunnery on the B29 Superfortress, he was assigned to the 58th Bomb wing in the 20th Air Force. He flew 33 combat missions over Japan and, among other medals, received the Distinguished Flying Cross. He is pictured in 1944 at the extreme right in the front row with the crew of his plane in India. (Courtesy of Francis Wiese.)

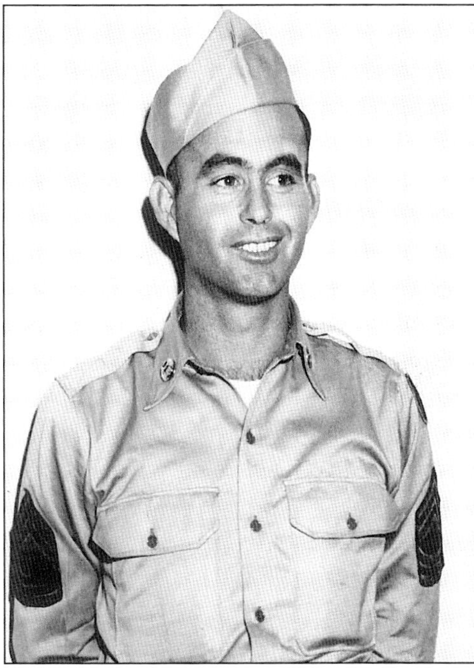

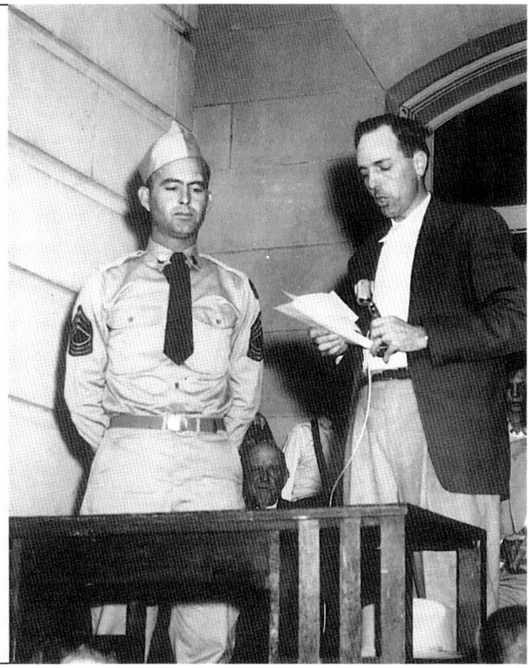

Twenty-six-year-old Master Sgt. William Arnold was the only P.O.W. from Cooke County taken during the Korean War. After his release in September 1953, he returned home to a hero's welcome. The first photograph shows Sgt. Arnold as he looked in 1953. In the second, he is shown at the courthouse where a ceremony was performed following a parade held in his honor. In the bottom photograph he is shown in back of a car during the parade. (Boyd & Breeding Collection, Morton Museum of Cooke County.)

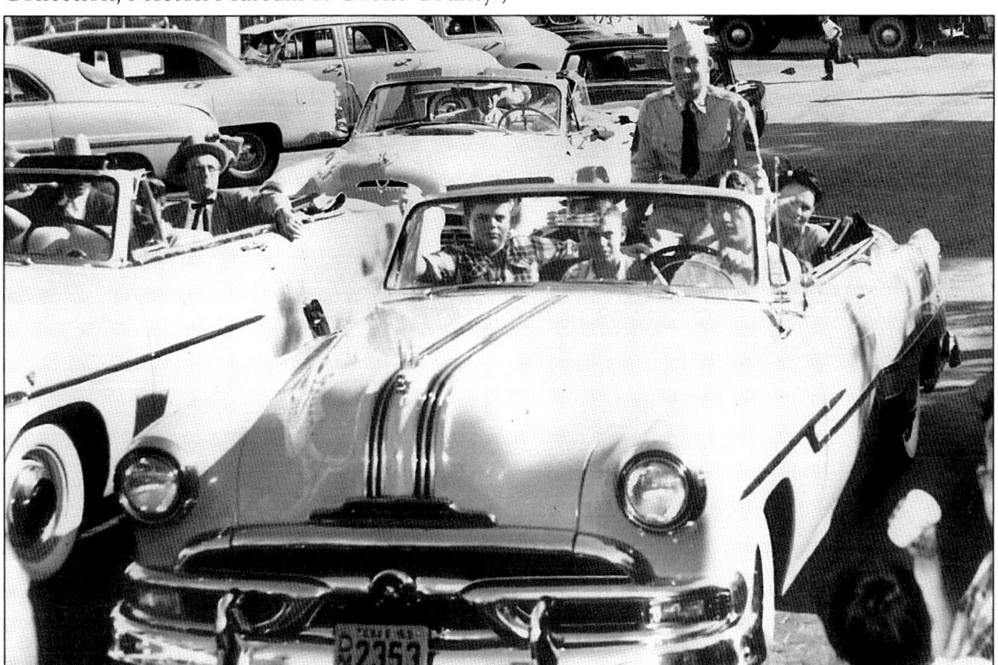

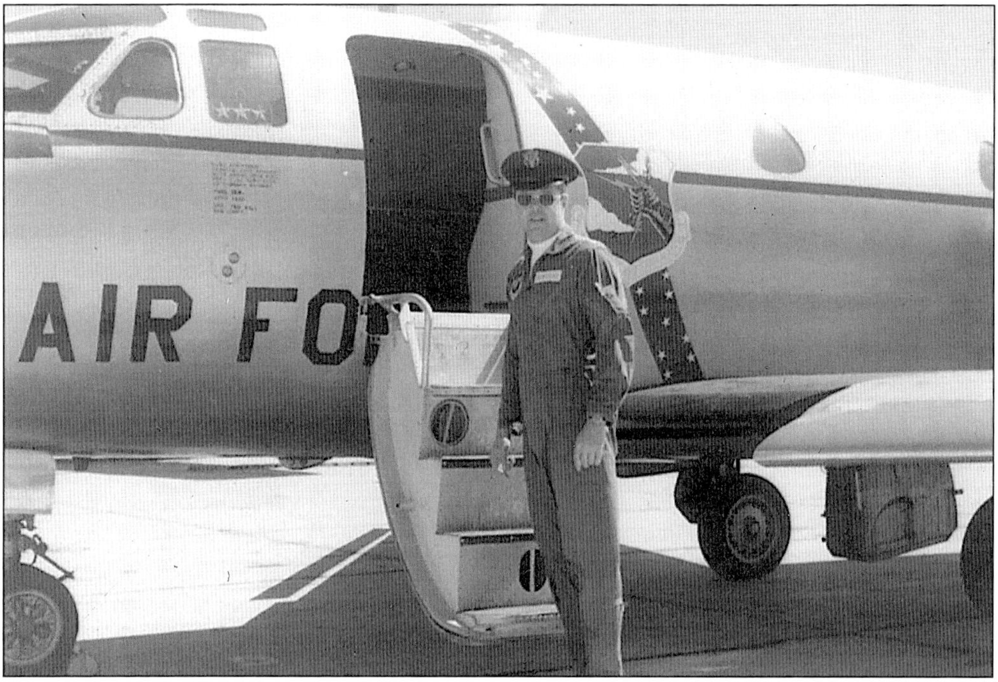

Lieutenant Colonel Guy Winstead prepares to step into a T39 plane in 1968. Lieutenant Colonel Winstead flew bombing missions over Vietnam throughout the war. Winstead served as a squadron commander, and from 1972–73 as director of operations. Winstead received a promotion to colonel. (Courtesy of Pat Winstead.)

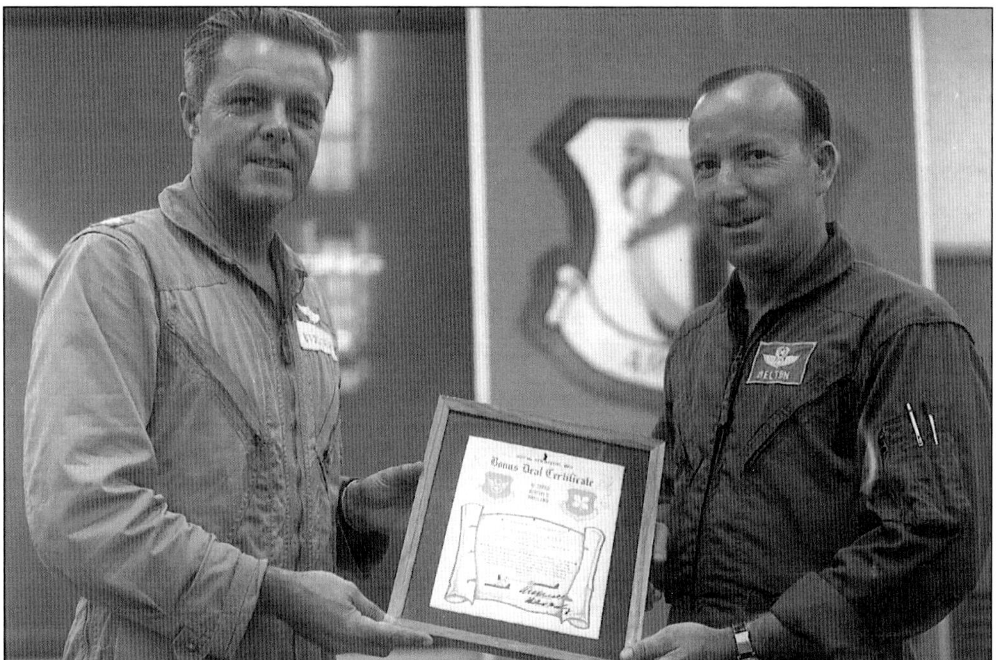

Lieutenant Colonel Guy Winstead is shown presenting an award to his tailgunner Sgt. Melton. (Courtesy of Pat Winstead.)

Six

Having a Good Time

"Where could respectable businessmen and community leaders smear greasepaint across their faces, don baggy suits and oversized floppy shoes, and not lose their respectability?" In Gainesville, as members of the hometown circus, which was just one form of amusement available to local residents.

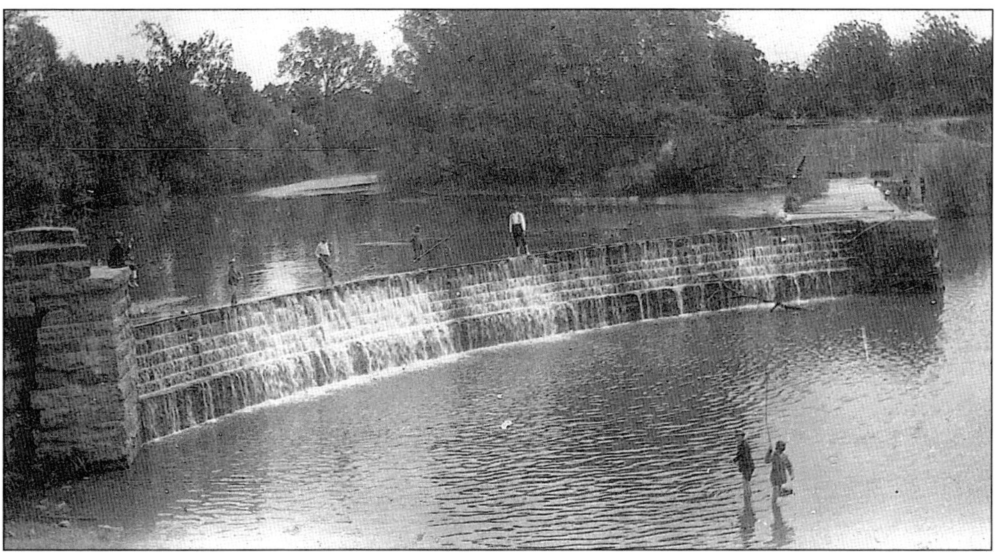

A dam was built across Elm Creek west of the "future Leonard Park in 1883 in order to provide a satisfactory reservoir for the water system." Many people remember fishing and swimming near the dam. Boating was popular and "row boats were kept in readiness at all times along Elm Creek." This photograph was taken in 1898. (Donated by Mary Agnes Stone, Morton Museum of Cooke County Collection.)

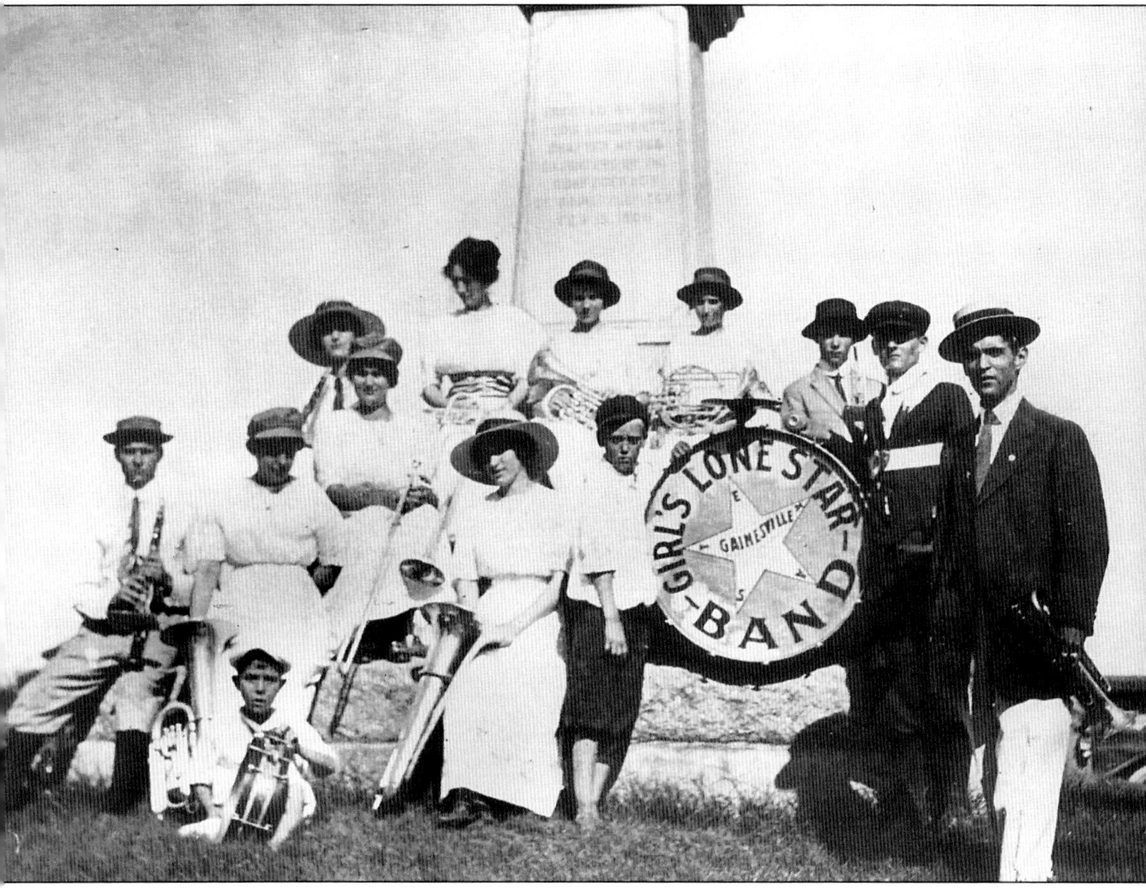

"The Lone Star Girls Band was a new musical group in Gainesville in 1915, organized by Joe Pineda. Members of the band were Misses Nell Bertram, Ascha Dee Gibson, Lettie Phipps, Stella Leach, Virgie Mahan, Mamie Lashmet, Mabel Beckelman, Sallie Lou Massey, Minnie Williams, Ruth Carter, Ora Williams, Capitola Johnson, Viola Massey, and Mrs. Jake Stamm. The band participated in a number of parades as well as playing for special events." (Morton Museum of Cooke County Collection.)

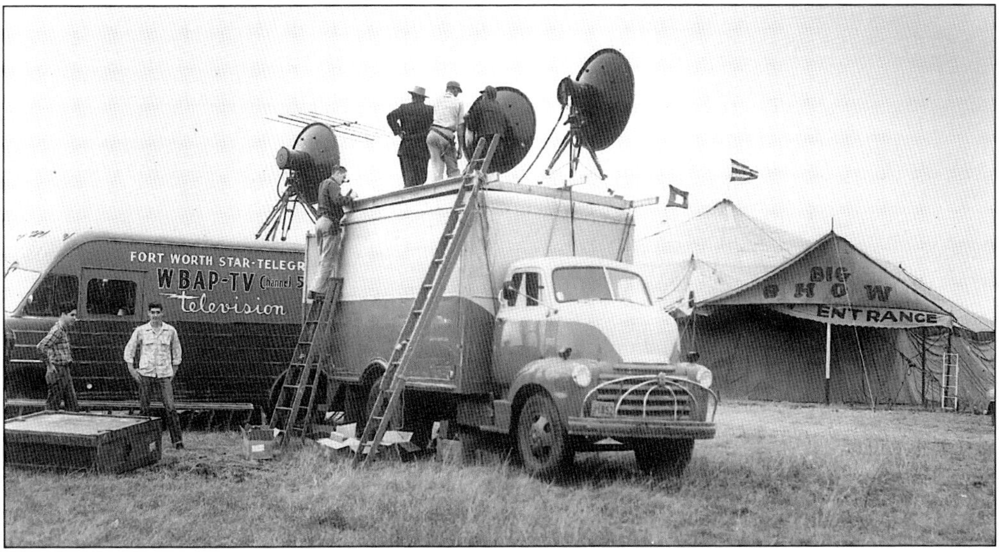

The Gainesville Community Circus represents a vital part of the history of Gainesville and the memory of it remains fresh in the minds of many people who performed in it or who saw a performance. In March 1956, WBA-TV, Channel 5, helped to create memories of the circus for many individuals by coming to Gainesville to televise a performance of it. (Boyd & Breeding Collection, Morton Museum of Cooke County.)

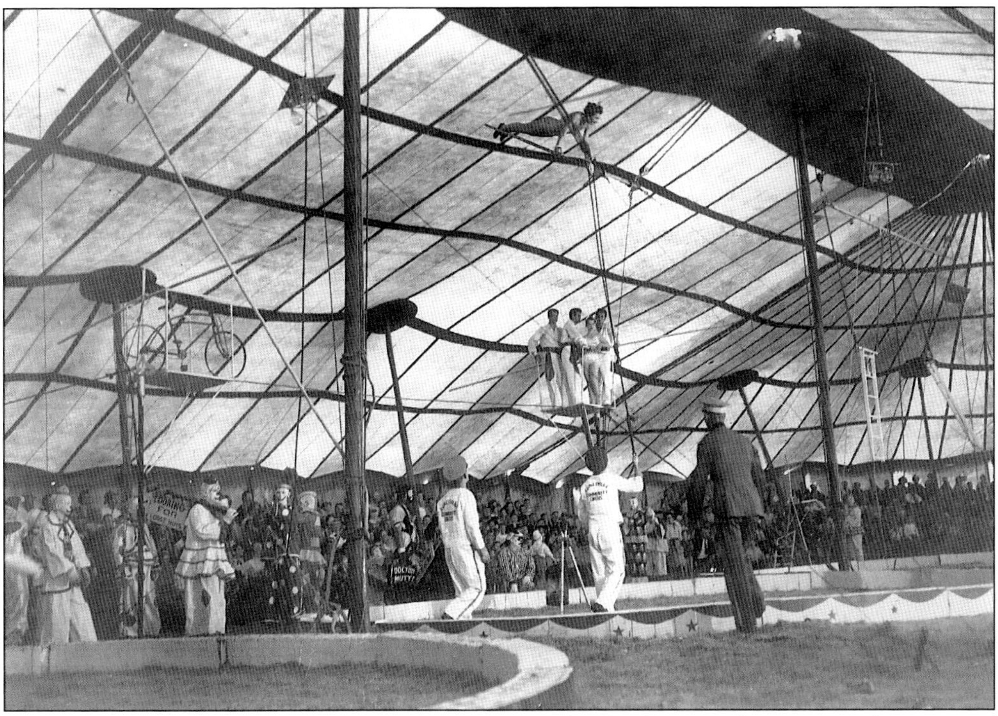

In March 1956, this photograph took viewers inside the big top during a performance of the Gainesville Community Circus. (Boyd & Breeding Collection, Morton Museum of Cooke County.)

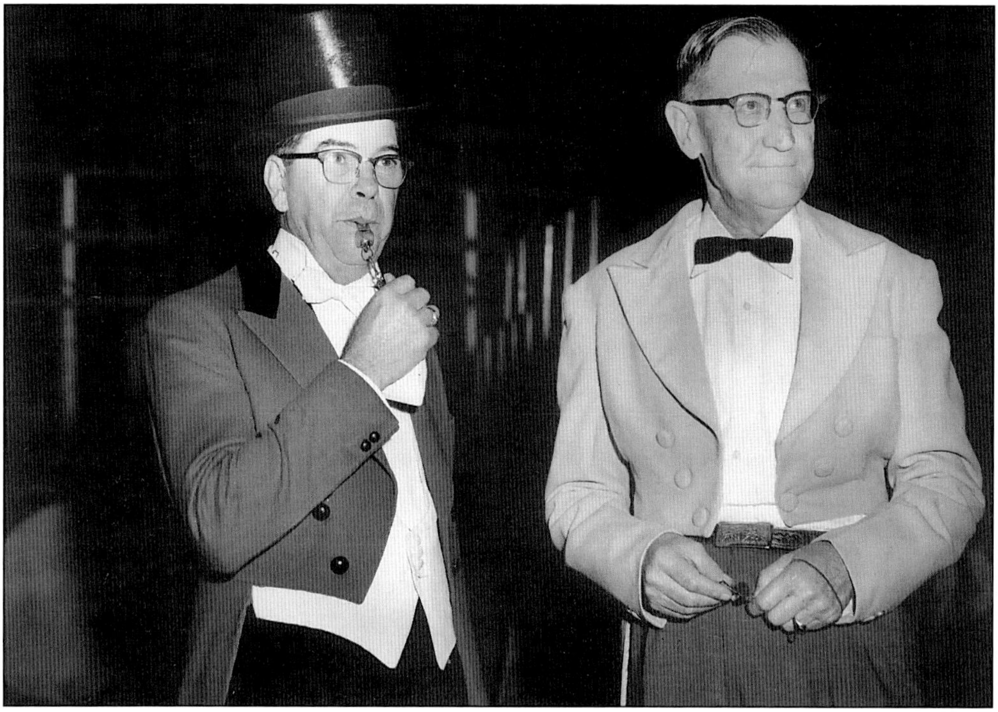

Dr. A.A. Davenport, in his role as ringmaster of the Gainesville Community Circus, is the man on the left blowing the whistle during a performance of the circus. (Boyd & Breeding Collection, Morton Museum of Cooke County.)

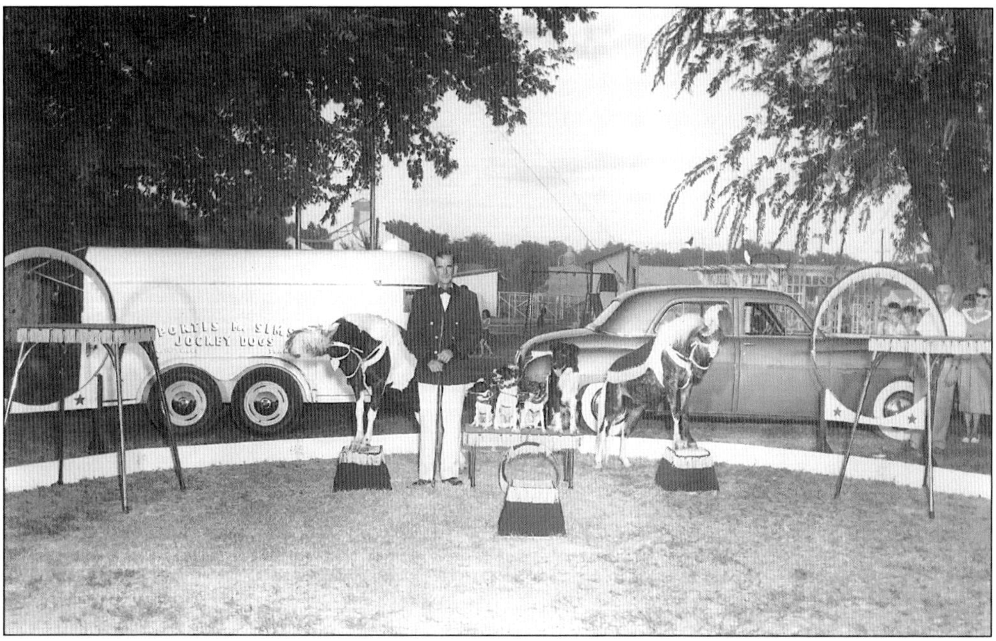

Portis Sims was a member of the Gainesville Community Circus. Here, in this July 1951 photograph, he is shown with his "dog & pony" act. (Boyd & Breeding Collection, Morton Museum of Cooke County.)

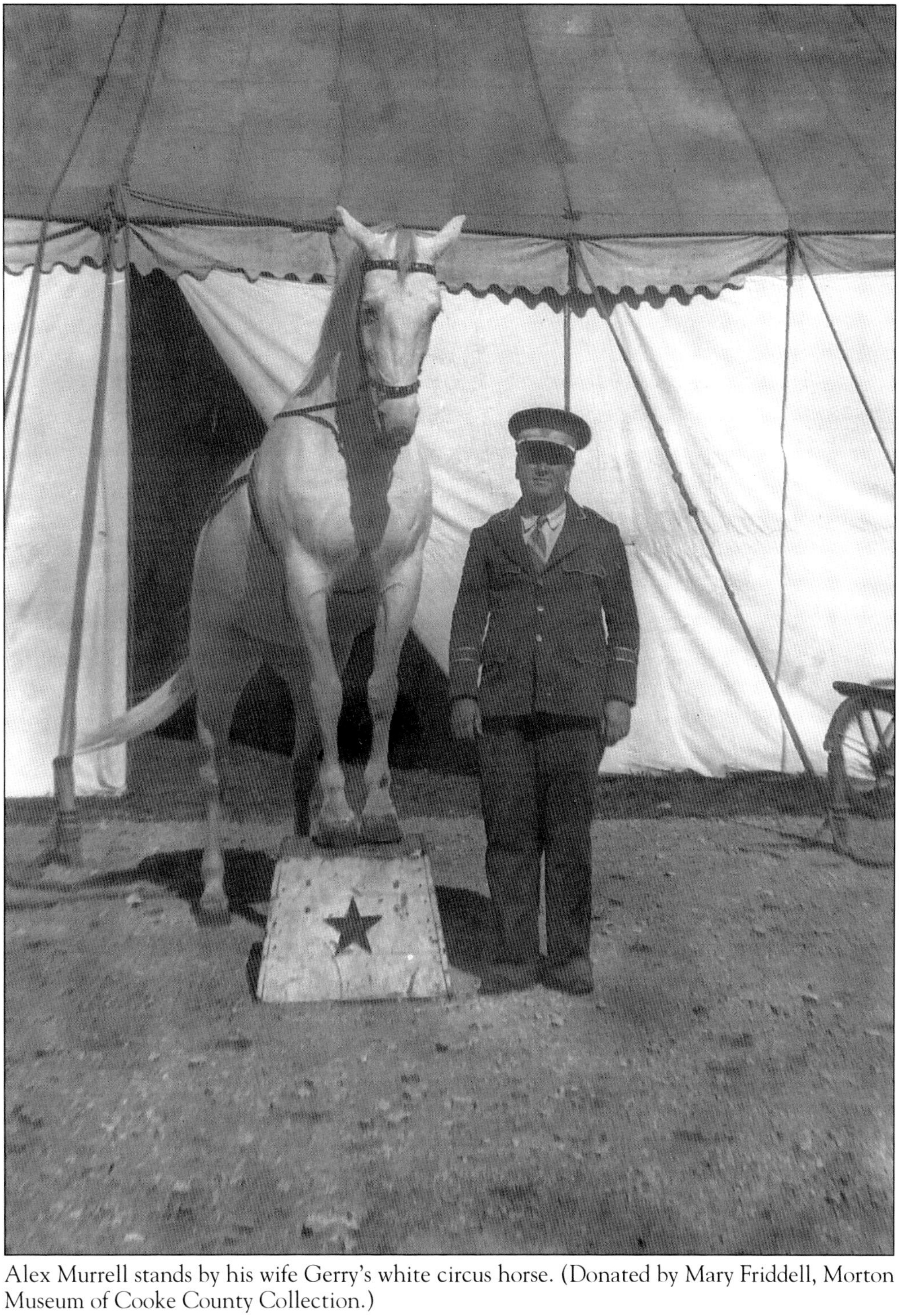

Alex Murrell stands by his wife Gerry's white circus horse. (Donated by Mary Friddell, Morton Museum of Cooke County Collection.)

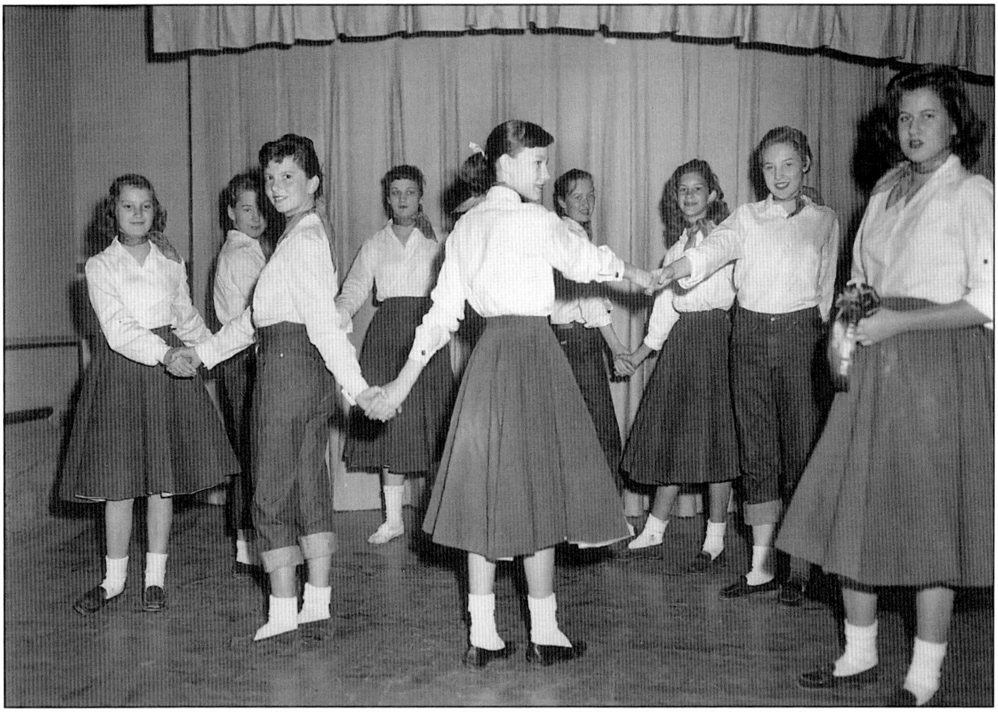

Members of the Valley View 4-H club practice their square dance steps in 1957. (Boyd & Breeding Collection, Morton Museum of Cooke County.)

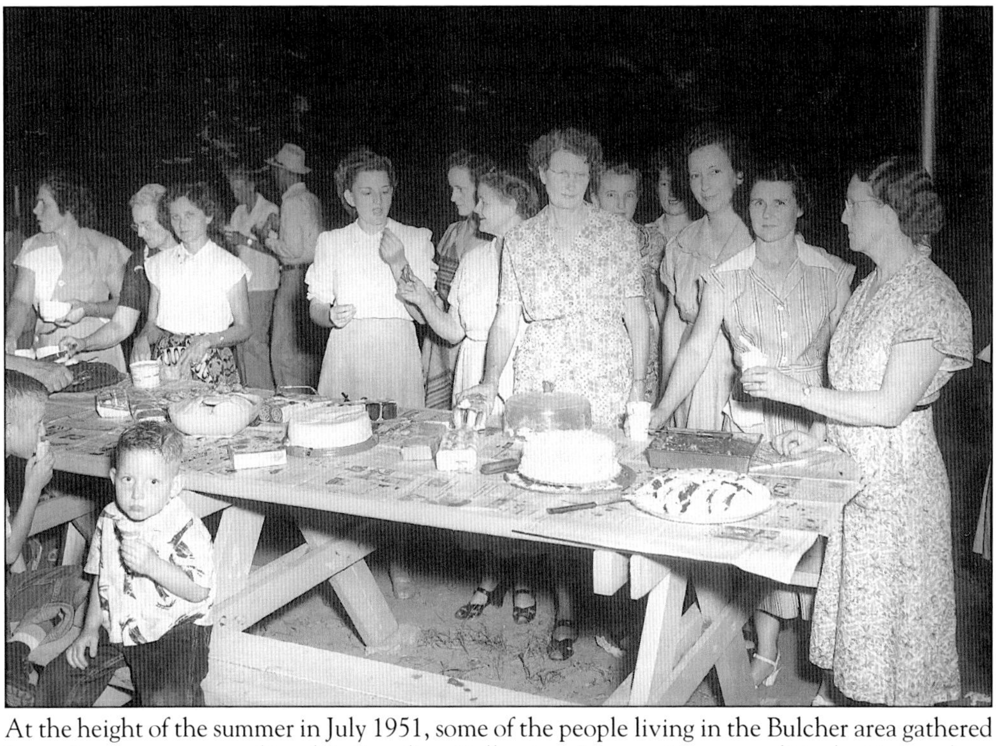

At the height of the summer in July 1951, some of the people living in the Bulcher area gathered for an ice cream supper. (Boyd & Breeding Collection, Morton Museum of Cooke County.)

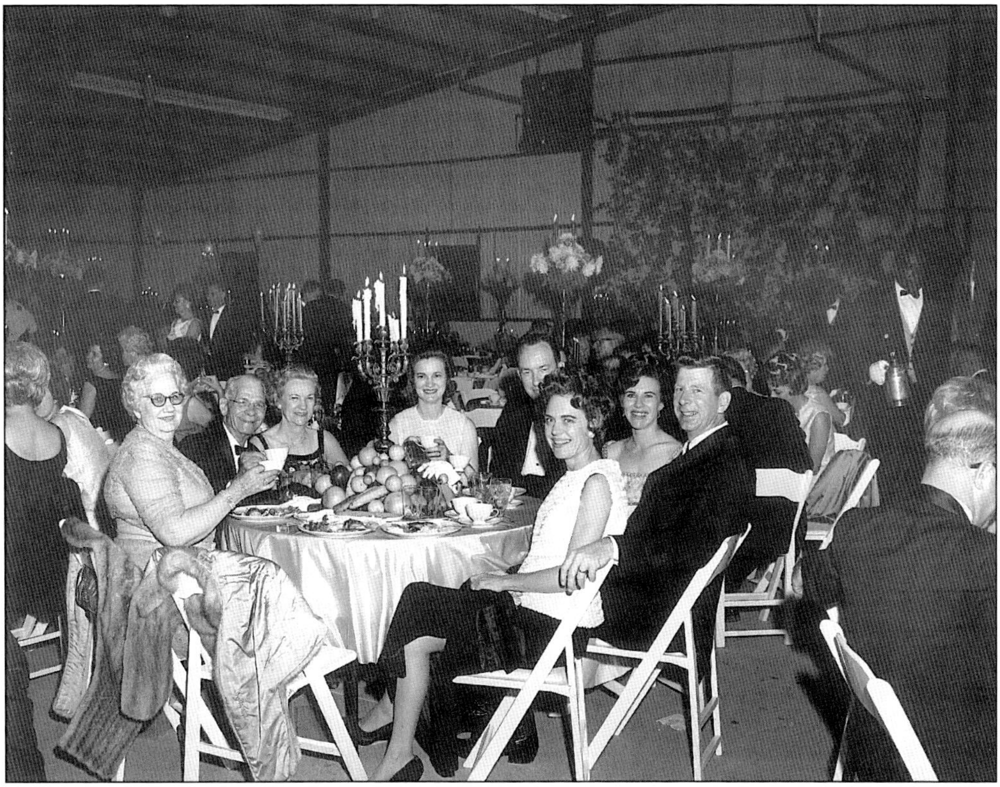

Everyone is having fun at this party at the Showbarn at the Medders' home in Muenster. (Boyd & Breeding Collection, Morton Museum of Cooke County.)

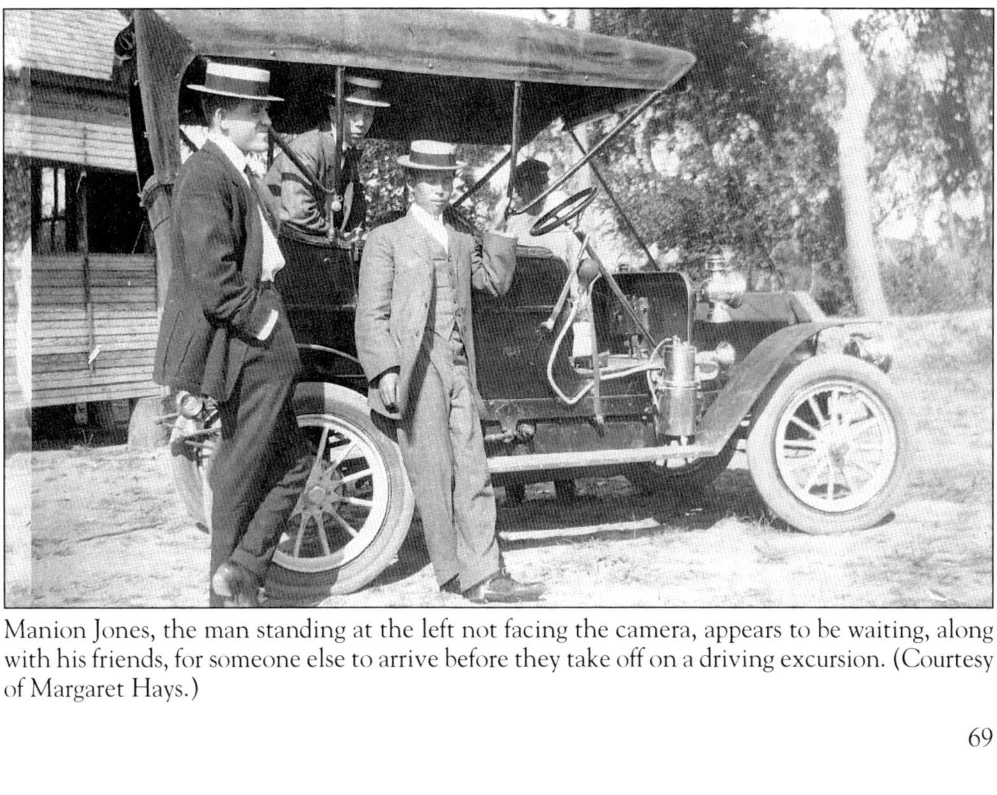

Manion Jones, the man standing at the left not facing the camera, appears to be waiting, along with his friends, for someone else to arrive before they take off on a driving excursion. (Courtesy of Margaret Hays.)

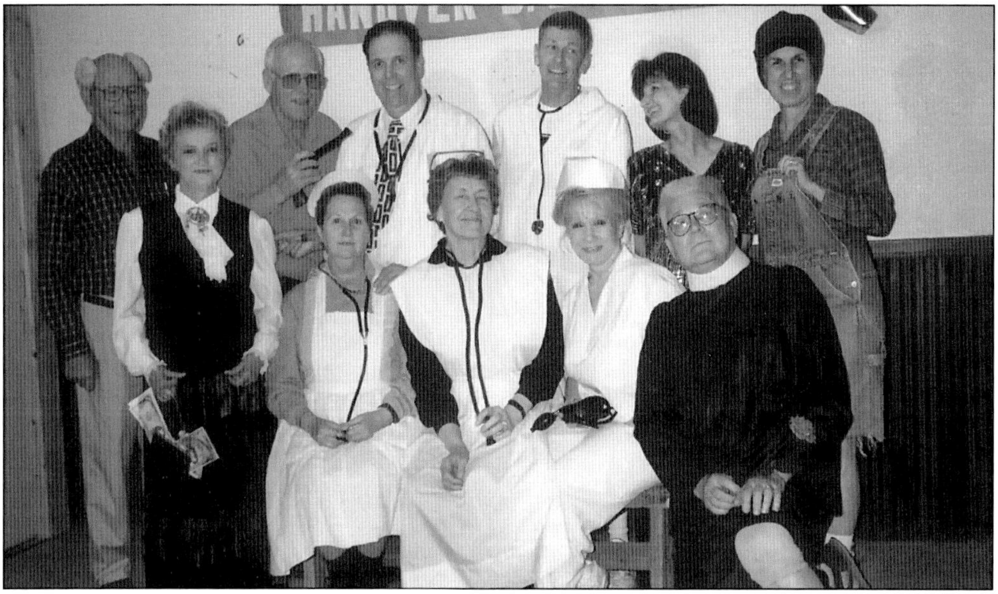

For 17 years the Mt. Springs Mellowdrummers have entertained the county with their joyous productions. Performances are held once a year. In 1998, some of the Mellowdrummers stopped for a moment and they were captured in this photograph. Pictured in the front row, from left to right, are as follows: Linda Bevers, Sherry Isbell, Delsie Lillard Lance, Kay Fuller, and Floyd Jenkins. Pictured in the back row, from left to right, are L.D. Lance, Spencer Bevers, David Isbell, Jerry McKown, Sandy Vann, and Marilyn McKown. Nadine Pitzinger has been the director for the group from the beginning, and two members—Delsie Lance and Kay Fuller—have been in the group since the organization started. (Courtesy of Delsie Lillard Lance.)

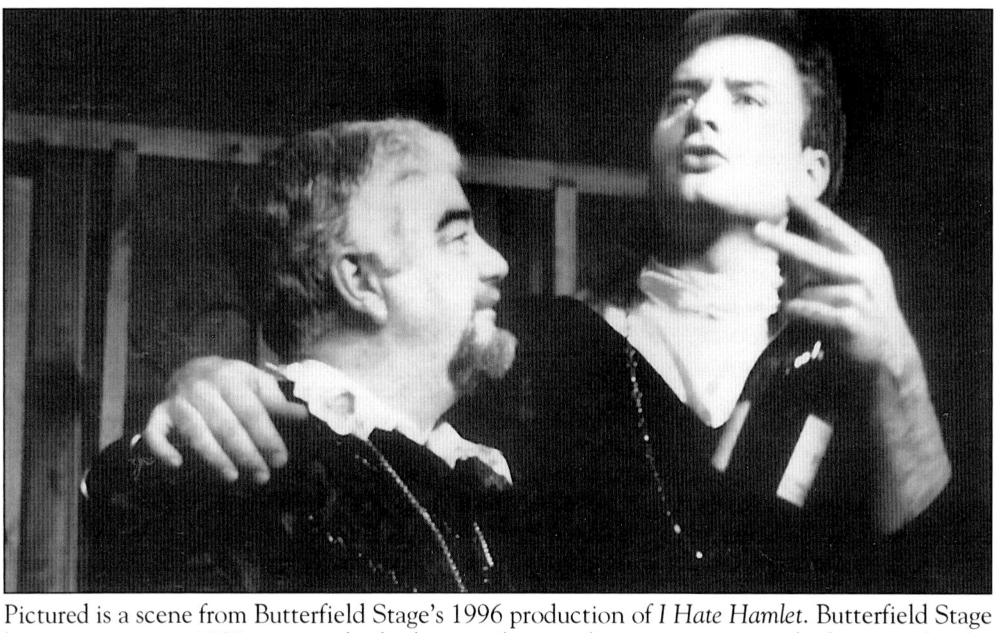

Pictured is a scene from Butterfield Stage's 1996 production of *I Hate Hamlet*. Butterfield Stage began its quest in 1979 to provide the best in theatrical entertainment and education for the people of Cooke County and the surrounding area. Pictured, from left to right, are David Chapman and Jim Fuller. (Courtesy of Butterfield Stage.)

Seven

Sports

Sports activities always enjoyed widespread county participation. Important voices included Dr. Charles Johnson who, among other things, worked to get the city council in Gainesville to approve Sunday baseball; J.D. Leeper, for whom the Gainesville football stadium is named; and Dr. Herbert Locke, who forcefully promoted the Gainesville Owls baseball team. Well-known athletes from the area include Kevin Mathis, Charles Paddock, John Mahon, and one who briefly attended the local community college—Dennis Rodman.

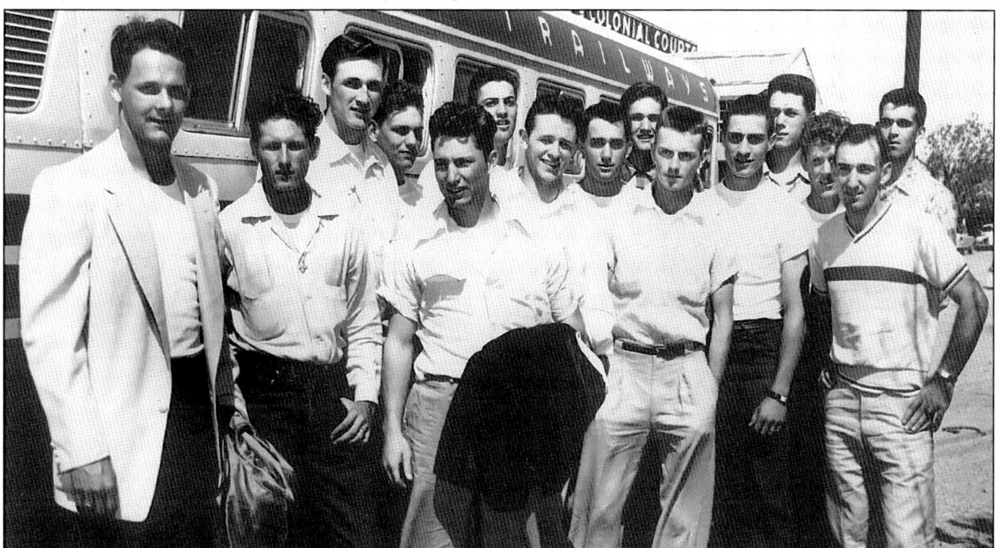

Owl baseball players are pictured arriving in town on April 13, 1954. (Boyd & Breeding Collection, Morton Museum of Cooke County.)

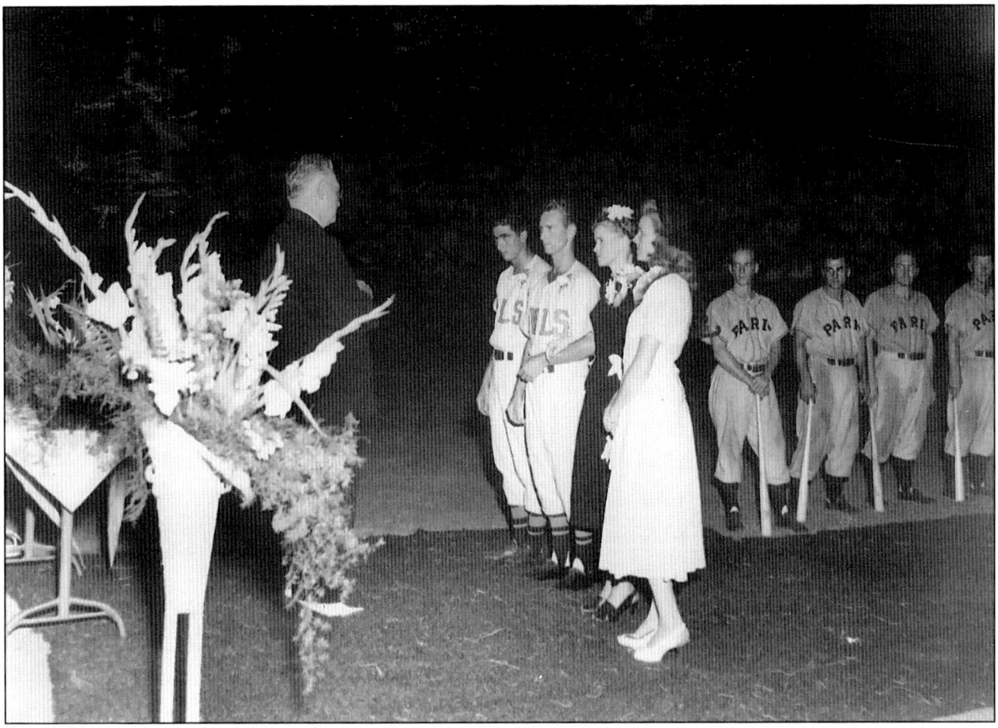

These two scenes depict the wedding ceremony of Gainesville Owls baseball player Herbert Moore to Mary Vanhuss in July 1948. During a break in a game between the Owls and the Paris, Texas team, the wedding party gathered on the pitcher's mound and the Reverend C.M. Thomas, pastor of the First Baptist Church, performed the ceremony. (Boyd & Breeding Collection, Morton Museum of Cooke County.)

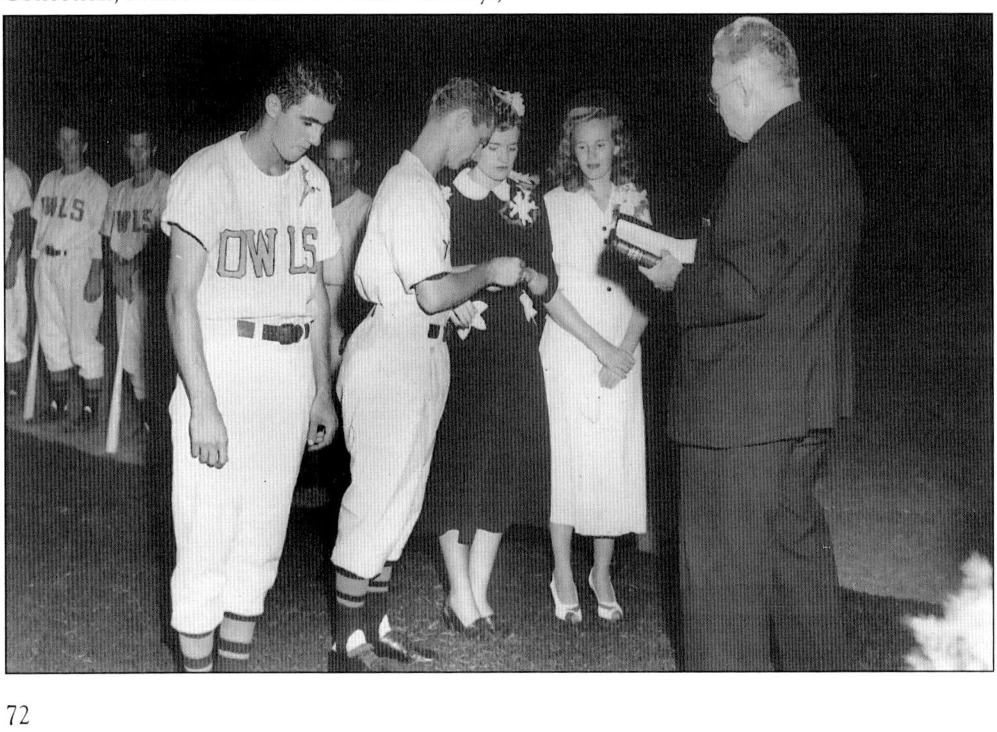

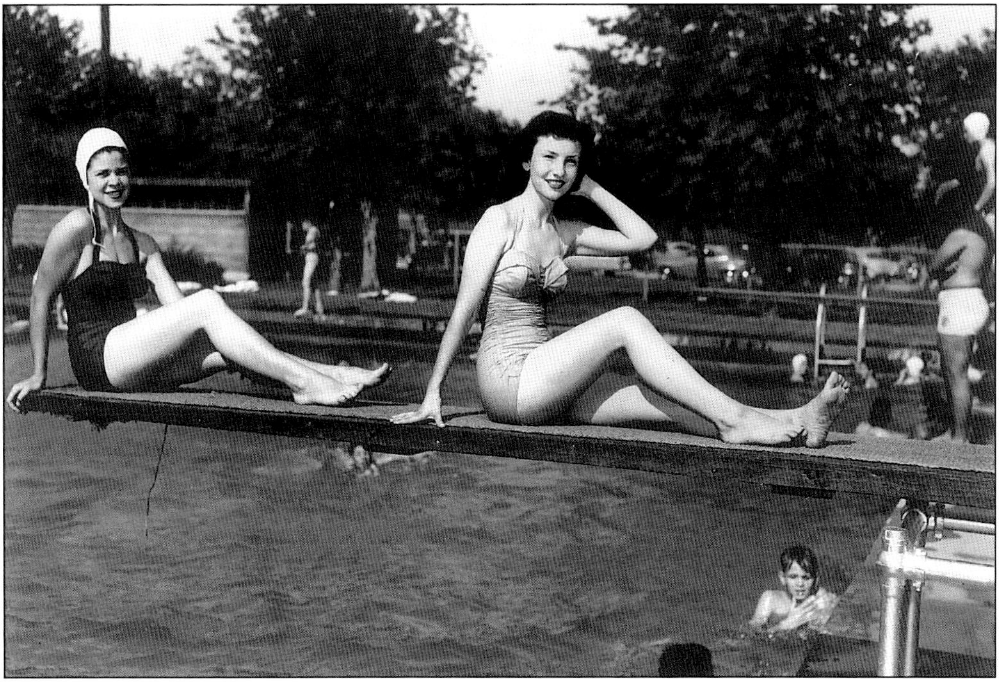

These bathing beauties posed on opening day—May 27, 1955—at the public swimming pool in Leonard Park. (Boyd & Breeding Collection, Morton Museum of Cooke County.)

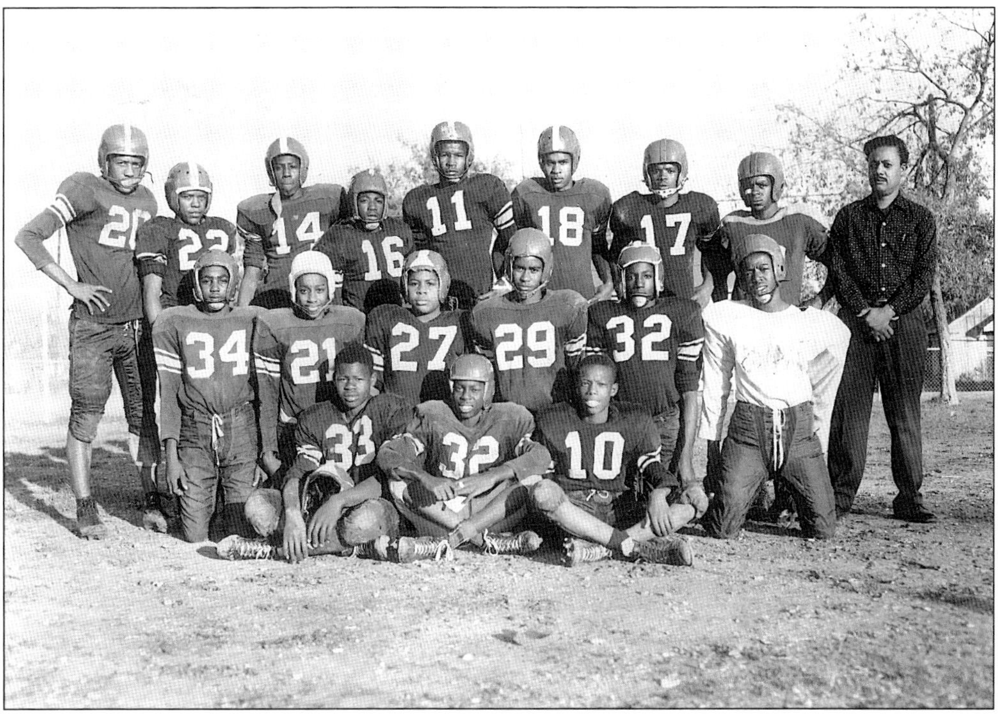

The Booker T. Washington football team is shown here on November 8, 1956. The coach was John Coleman. (Boyd & Breeding Collection, Morton Museum of Cooke County.)

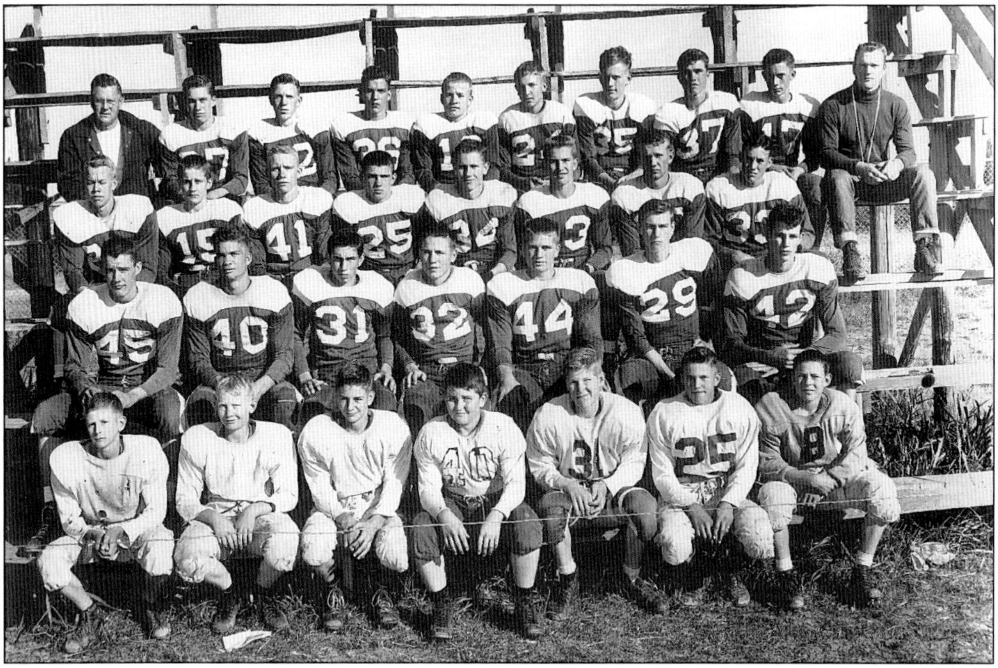

In 1955, the Sacred Heart Football team in Muenster took time from practice to sit and have this photo snapped. (Boyd & Breeding Collection, Morton Museum of Cooke County.)

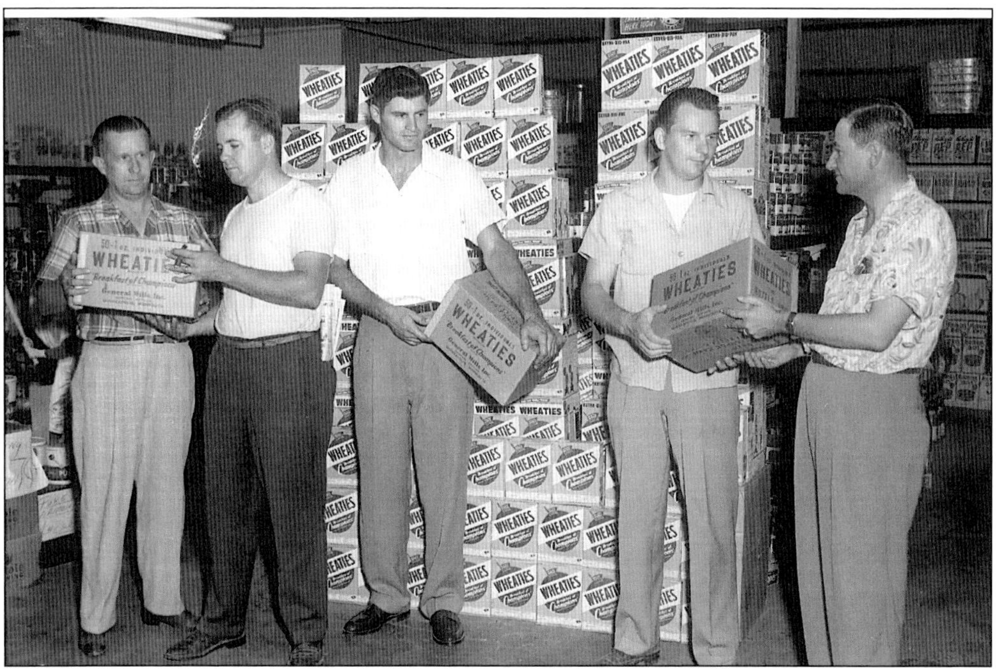

As the saying goes, "If You Are An Athlete, You Always Want to Eat Your Wheaties." General Mills, Inc., gave "cases of Wheaties to every member of the Gainesville Owls baseball team who made home runs during the 1951 season." Here, in this September 1951 photograph, three members of the club accepted the gifts for their fellow players. The photo was taken inside the Temple Cash grocery store. (Boyd & Breeding Collection, Morton Museum of Cooke County.)

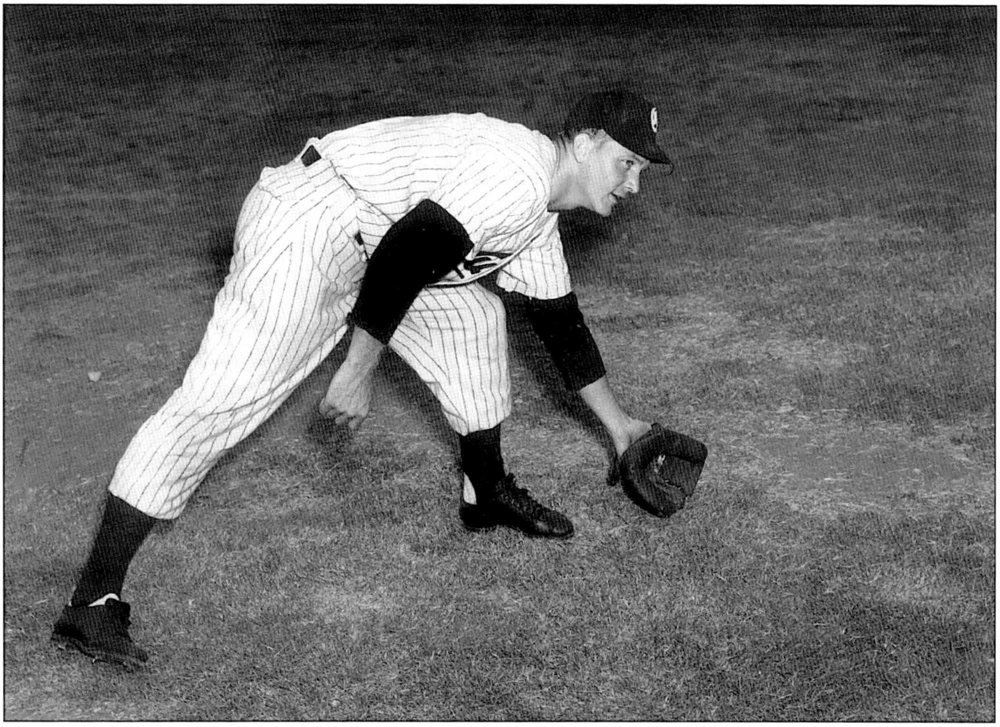

John Gardner, member of the Gainesville Owls, prepares to catch a baseball during practice in 1950. (Boyd & Breeding Collection, Morton Museum of Cooke County.)

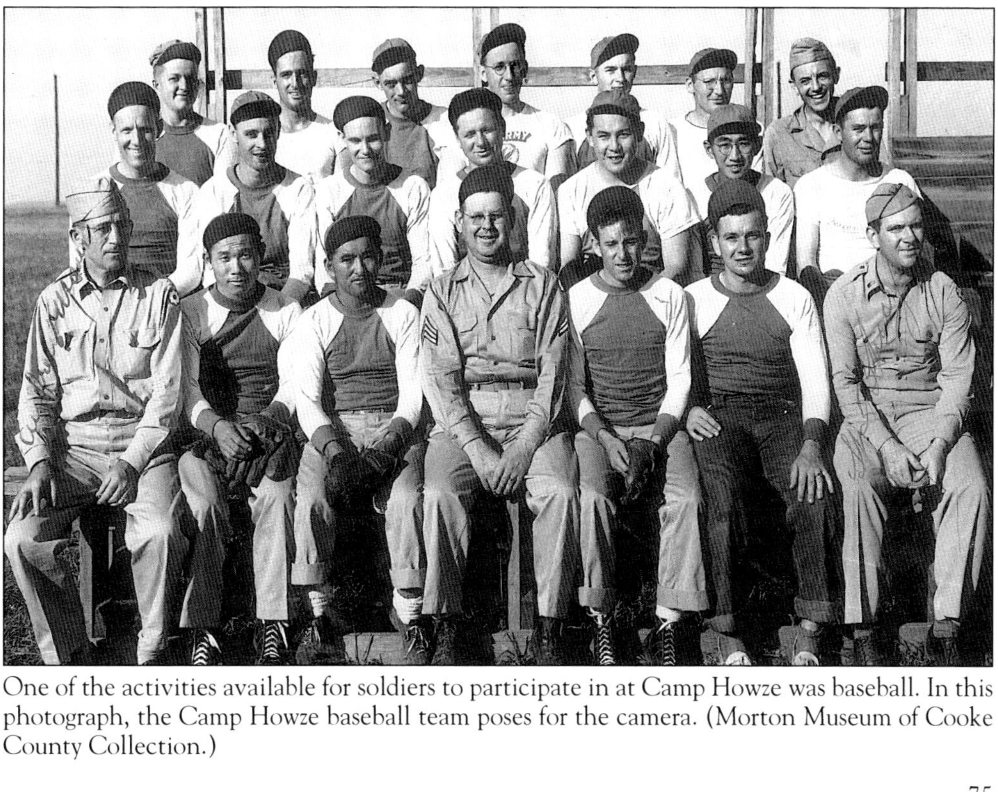

One of the activities available for soldiers to participate in at Camp Howze was baseball. In this photograph, the Camp Howze baseball team poses for the camera. (Morton Museum of Cooke County Collection.)

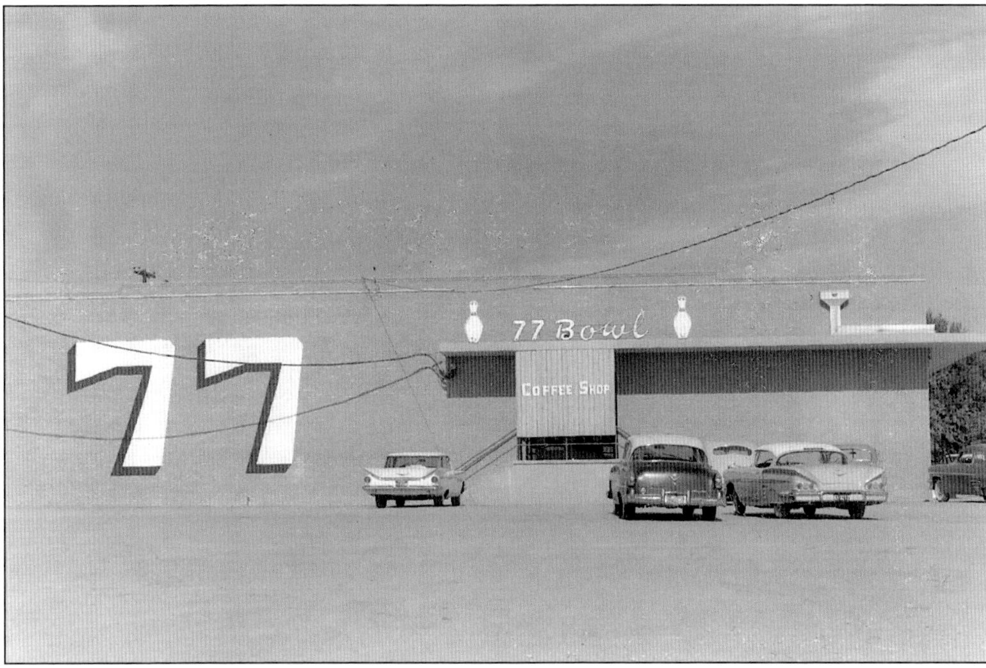

Bowling leagues thrive in Gainesville. In 1960, those wishing to bowl headed for the 77 Bowl. (Boyd & Breeding Collection, Morton Museum of Cooke County.)

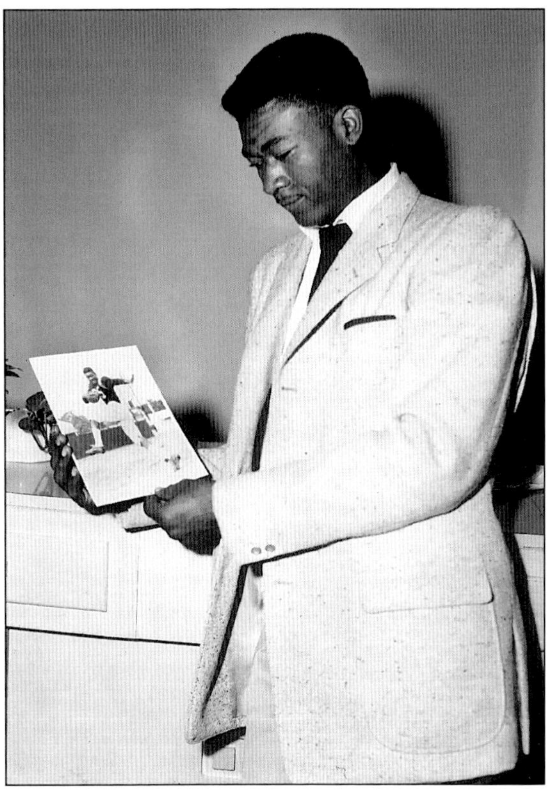

R.M. Moore holds a photograph of himself in his football uniform. Mr. Moore received a scholarship to the University of California after serving in the special services branch of the army where he played both football and baseball. (Boyd & Breeding Collection, Morton Museum of Cooke County.)

Eight

Children

While struggling with different issues over the decades, a child of the 21st century often still shares many of the same traits as a child of the 19th century.

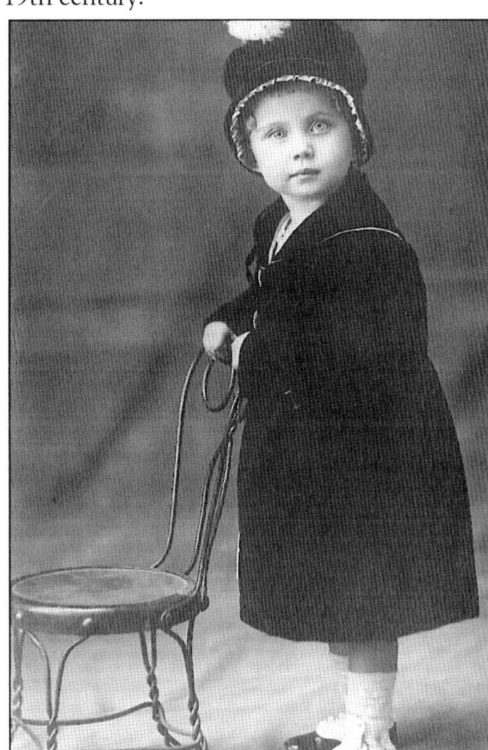

Dressed in her Sunday best, this young girl would be an adorable addition to anyone's home. The child's identity is unknown. (Morton Museum of Cooke County Collection.)

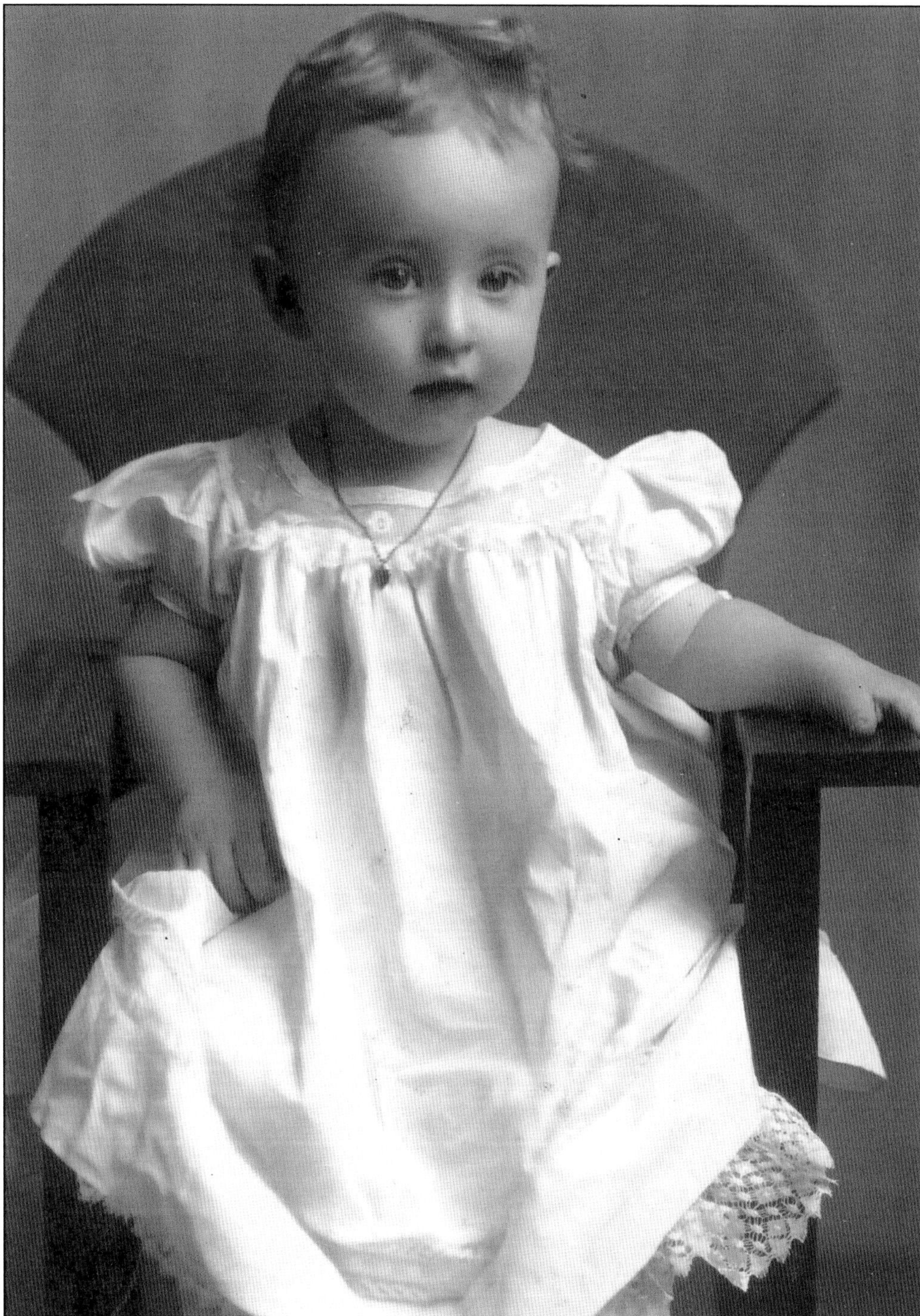

Many people look at this child and see a little girl—long dress, necklace, frilly socks, and a lacy slip all reinforce that idea. In reality, this child was a boy—Wilford Decay. For many years, a common practice involved dressing young boys to look like girls until they reached a certain age. Such was the case with Wilford. (Boyd photograph, Morton Museum of Cooke County Collection.)

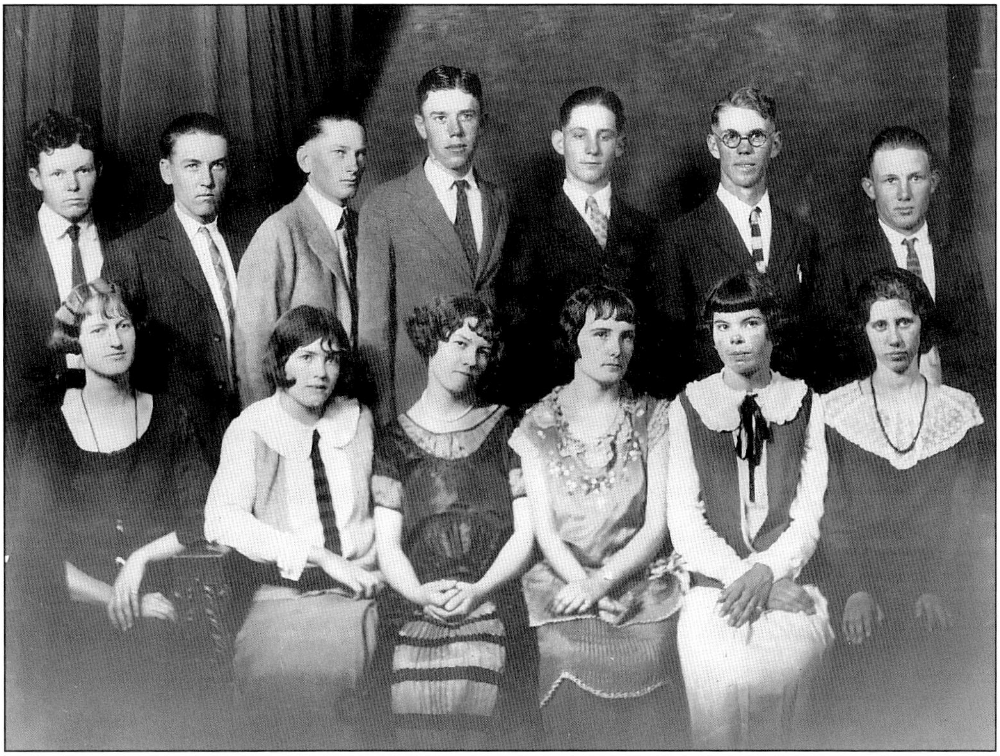

The Myra High School graduating class of 1924 included Hal Maxwell, the son of Dr. Maxwell, who operated the Palace Drug Store. Hal Maxwell is 4th from the left in the back row. (Donated by Dr. Hal Maxwell, Boyd & Breeding Collection, Morton Museum of Cooke County.)

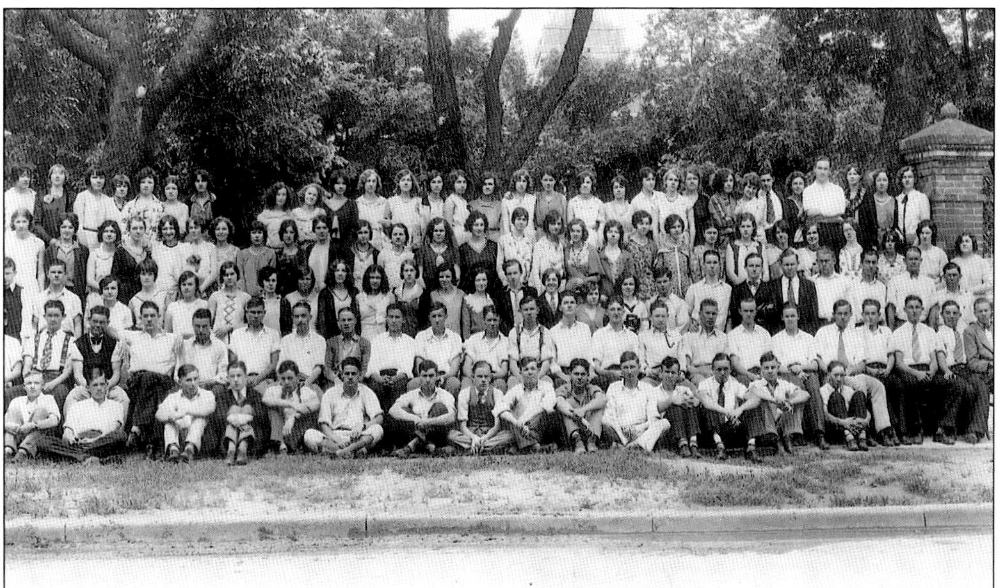

As the Great Depression began to spread across the country, the Gainesville High School graduating class of 1930 gathered outside the gate of the school for this group image. (Morton Museum of Cooke County collection.)

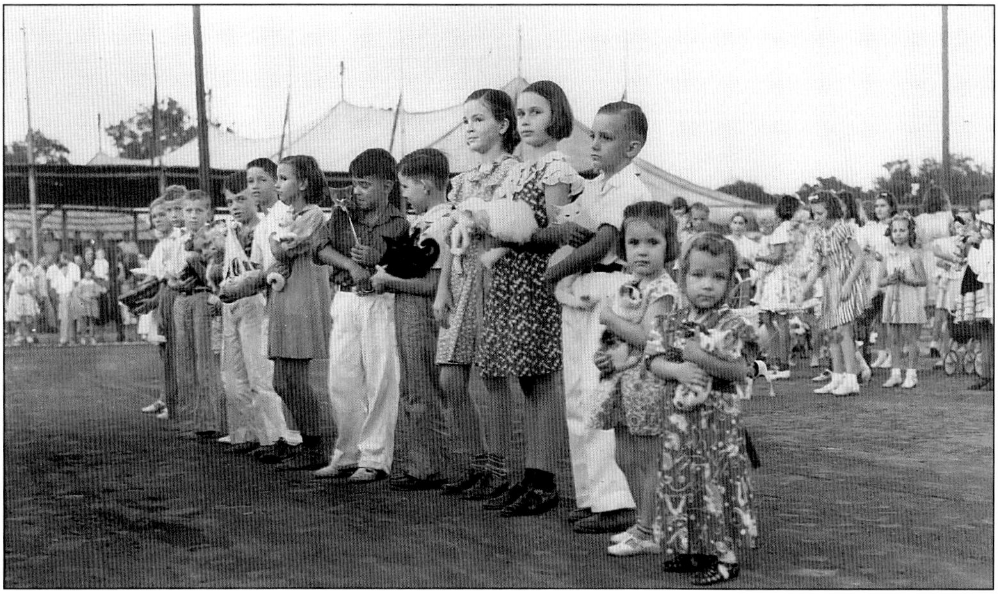

For many years during the Cooke County Fair, one of the common features was a pet and doll parade for children. In August 1939, it was reported that the "Cooke County children's Pet and Doll parade will have a true circus effect, with an elephant, Burma-horse-drawn circus wagons, and a brass band leading the long line of pets and doll entrants. All children 12 years of age or under who resided within the boundaries of the county were eligible to take part in the parade." Pictured are children preparing for the parade and judging in the 1930s. (Boyd & Breeding Collection, Morton Museum of Cooke County.)

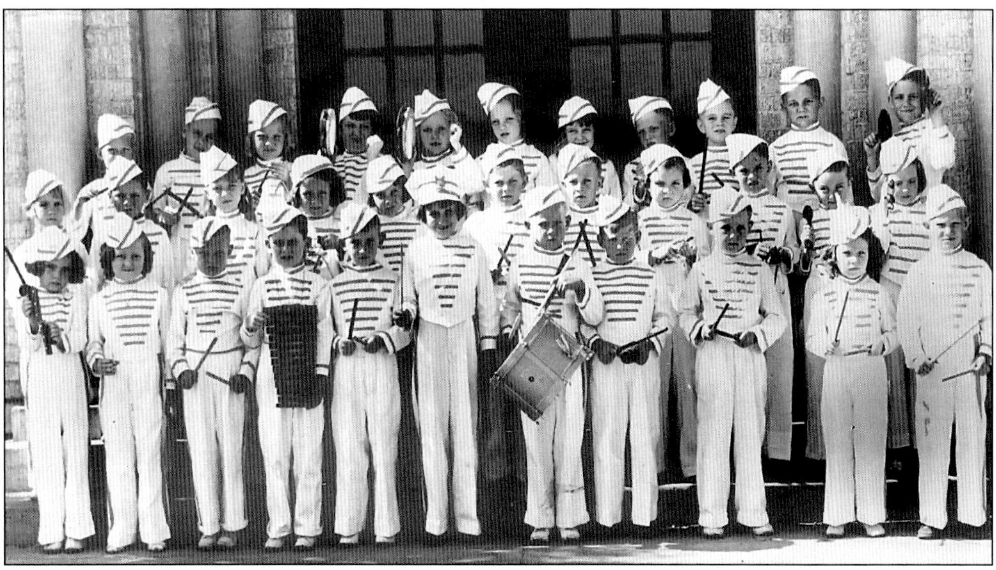

The rhythm band of Gainesville's Robert E. Lee Elementary school is pictured in this 1938 photo. Some of the members were Darlene Long, Delores Bewley, Jack Wages, Ralph Paclik, Weldon McWhirter, Maxine Hatcher, Buddy Homer, Buster Homer, ? Kitchens, Paul Booher, Dink Wilhoit, Peggy Gaston, Dorothy Ringgold, Janice Ward, Richard Helms, Pete Dennison, and Corky Holman. School rhythm bands remained popular in county schools for many years. (Donated by Paul Booher, Morton Museum of Cooke County.)

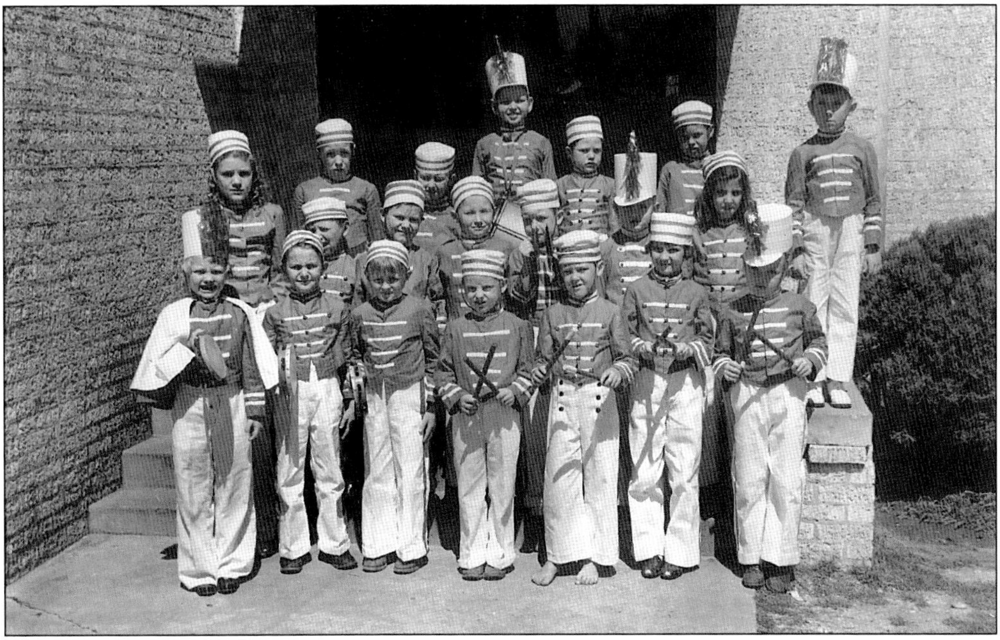

In 1942, this North School Rhythm Band in Gainesville was doing its patriotic duty. (Boyd & Breeding Collection, Morton Museum of Cooke County.)

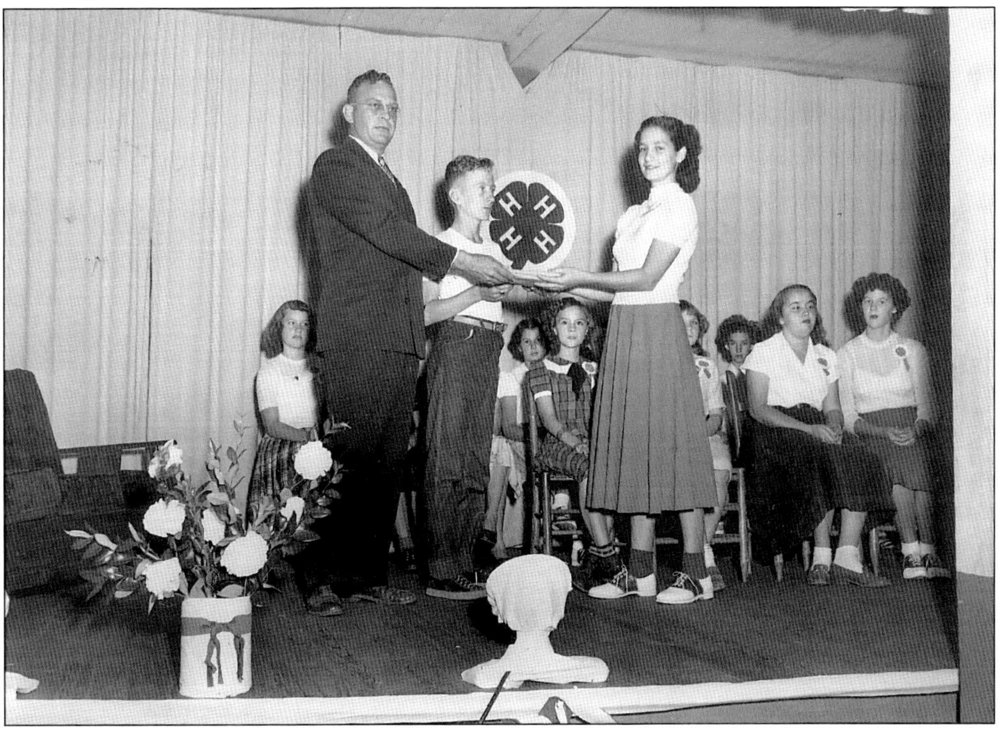

Miss Jacqueline Gunter, president of the Rad Ware 4-H girls, is shown handing "a United Nations flag made by the girls to Austin Fischer, principal of Rad Ware school and to Jerry Carroll McDaniel, president of the 4-H boys." This was part of a larger event celebrating United Nations day in October 1950. (Boyd & Breeding Collection, Morton Museum of Cooke County.)

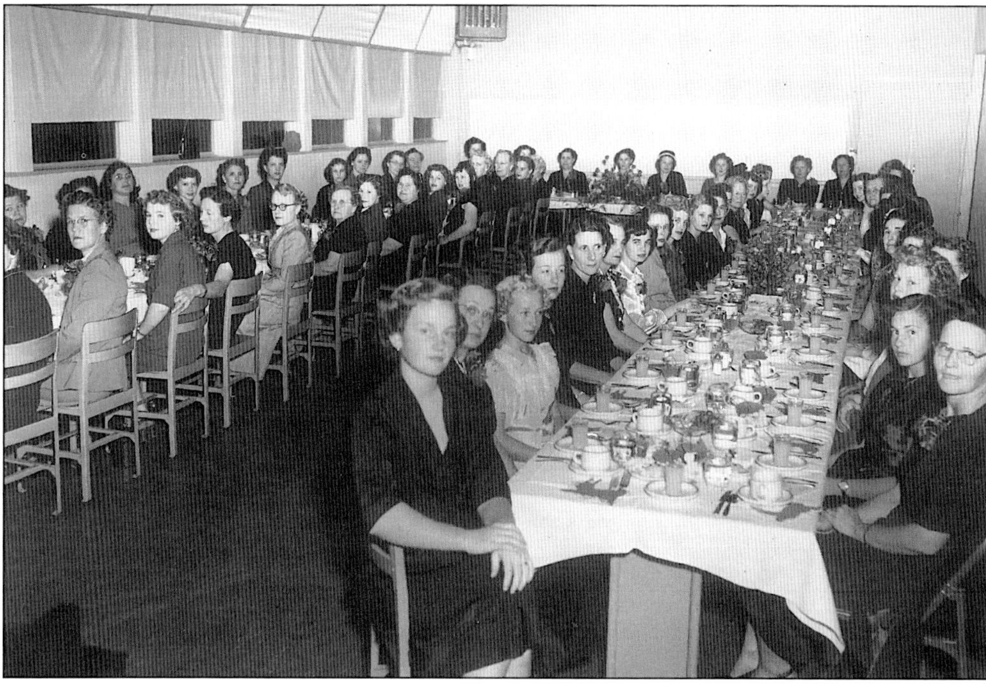

This mother-daughter banquet was held in Muenster on March 8, 1951. (Boyd & Breeding Collection, Morton Museum of Cooke County.)

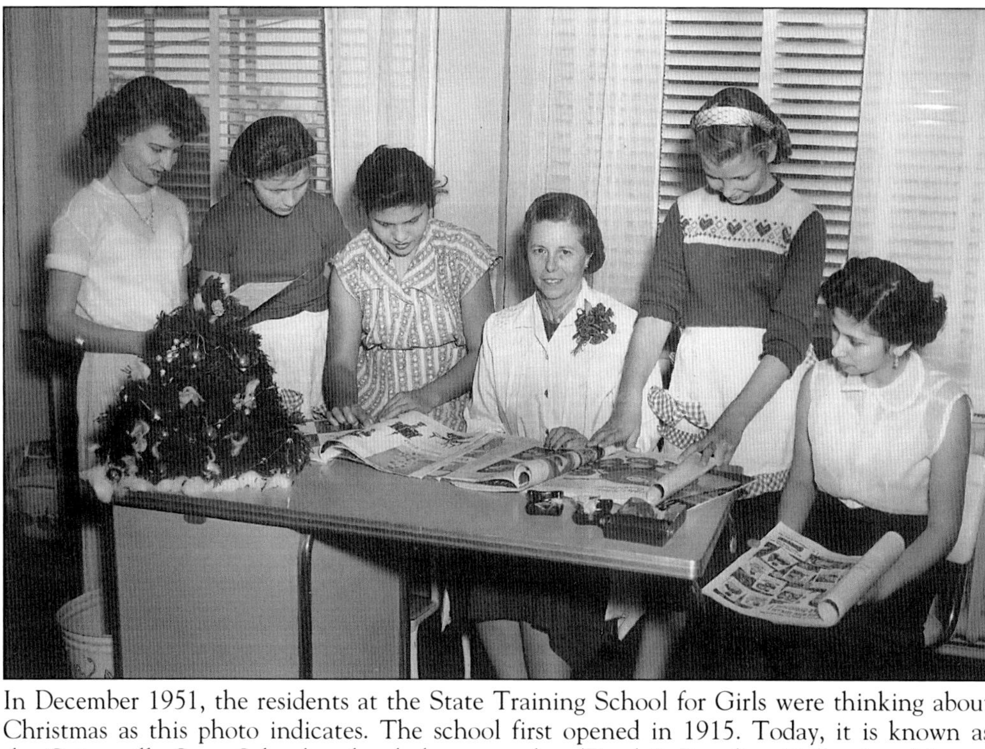

In December 1951, the residents at the State Training School for Girls were thinking about Christmas as this photo indicates. The school first opened in 1915. Today, it is known as the Gainesville State School and only houses males. (Boyd & Breeding Collection, Morton Museum of Cooke County.)

These children were two of the members of the Walnut Bend School's Rhythm Band in 1951. (Boyd & Breeding Collection, Morton Museum of Cooke County.)

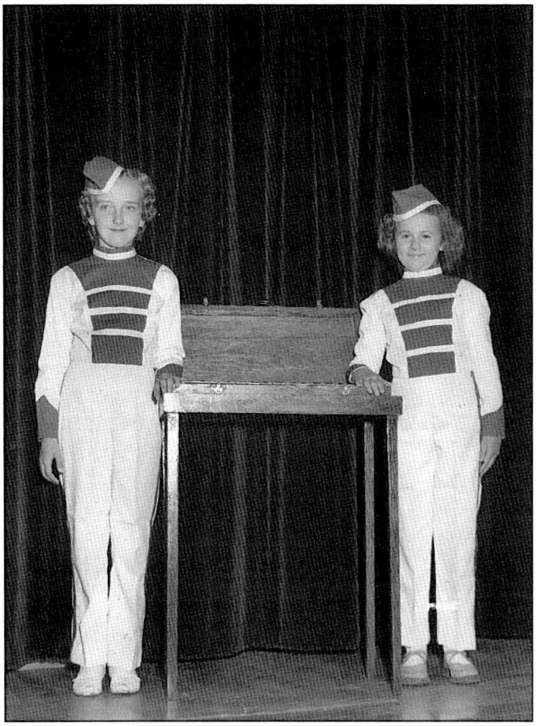

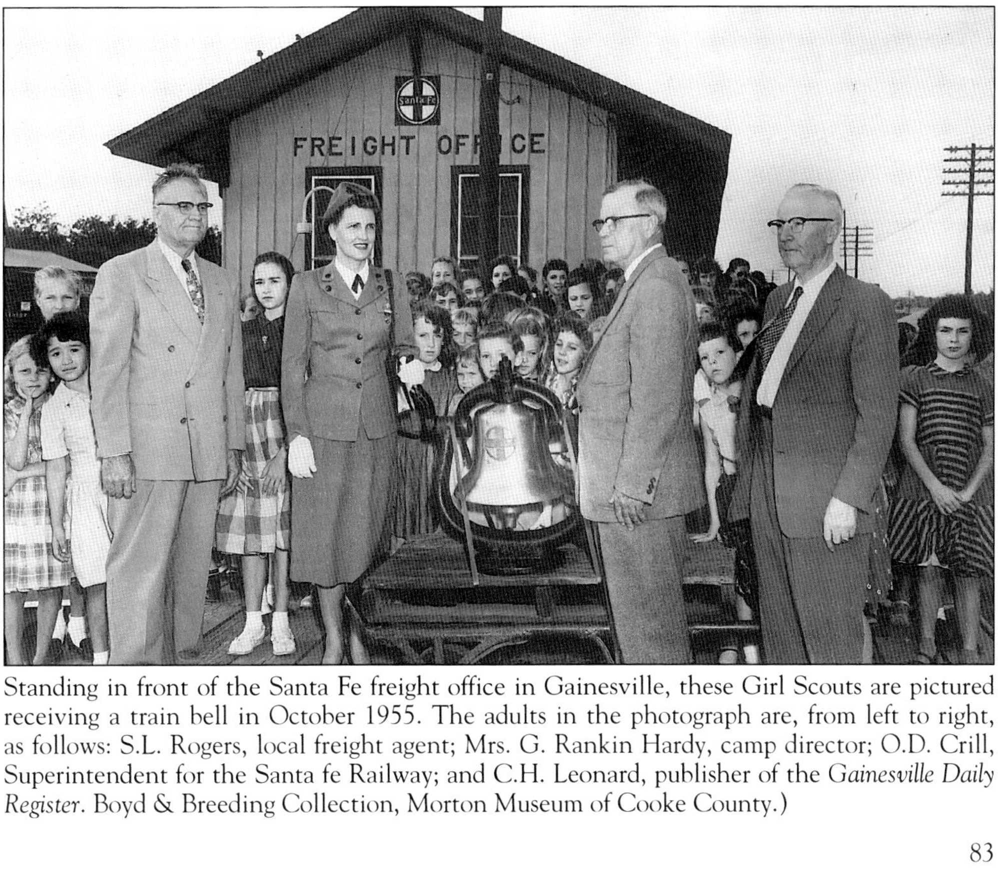

Standing in front of the Santa Fe freight office in Gainesville, these Girl Scouts are pictured receiving a train bell in October 1955. The adults in the photograph are, from left to right, as follows: S.L. Rogers, local freight agent; Mrs. G. Rankin Hardy, camp director; O.D. Crill, Superintendent for the Santa fe Railway; and C.H. Leonard, publisher of the *Gainesville Daily Register*. Boyd & Breeding Collection, Morton Museum of Cooke County.)

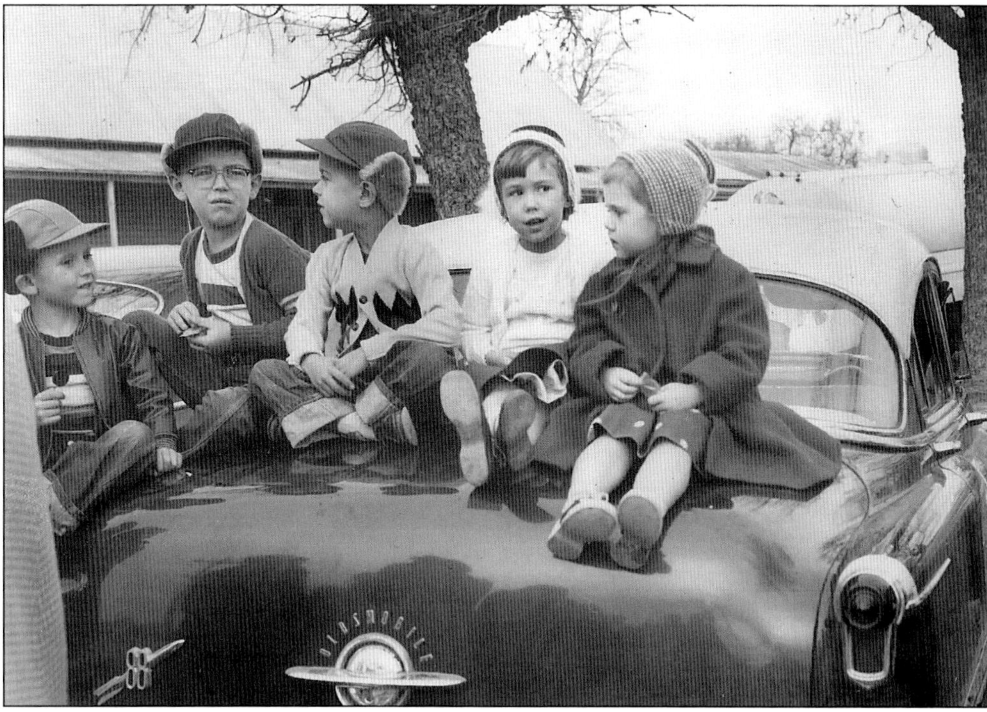

These children were eagerly awaiting the arrival of Santa Claus in Muenster in 1955. (Boyd & Breeding Collection, Morton Museum of Cooke County.)

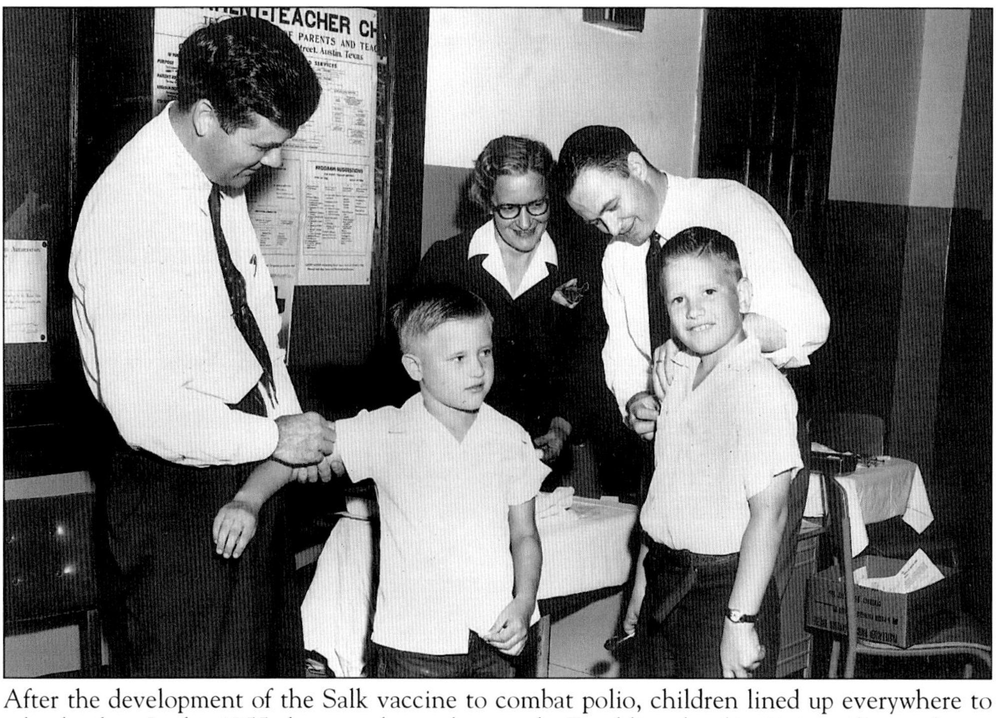

After the development of the Salk vaccine to combat polio, children lined up everywhere to take the shot. In this 1955 photograph, two boys at the Franklin school in Gainesville are shown receiving the vaccine. (Boyd & Breeding Collection, Morton Museum of Cooke County.)

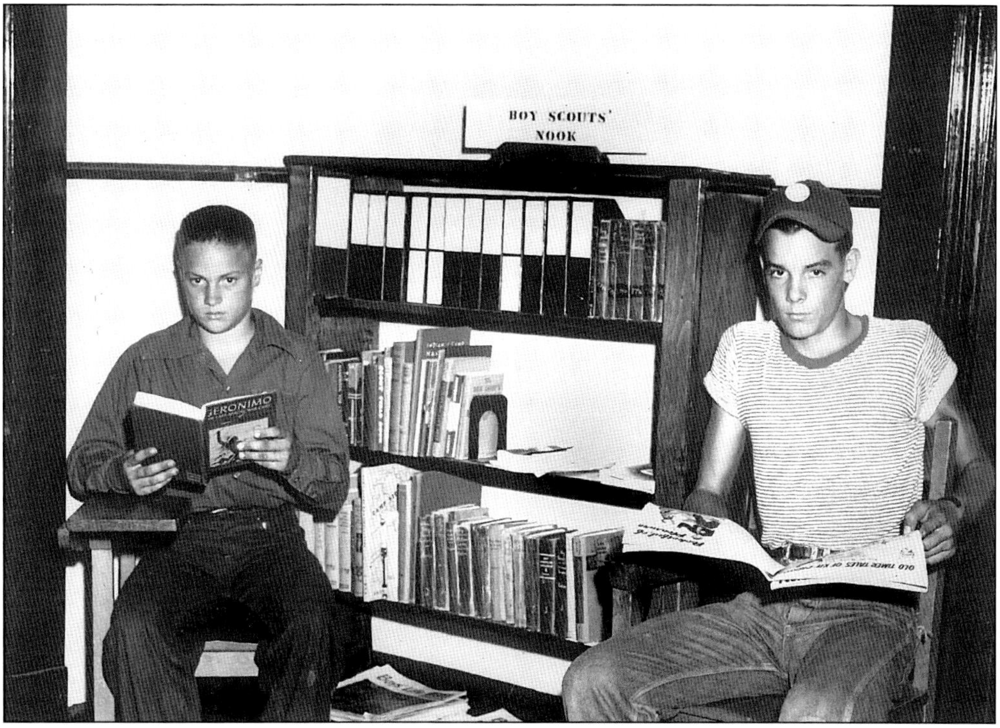

In 1955, these two boys were relaxing in the Boy Scouts' Nook in the Carnegie Public Library. (Boyd & Breeding Collection, Morton Museum of Cooke County.)

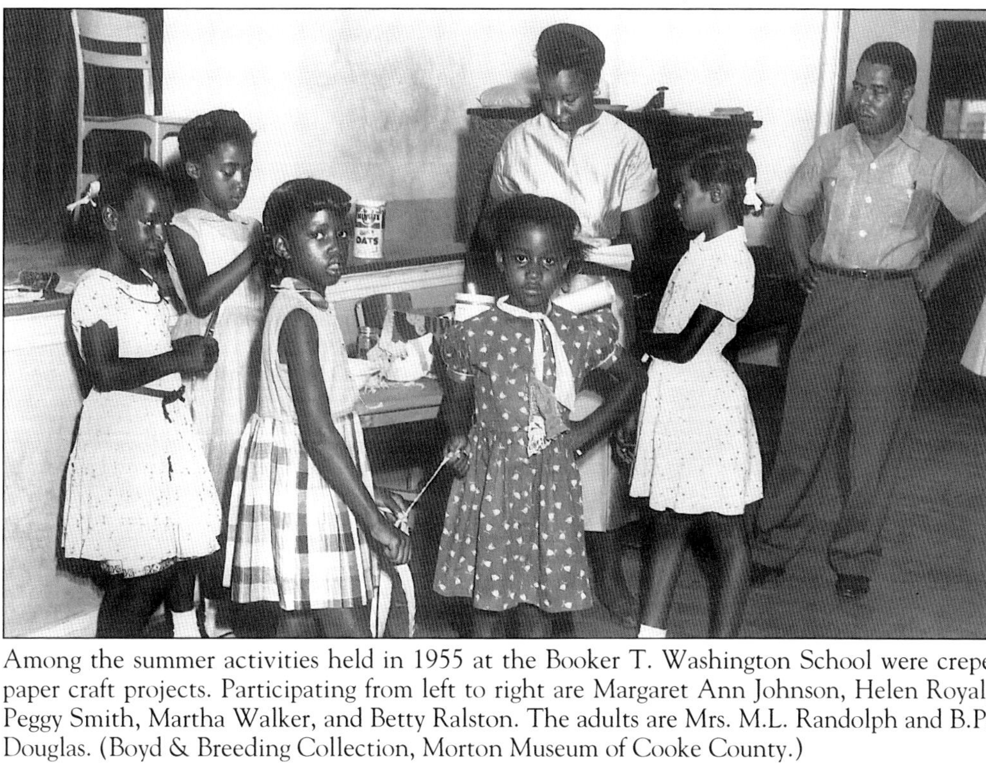

Among the summer activities held in 1955 at the Booker T. Washington School were crepe paper craft projects. Participating from left to right are Margaret Ann Johnson, Helen Royal, Peggy Smith, Martha Walker, and Betty Ralston. The adults are Mrs. M.L. Randolph and B.P. Douglas. (Boyd & Breeding Collection, Morton Museum of Cooke County.)

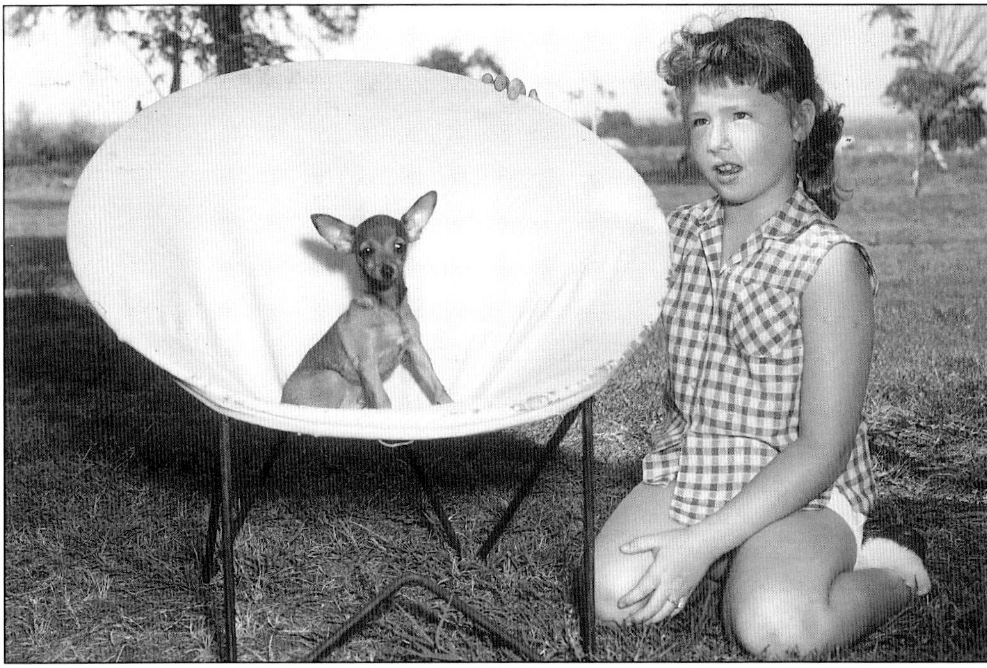

Priscilla Sallee won first prize with this puppy in a pet parade in 1957. (Boyd & Breeding Collection, Morton Museum of Cooke County.)

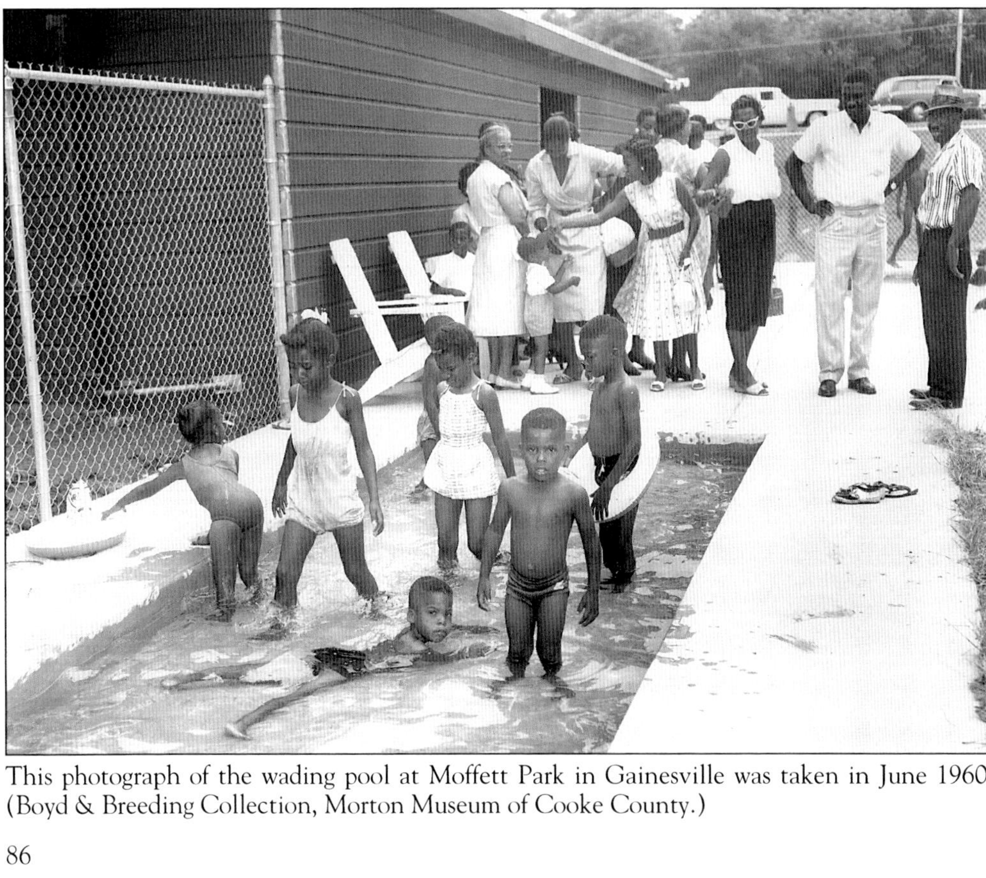

This photograph of the wading pool at Moffett Park in Gainesville was taken in June 1960. (Boyd & Breeding Collection, Morton Museum of Cooke County.)

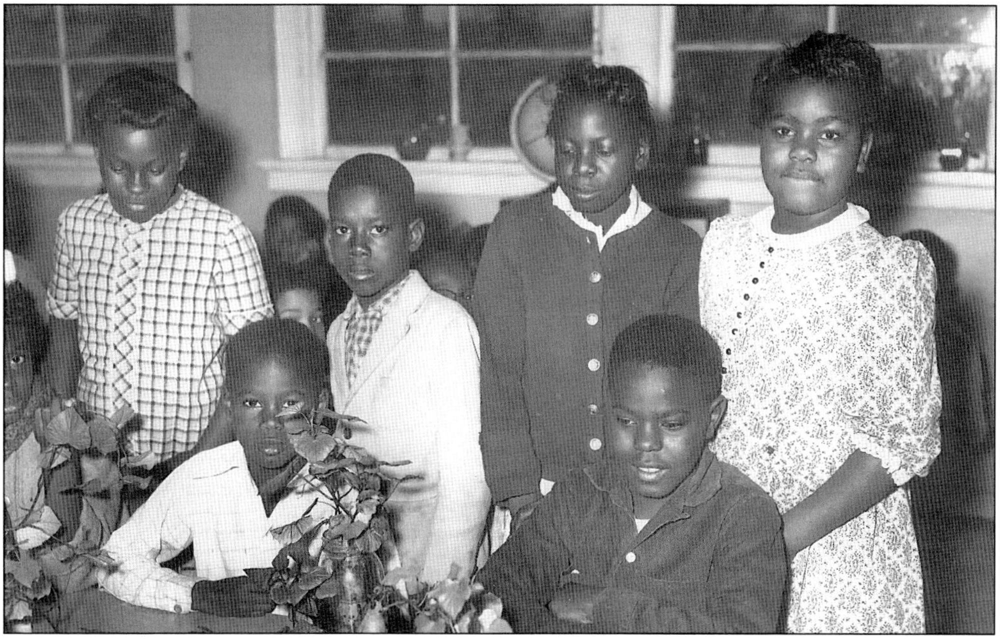

These Booker T. Washington students were studying nature in their science class in February 1960. (Boyd & Breeding Collection, Morton Museum of Cooke County.)

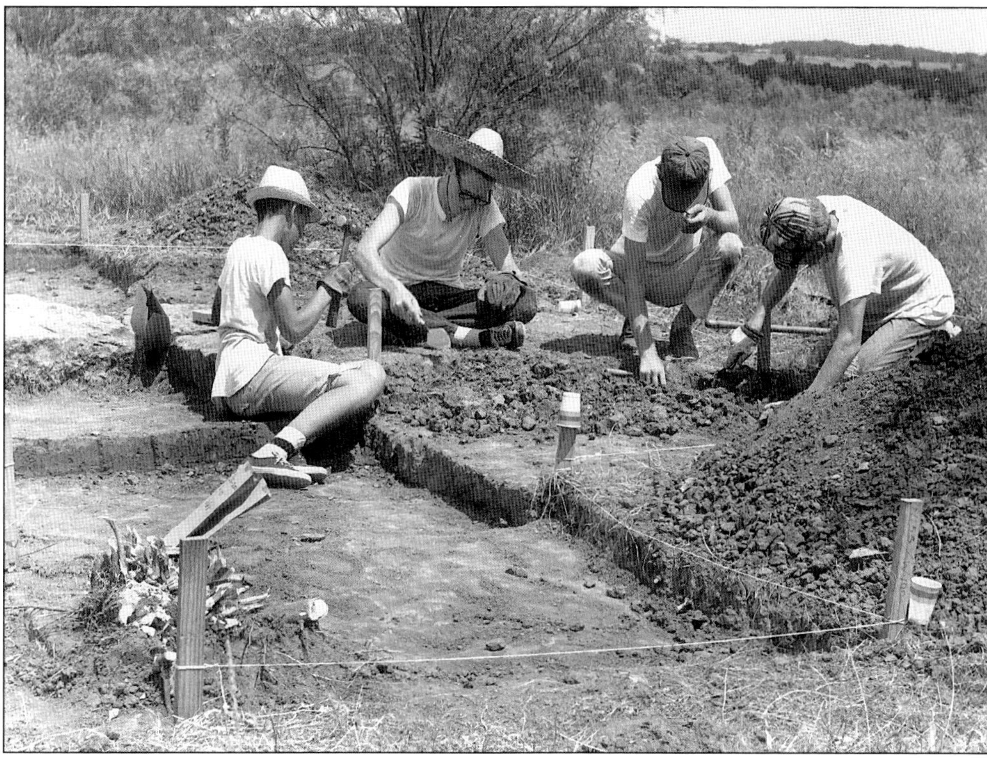

In the late 1960s, the Morton Museum of Cooke County sponsored an archaeological dig at the site of Fort Fitzhugh, the first site of settlement in what became Cooke County. The boys seen here were part of that project. (Morton Museum of Cooke County Collection.)

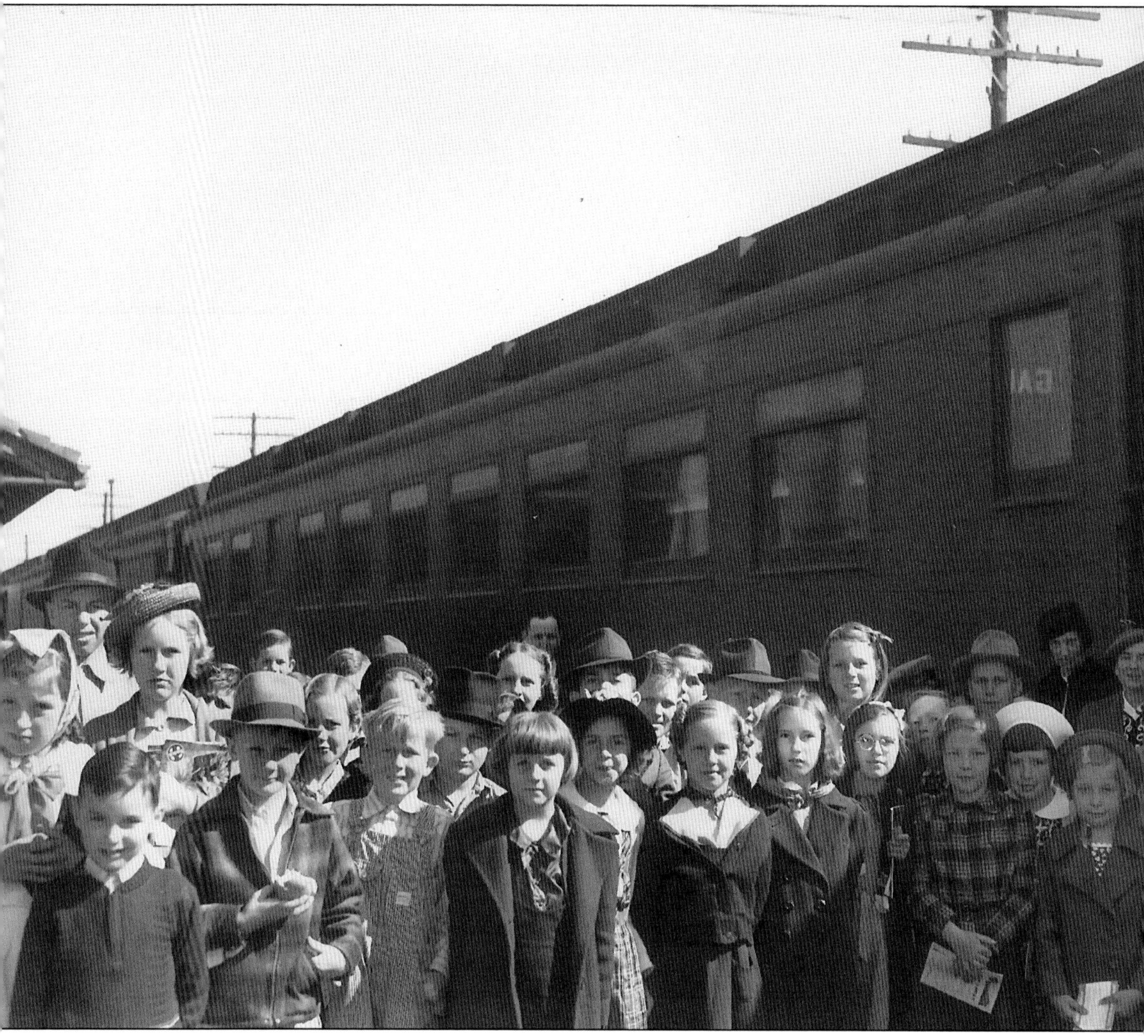

These children were on a field trip from school when they visited the Santa Fe depot in Gainesville during the late 1930s. (Morton Museum of Cooke County Collection.)

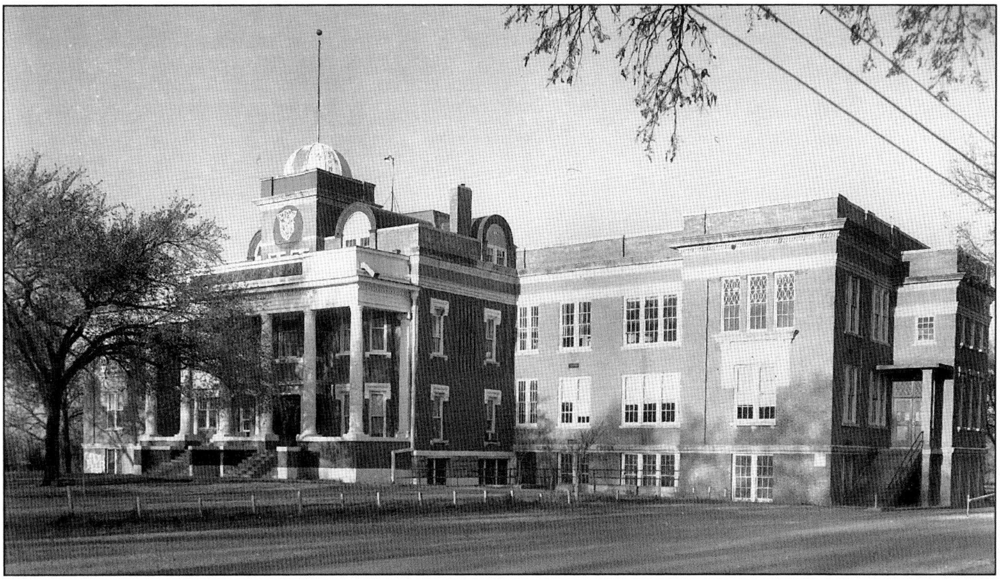

Originally erected as a private home by Senator Joseph Weldon Bailey, this house was later sold to W.H. Dougherty who, in turn, gave it to the city of Gainesville to be converted into a high school. At that point, wings were added to the house and it opened as the Newsome Dougherty Memorial High School. It served as the high school for almost 40 years. (Morton Museum of Cooke County Collection.)

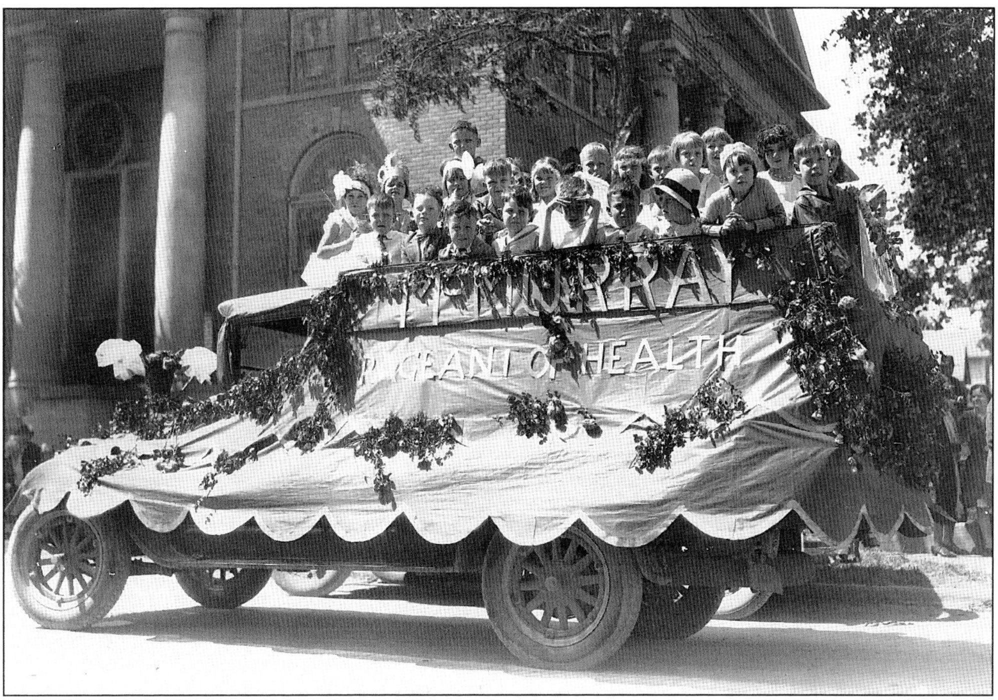

High atop a Model T, these children from McMurray Elementary School were traveling west on California street *c.* 1915, when this photograph was snapped. The words under McMurray read "Pageant of Health." The building in the background was the Whaley Memorial Methodist Church. (Courtesy of Margaret Hays.)

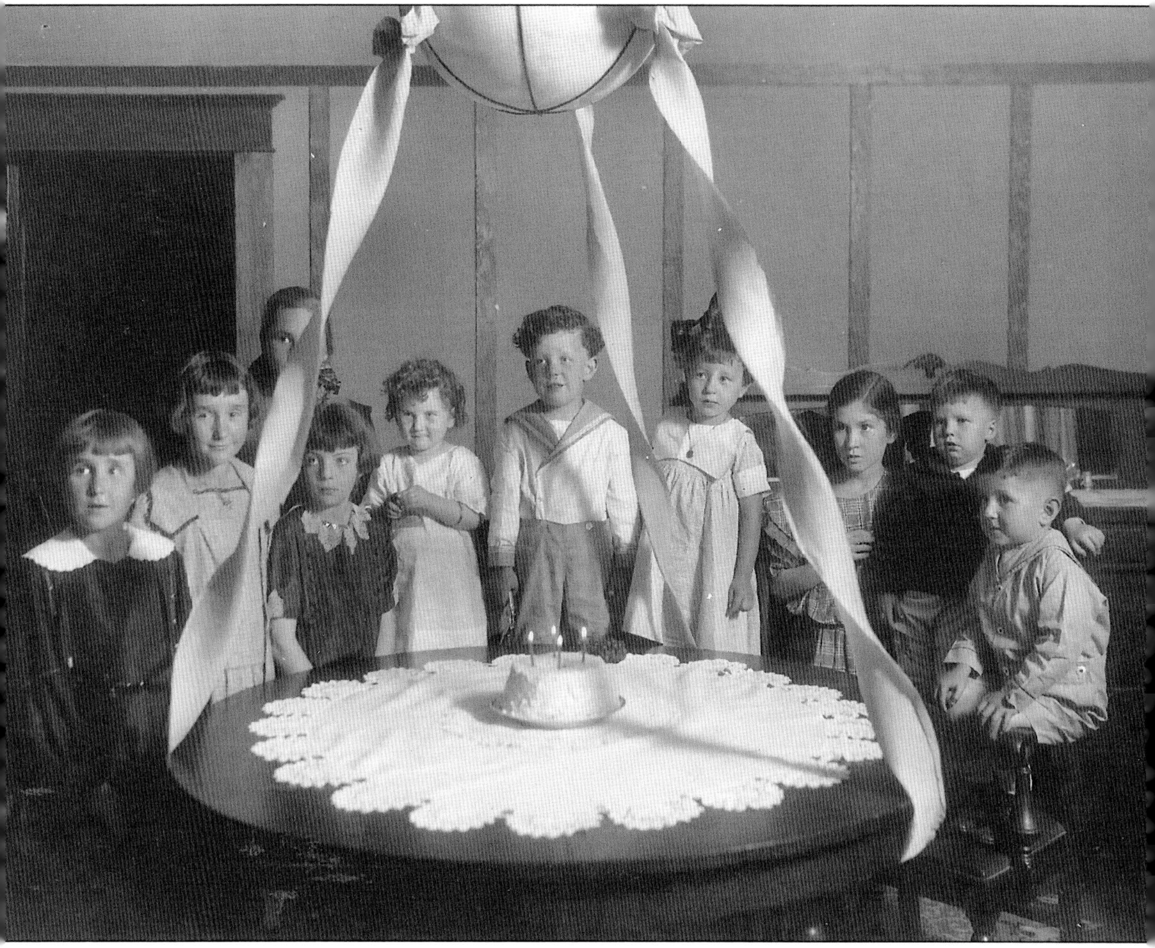

Young Mister Ralph Breeding stands in the center of this photograph. Helping him to celebrate his fourth birthday were, among others, Margaret, Estelle, and Louanna Hays, the girls at the extreme left. Ralph Breeding was the son of Guy Breeding. (Courtesy of Margaret Hays.)

Nine

The Ties that Bind Us Together

From the very beginning, residents joined together to improve life in the county. Over time, people constructed churches, organized libraries, theaters, a museum, a community college, a zoo, a hometown circus, planned centennial celebrations, parks, and more. A variety of activities, concerns, passions, and enterprises continue to bind county residents together.

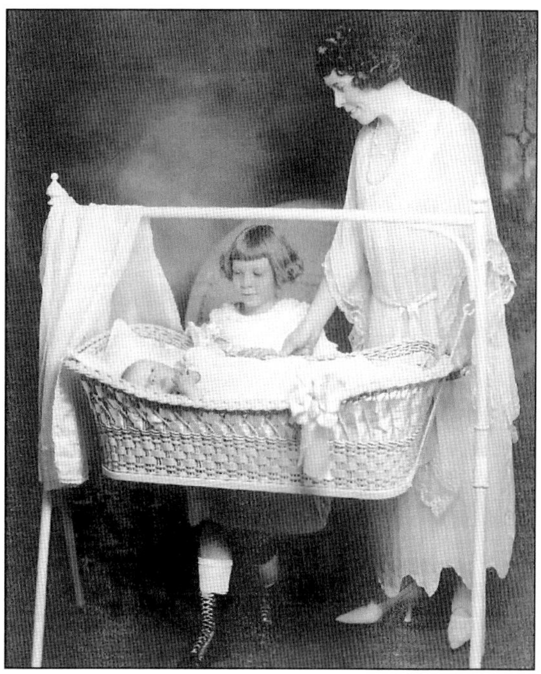

In this early 20th century scene, a young mother and child stare lovingly at a baby in a wicker bassinet—a scene anyone could relate to no matter what century in which they reside. The identities of the people are unknown. (Morton Museum of Cooke County Collection.)

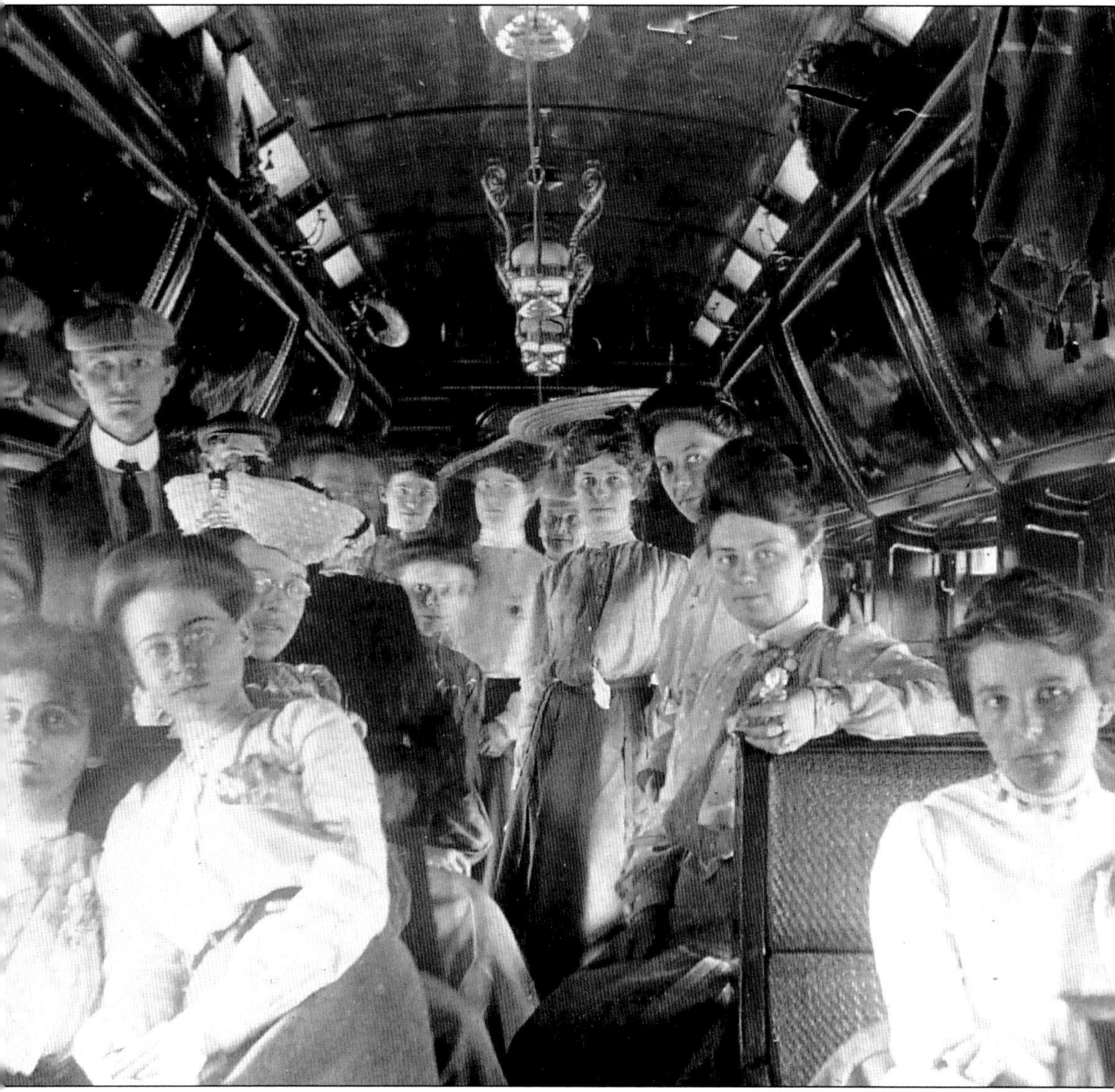

The Epworth League was the young peoples' group of the Methodist Episcopal Church South. From July 16–19, 1903, a national meeting of the Epworth League was held in Detroit. Members of the local group boarded a train to attend that convention. One member was Ianna Jones, and this photograph was taken during that journey. She is pictured in this photo, sitting by herself and staring into the camera. (Courtesy of Margaret Hays.)

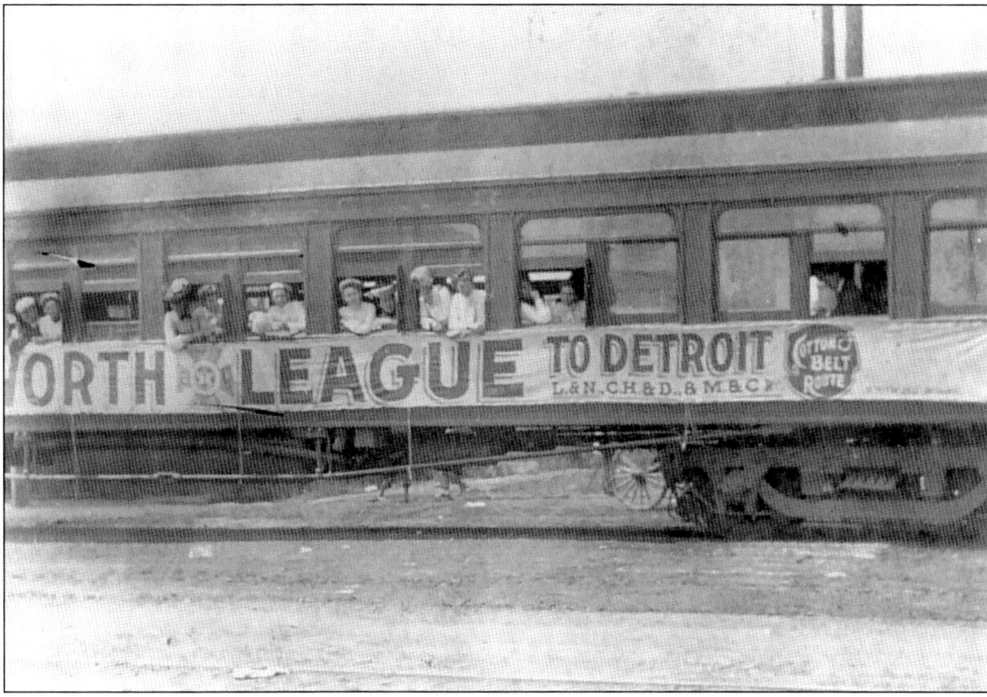

These photographs were taken during the train trip made by Ianna Jones, en route to the Epworth League Convention in Detroit in 1903. (Courtesy of Margaret Hays.)

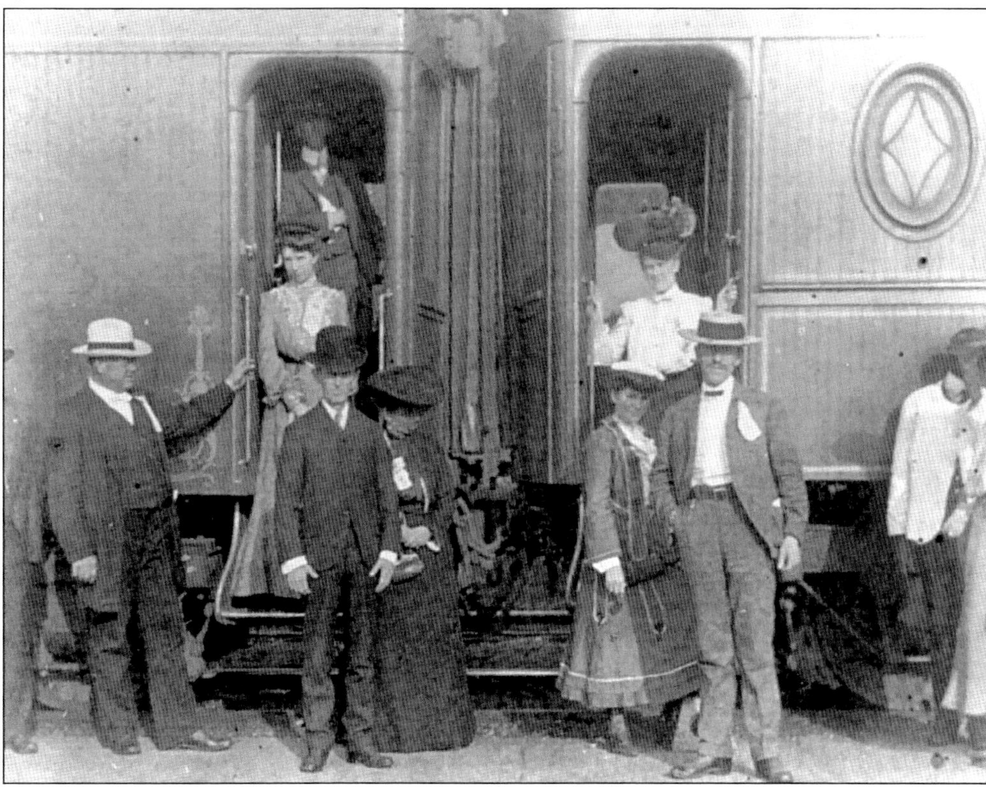

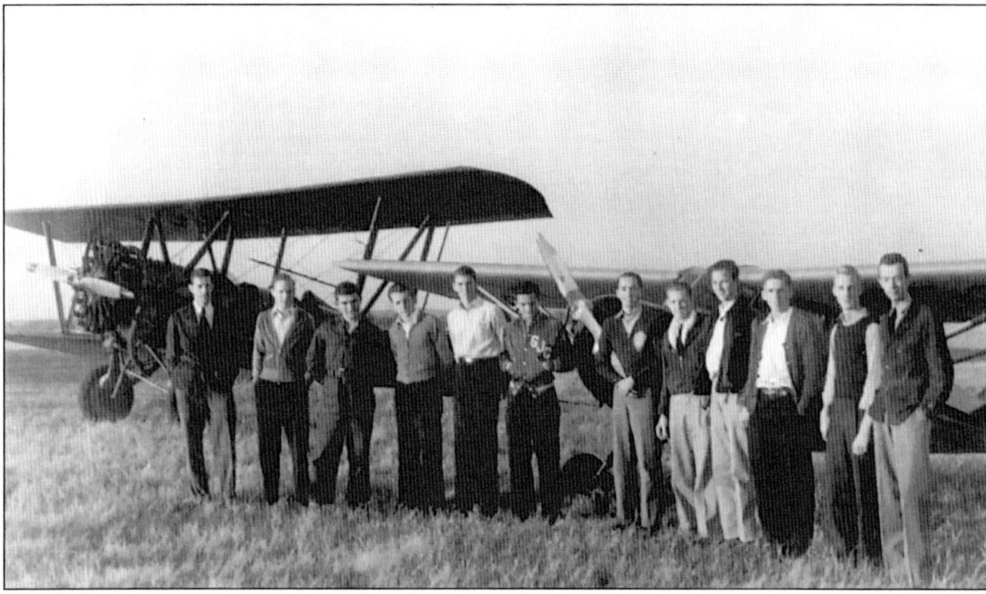

In this photograph, the men standing in front of the planes were members of the first Civilian Pilot Training Program class at the Gainesville Junior College. The class was conducted between the fall of 1939 and May, 1940. Pictured, from left to right, are as follows: John Parker (Instructor Ground School), Hugh McCain Jr., Clyde Cribley, Jack Merrick, Bob Werse, Dean Copeland, unknown, Verne Bivin, Bob Solomon, Paul Giraudin Jr., Wallace McDaniel, and Eugene G. DeBullet (Flight Instructor and owner of Red River Flying Service). (Courtesy of Jack Merrick.)

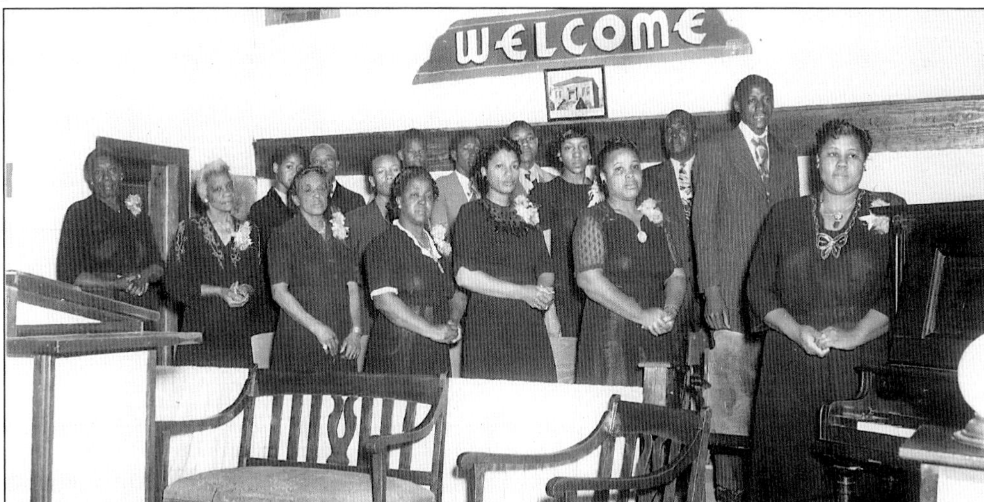

In 1948, the Mt. Olive First Baptist Church radio choir did a broadcast every Sunday afternoon from 1:00 to 1:30. Pictured from left to right, are as follows: (first row) Frankie Kendrick, Allie M. Terrell, Malissa Walla, Jennie M. Adams, Daisy Dennis, Bertha Pollard, and Violan Carbin (the minister's wife and a musician). In the back row, from left to right, are: Floyd Manuel, Travis Gooden, Donald Woody, Weldon Monroe, Alonzo Williams, Andrew Groner, Pinky Franks, Soloman Pollard, and Milton Proby. (Boyd & Breeding Collection, Morton Museum of Cooke County.)

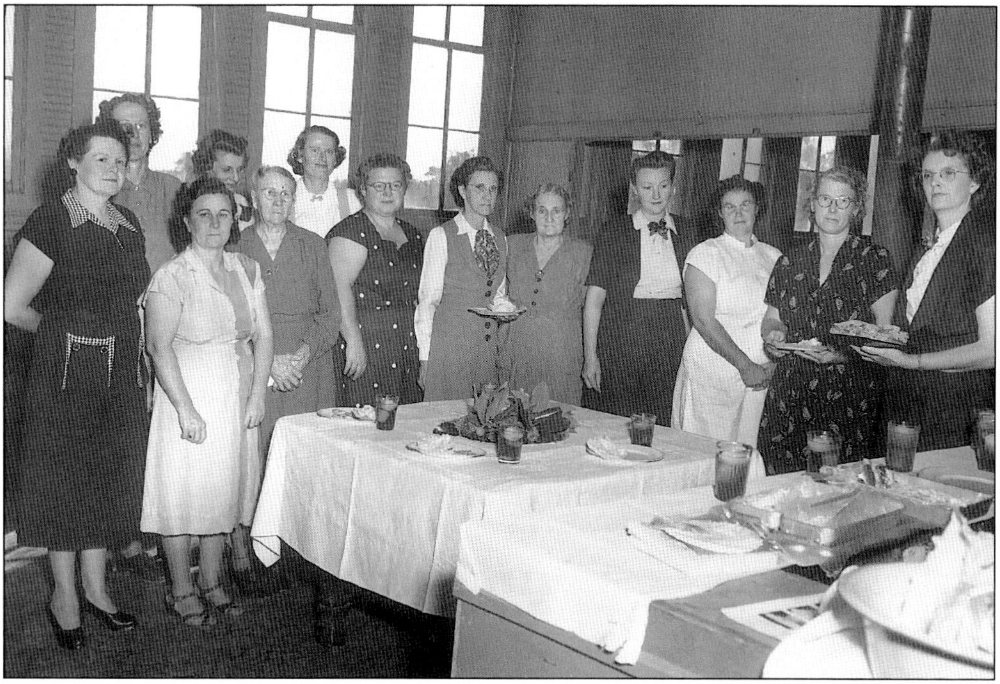

In 1951, these ladies of the Dye School Home Demonstration Club gathered for a meeting and refreshments. (Boyd &Breeding Collection, Morton Museum of Cooke County.)

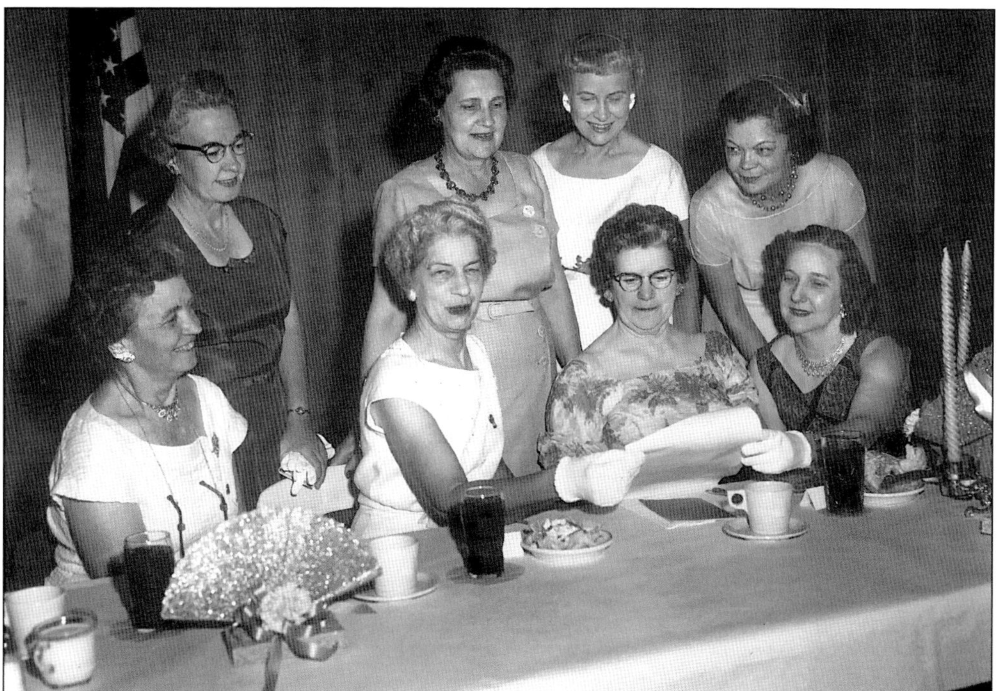

In July 1954, the new officers of the Soroptimists were installed. Mrs. Frank Dustin was president. Note that the women are either wearing or carrying gloves—a must in that time period for women. (Boyd & Breeding Collection, Morton Museum of Cooke County.)

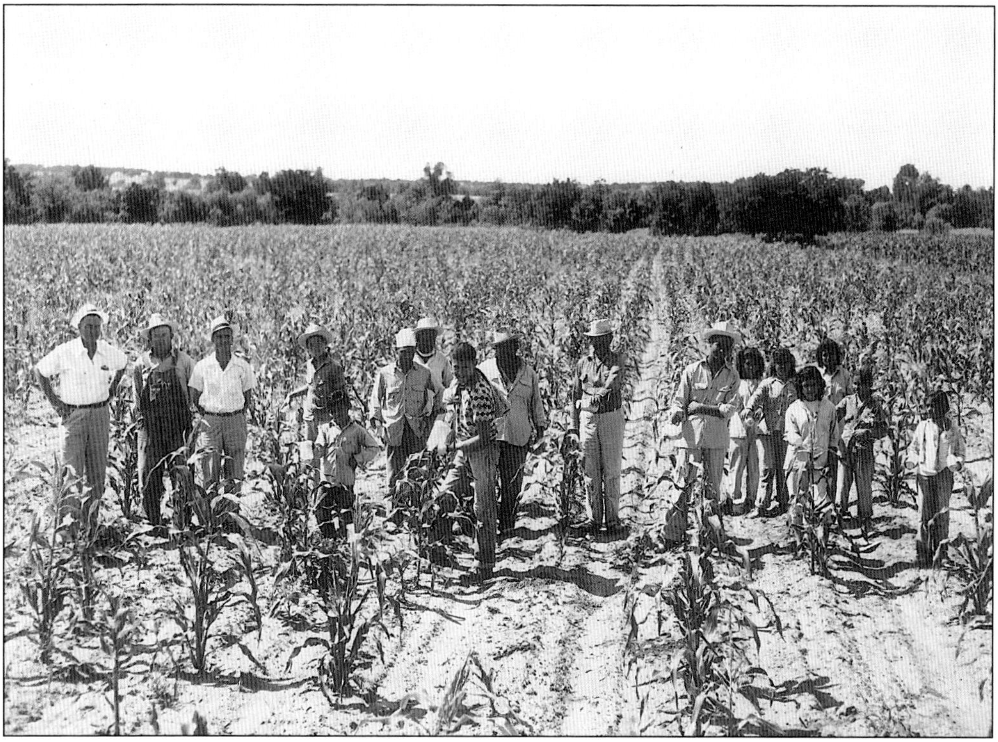

Farming represents one thread that ties Cooke County in the 21st century to its past in the 19th century. In 1952, as shown in these snapshots, Mexican farm laborers were at work in one of the fields in the county. (Boyd & Breeding Collection, Morton Museum of Cooke County.)

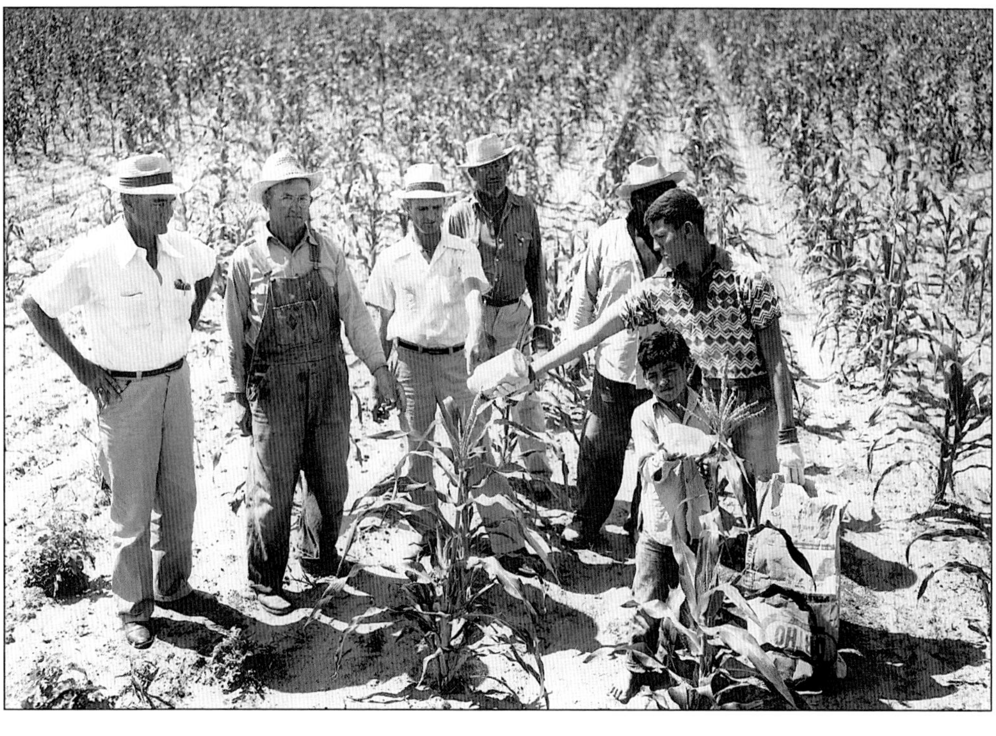

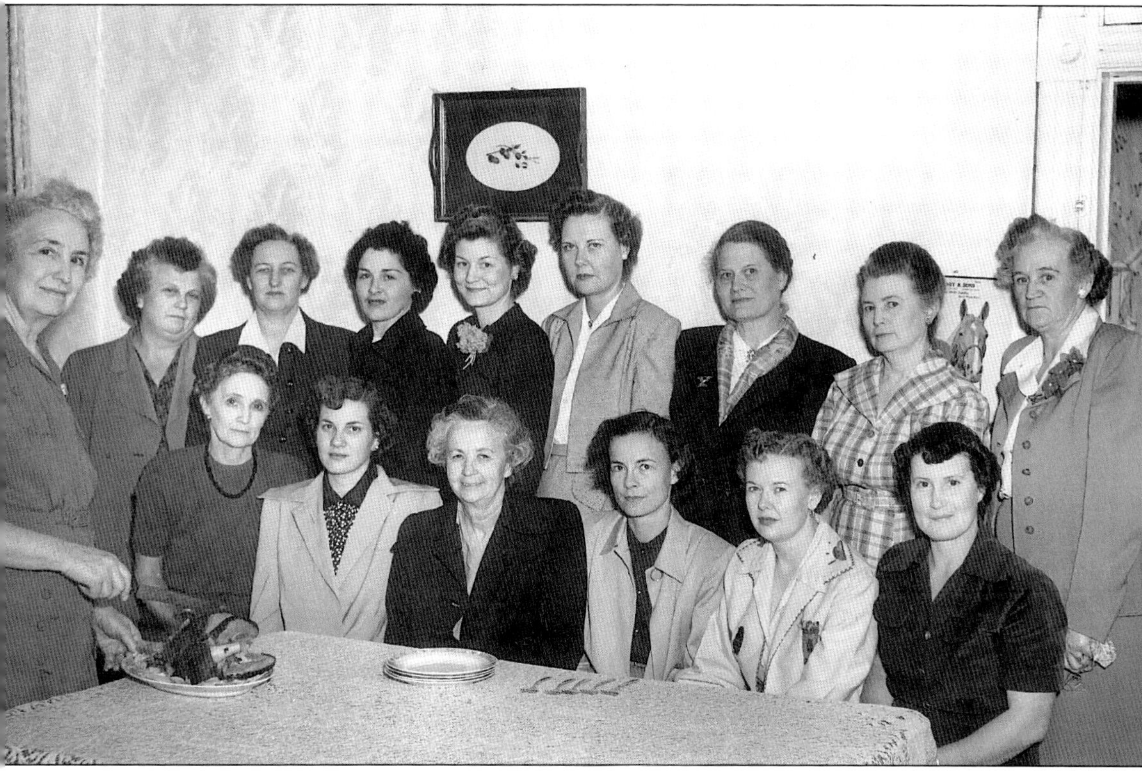

These members of the Valley View Home Demonstration Club posed for this photograph in 1952. (Boyd & Breeding Collection, Morton Museum of Cooke County.)

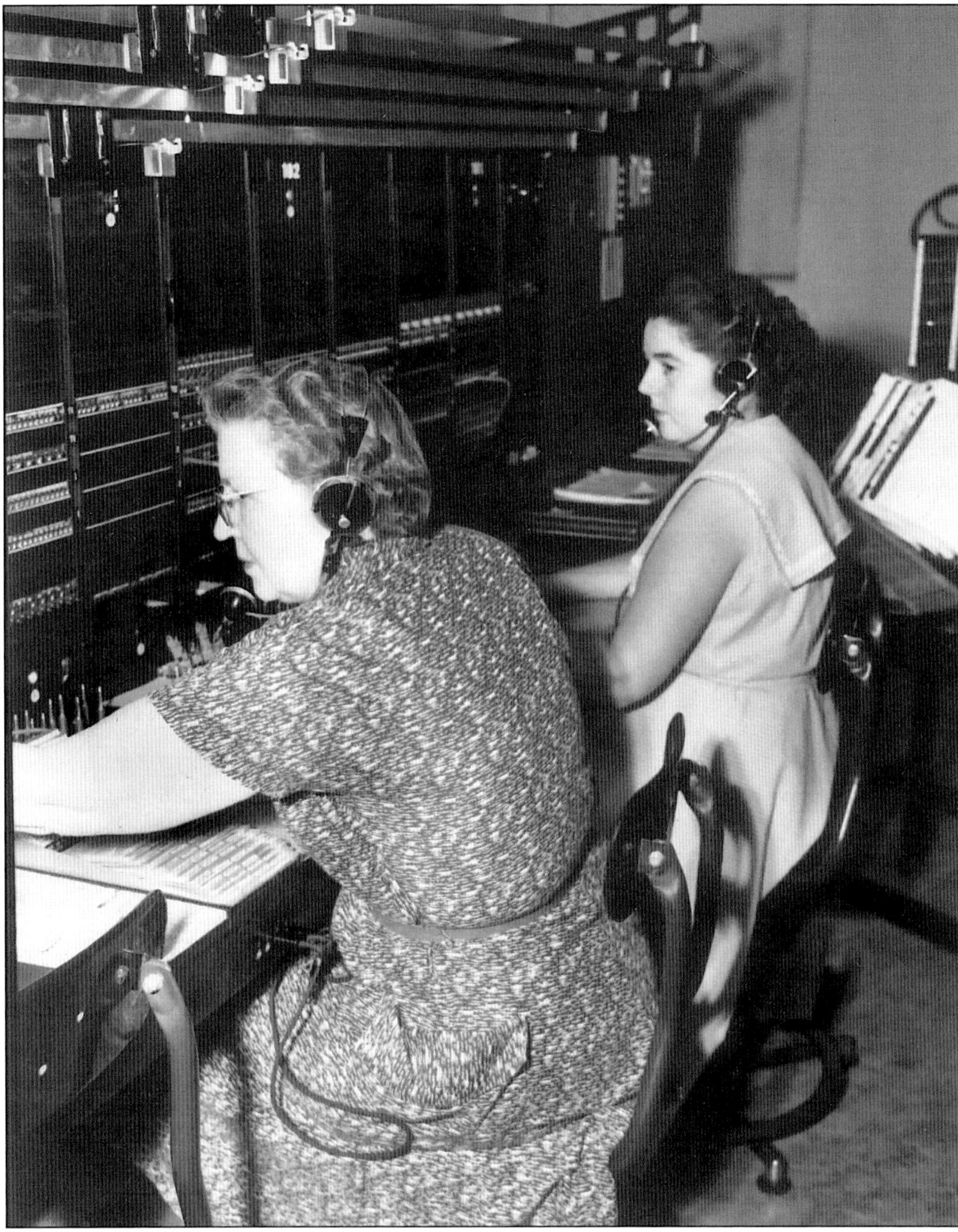

These telephone operators—Miss Freida Johnson and Mrs. Betty Wheelock—were hard at work binding the county together in 1955 when they were captured at their job in this picture. (Boyd & Breeding Collection, Morton Museum of Cooke County.)

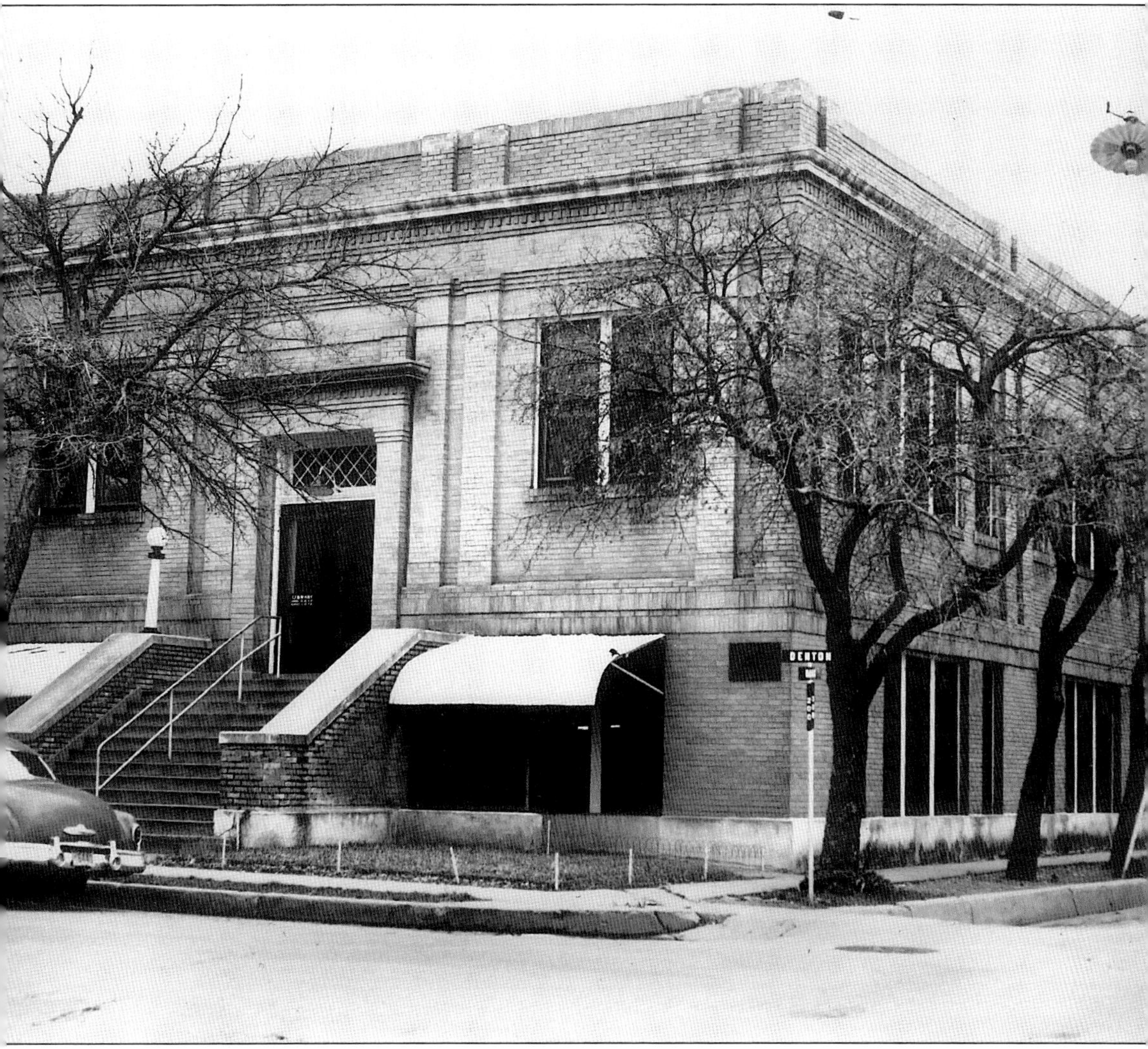

The Carnegie Library in Gainesville was constructed in 1914, primarily through the hard work of Lillian Gunter and the XLI club. It served as the public library for many years before a new structure was constructed. Currently, the old Carnegie Library houses the Butterfield Stage Theater and the Arts Council. (Boyd & Breeding Collection, Morton Museum of Cooke County.)

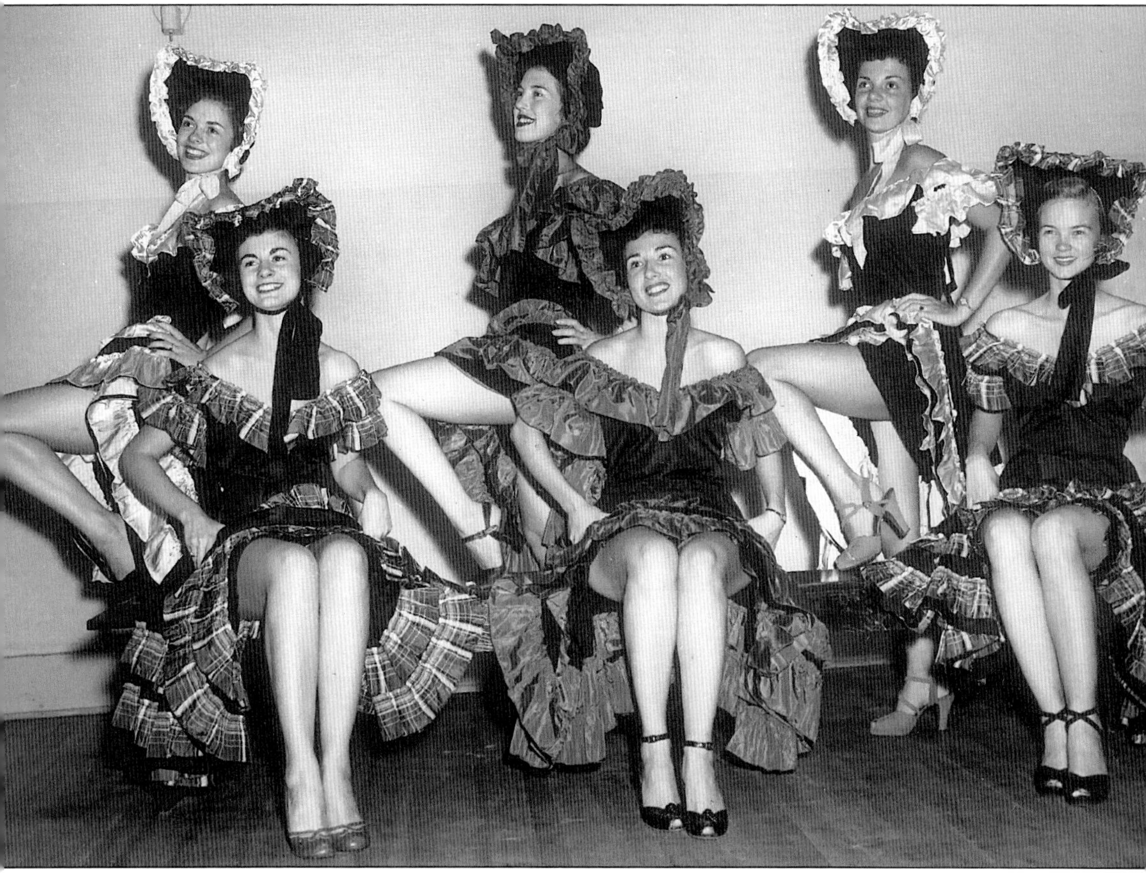

During the Gainesville Centennial celebration in 1950, these Can Can girls performed in the Progressorama, a pageant celebrating and telling the story of Gainesville's history. The Can Can girls were, from left to right, as follows: Paula Collins, Betty Collins, Mary McCann, Barbara Lynch, Margaret Lynch, and Betty Gunter. (Boyd & Breeding Collection, Morton Museum of Cooke County.)

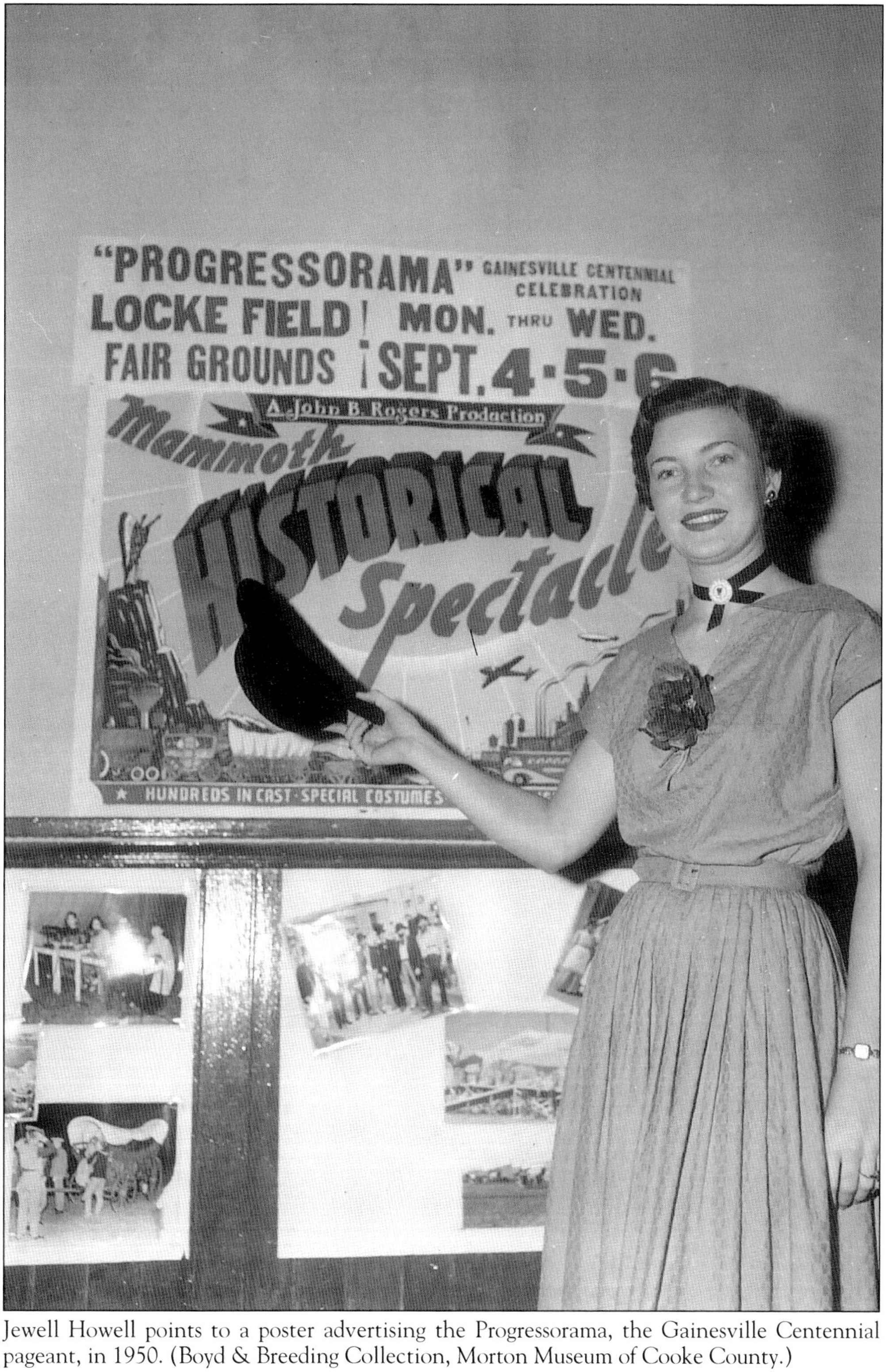

Jewell Howell points to a poster advertising the Progressorama, the Gainesville Centennial pageant, in 1950. (Boyd & Breeding Collection, Morton Museum of Cooke County.)

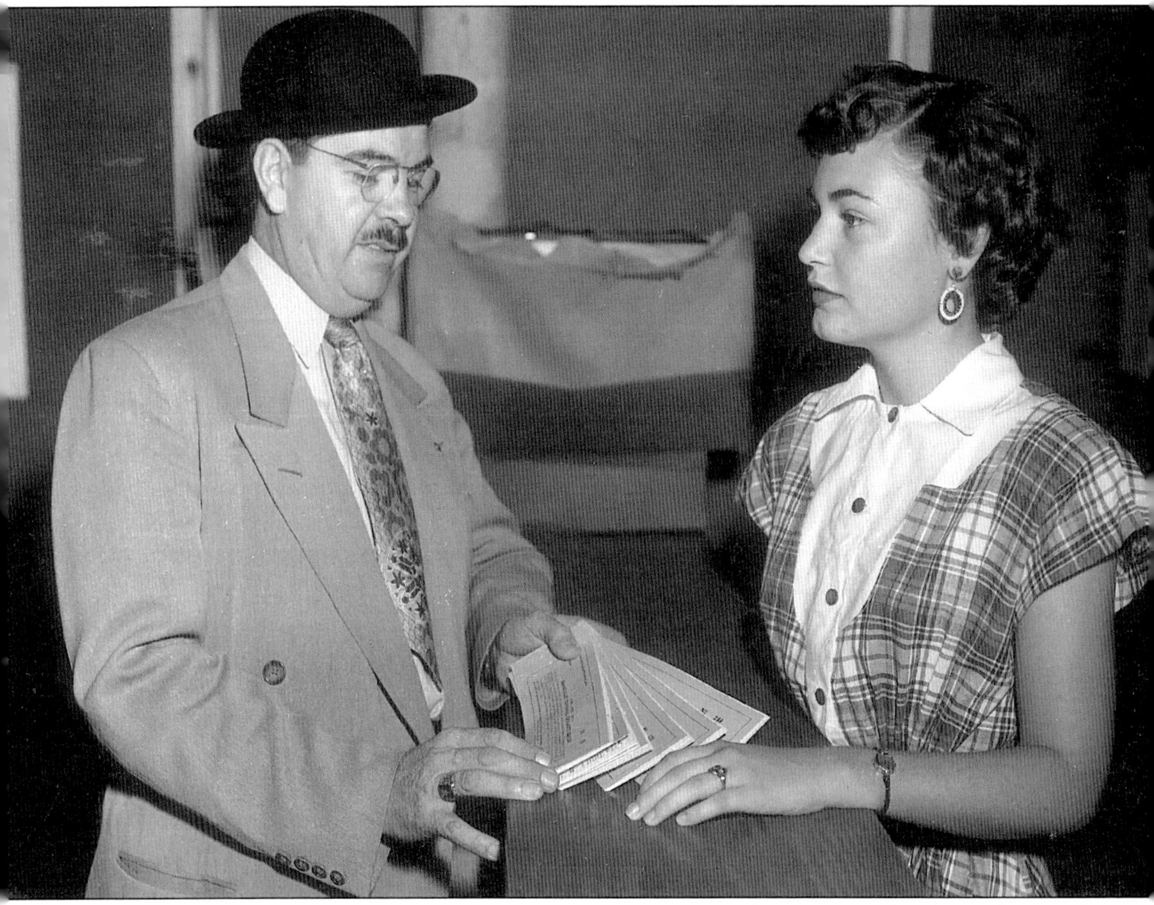

Dr. A.A. Davenport, sporting the black derby hat worn by many individuals during the centennial celebration, discusses centennial preparations with Jewell Howell. (Boyd & Breeding Collection, Morton Museum of Cooke County.)

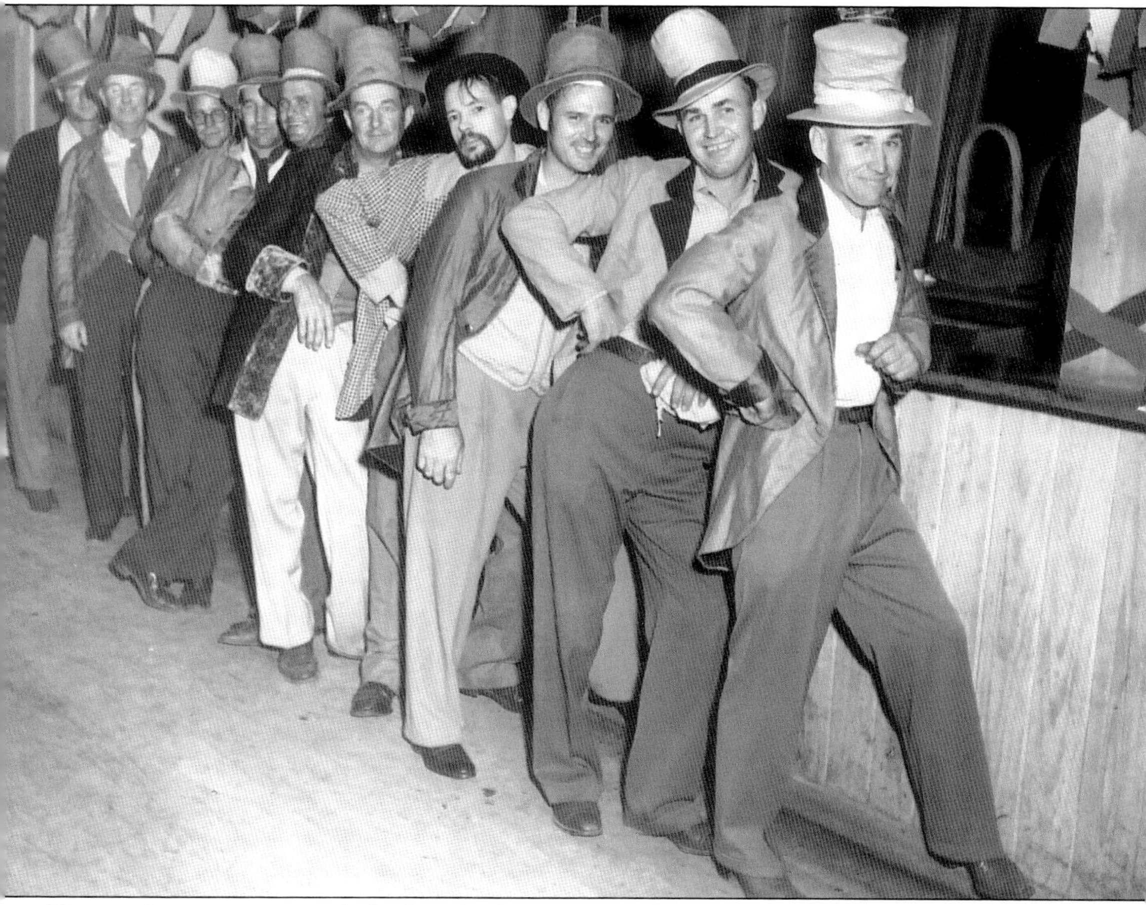

This motley crew, apparently harking back to Gainesville's saloon days, steps up to the bar probably during the costume ball held during Gainesville's centennial. (Boyd & Breeding Collection, Morton Museum of Cooke County.)

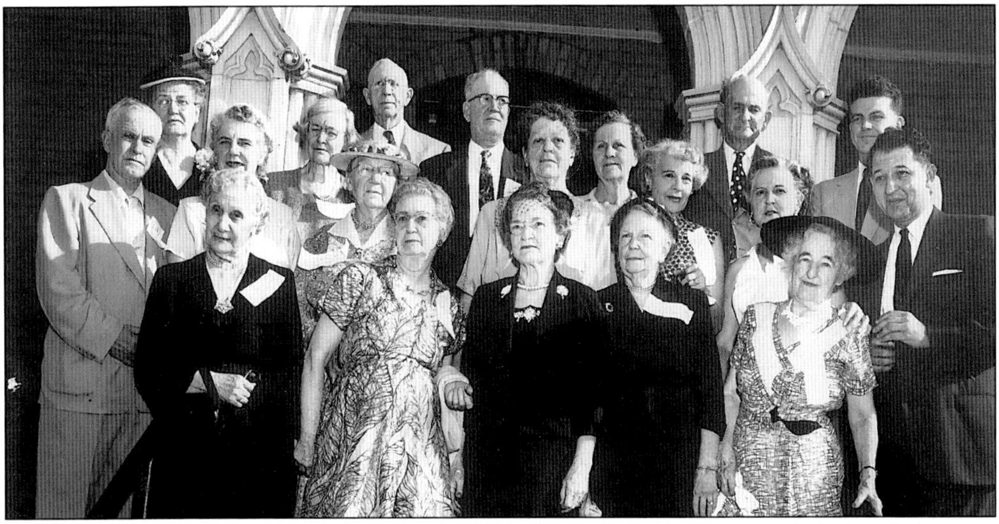

These members of the First Presbyterian Church in Gainesville attended the dedication ceremony of the present church building in 1913, and also witnessed the 75th anniversary of the church's founding in June 1954 when they gathered on the front steps of the church. Pictured in the first row, from left to right, are: Mrs. R.S. Timmerman, Mrs. A.C. Schoppaul, Mrs. Louis House, Mrs. Y.L. Griffin, and Mrs. W.D. Garrett. In the second row, from left to right, are: F.C. Beattie, Mrs. Ruth Tyler Johnston, Mrs. G.W. Wingent, Mrs. C.L. Sarles, Mrs. Roy Blanton, Mrs. John Bray, and Dr. Harry Sarles. In the back row, from left to right, are: Mrs. Brien Bonner, Miss Elgie Hailey, R.S. Timmerman, Wylie Brown, Mrs. E.C. Leonard, C.L. Sarles, and Reverend Edwin E. Hancock, the pastor at that time. (Boyd & Breeding Collection, Morton Museum of Cooke County.)

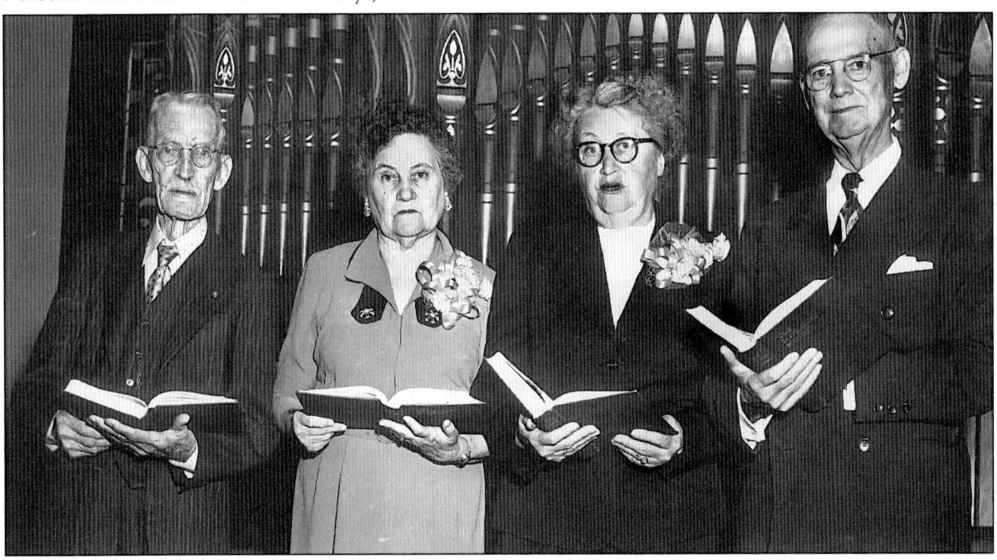

Members of the First Methodist Church mixed quartet held a reunion and sang for the 100th anniversary services of the church in Gainesville in March 1954. For more than 35 years, this quartet sang together until one member moved out of town. The members are, from left to right, C.M. Buckingham, Mrs. Hugh Hamilton, Mrs. Pauline McArdle (who also sang in performances of the Gainesville Community Circus), and William H. Rue. (Boyd & Breeding Collection, Morton Museum of Cooke County.)

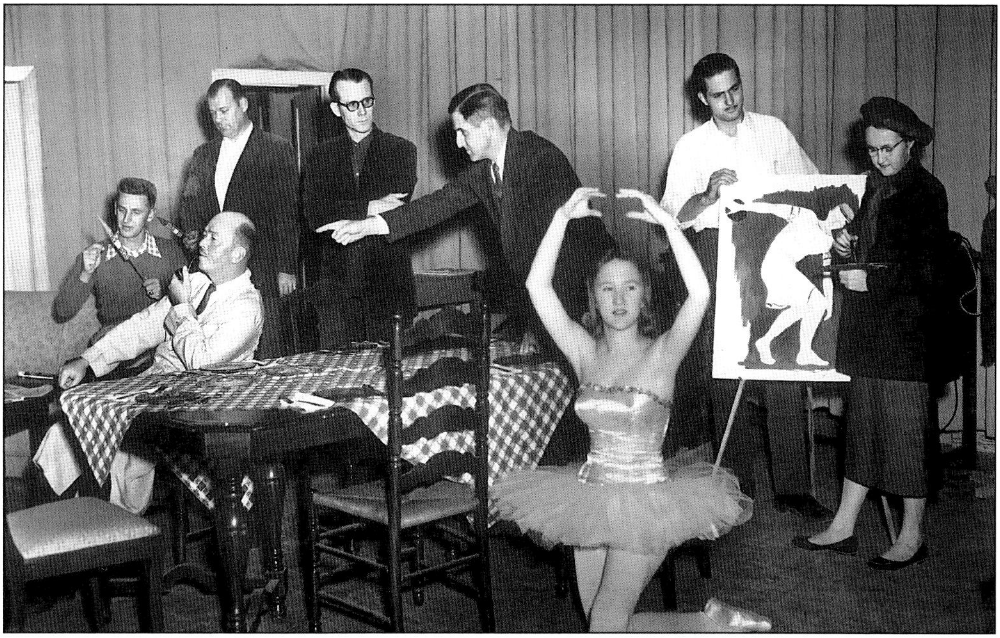

The Civic Theater cast performed "You Can't Take It With You" in Gainesville's junior high auditorium in November 1955. Seated in this shot, during a scene from the second act, are, from left to right, as follows: Tim McPherson and Charles Cuthrell, with Joyce Hinsley as the ballerina. Standing, from left to right, are Pete Brazile, Tommy Tomlinson, Frank Blagg, Glenn Gaston, and Barbara Shafer. (Boyd & Breeding Collection, Morton Museum of Cooke County.)

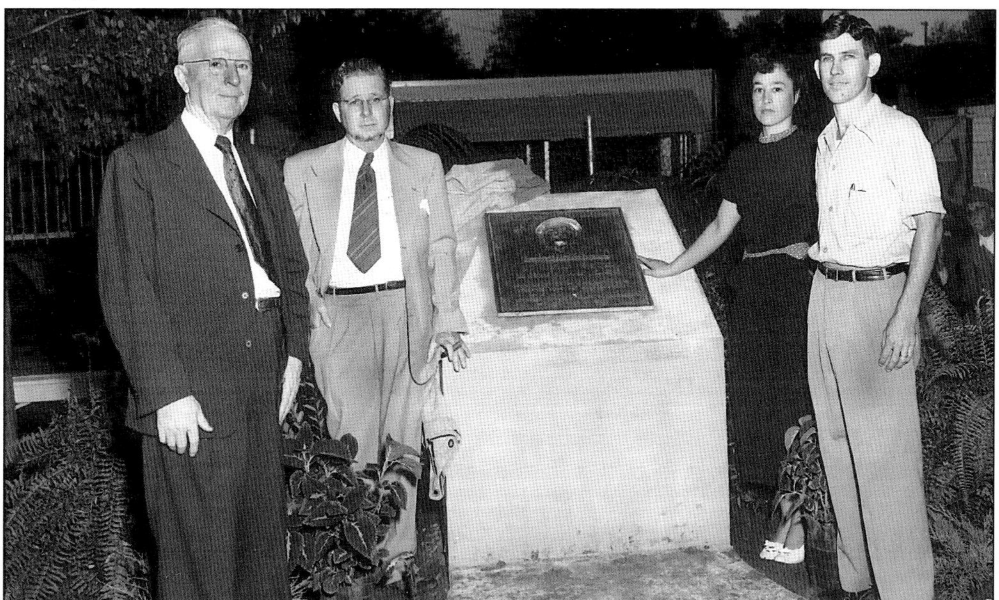

In 1950, the Frank Buck Zoo in Gainesville was officially established. Here, among others, Clarence Leonard and Frankie Schmitz unveil the plaque. (Boyd & Breeding Collection, Morton Museum of Cooke County.)

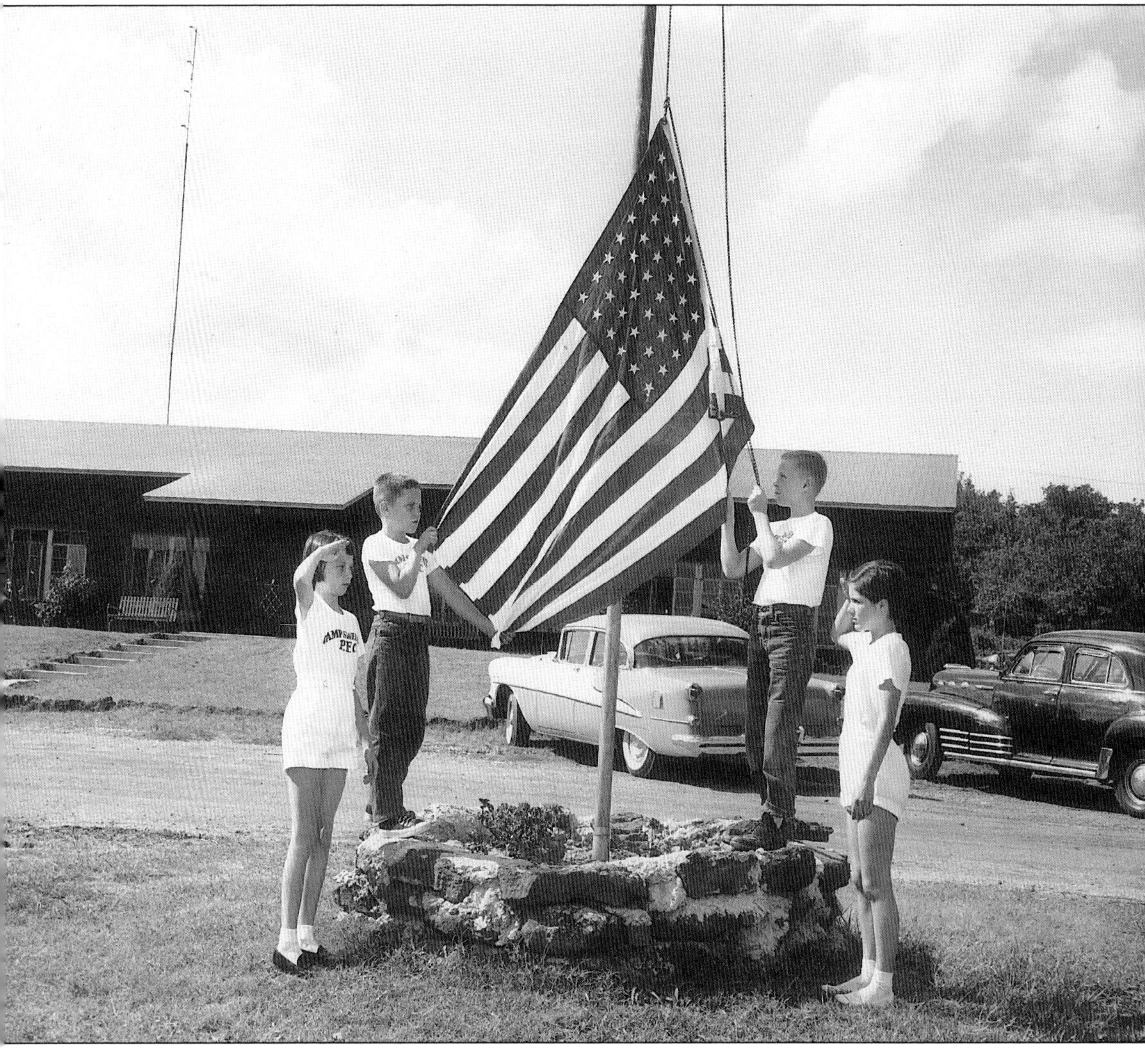

Camp Sweeney opened its doors to young diabetic campers in 1950. Here, four of the children do the honors for the United States flag flying at the camp. (Boyd & Breeding Collection, Morton Museum of Cooke County.)

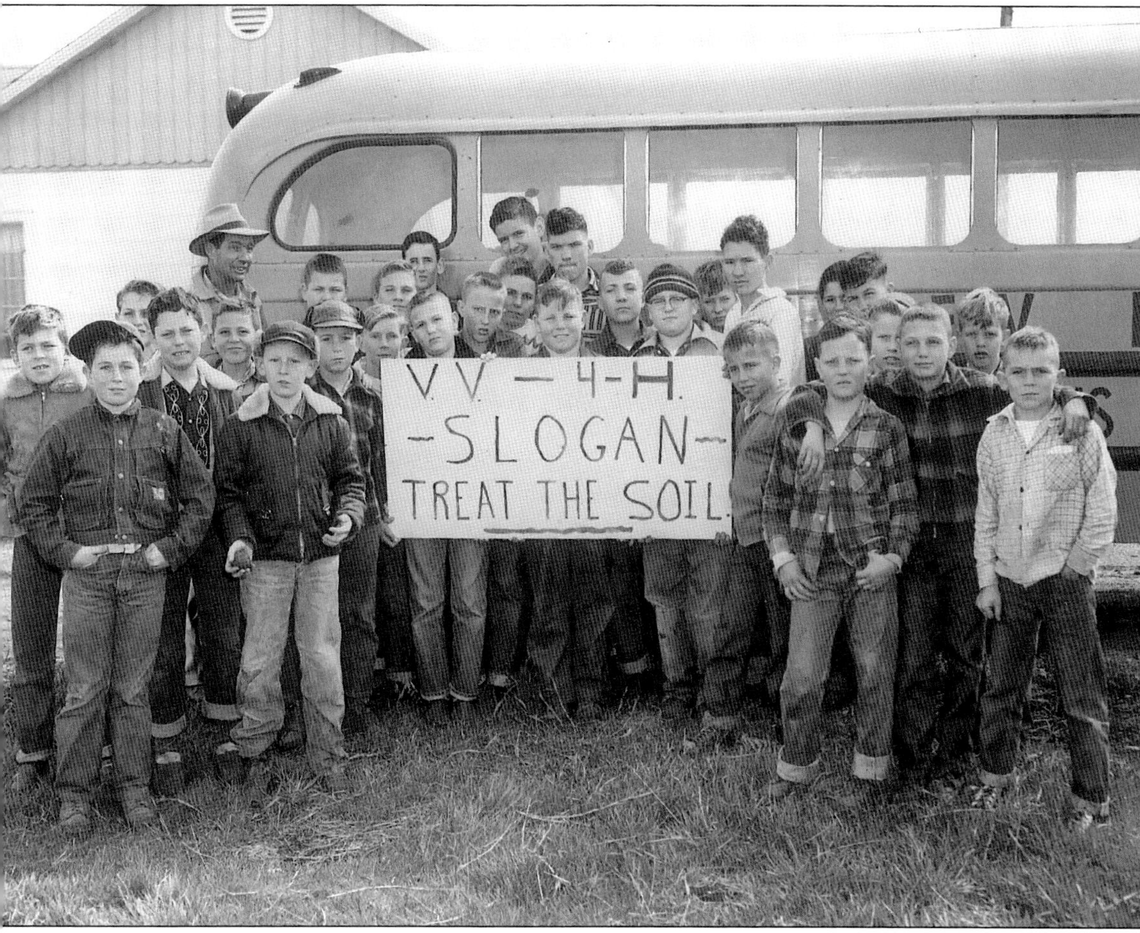

Members of the Valley View 4-H club posed in 1957 with their interest in farming clearly displayed. (Boyd & Breeding Collection, Morton Museum of Cooke County.)

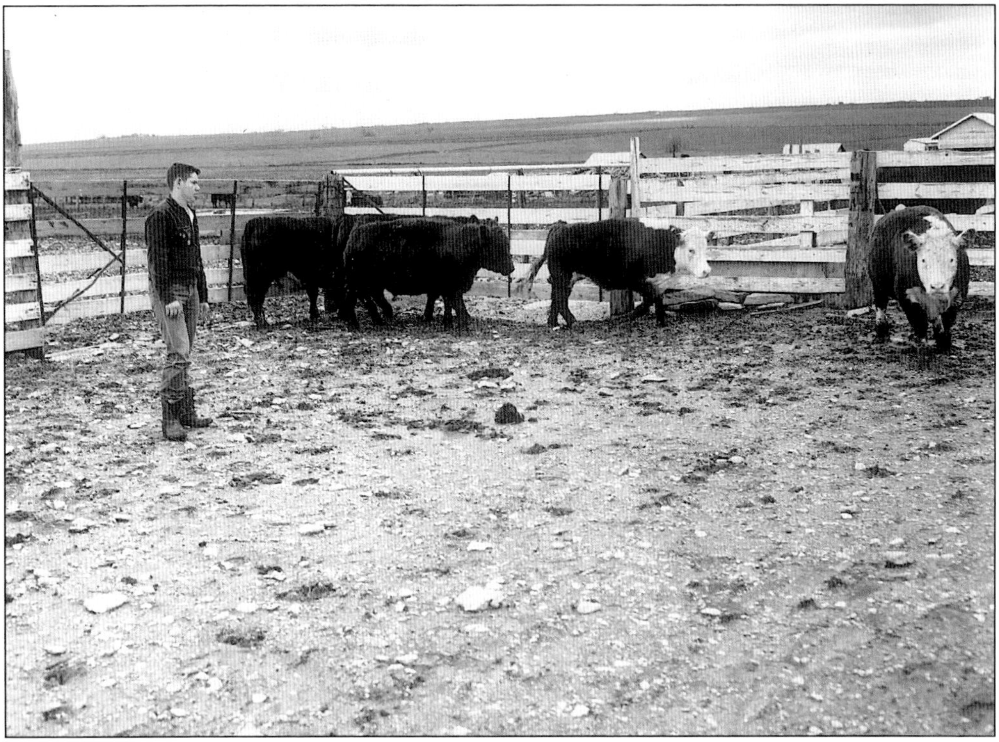

Anthony Dresser works cattle on a Cooke County farm in this 1957 photograph. (Boyd & Breeding Collection, Morton Museum of Cooke County.)

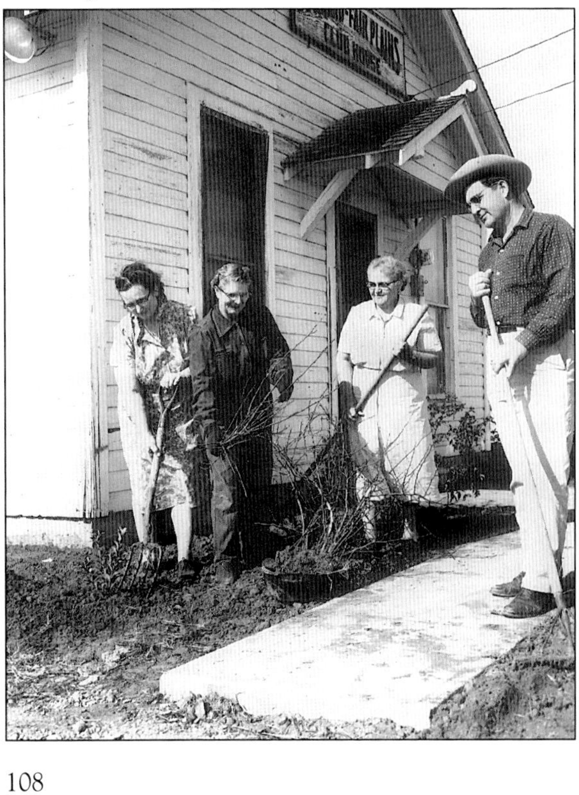

These members of the Downard-Fair Plains community club were busy planting shrubs at the club house in January 1959. (Boyd & Breeding Collection, Morton Museum of Cooke County.)

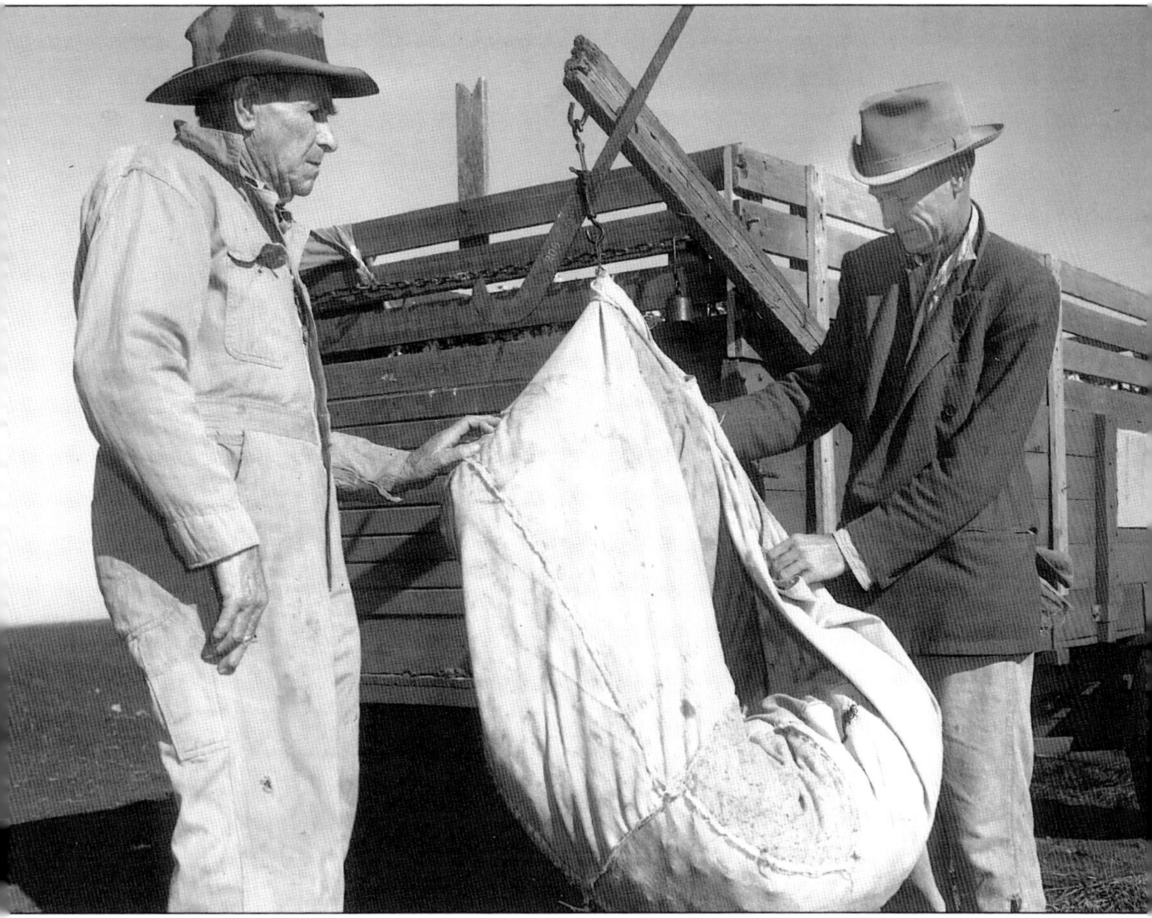

This scene of cotton farming and weighing cotton will bring back memories to many people. (Boyd & Breeding Collection, Morton Museum of Cooke County.)

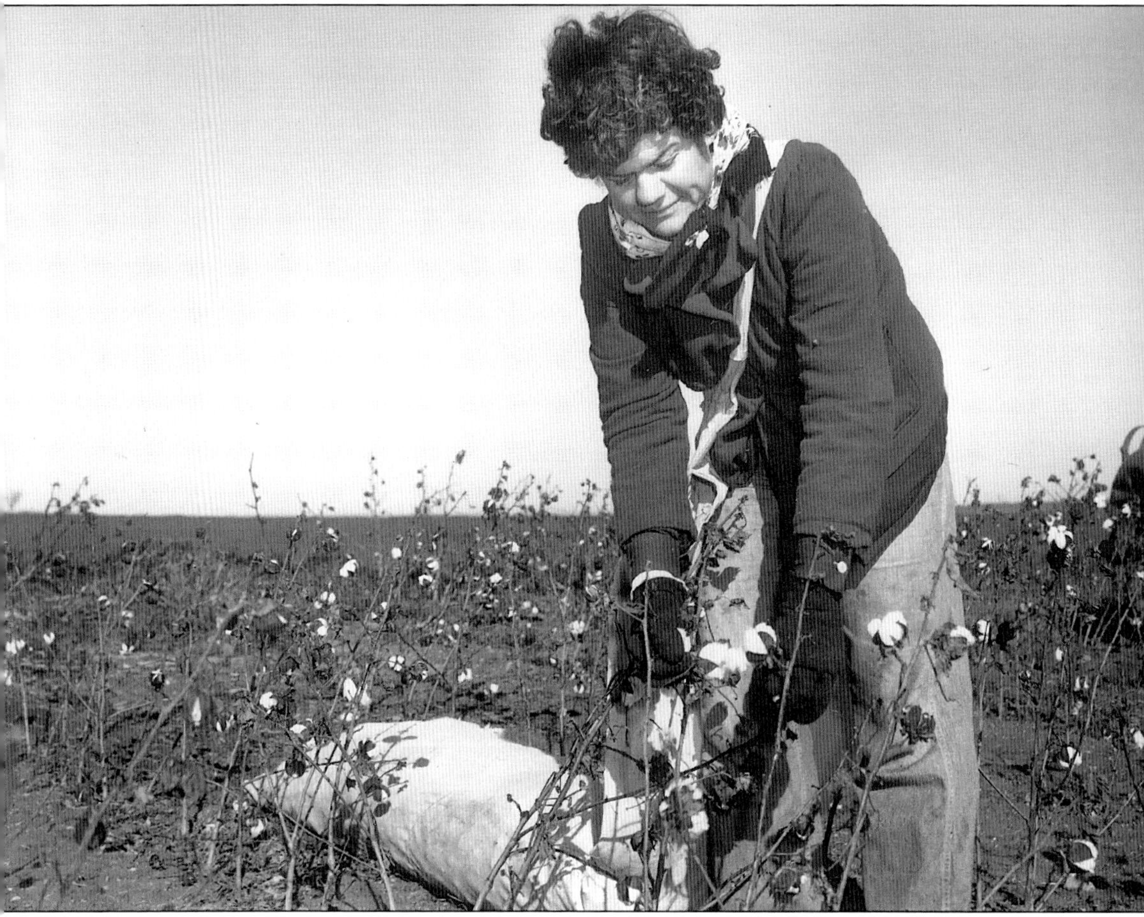

Cotton was a very important crop in Cooke County, and picking it was a chore that many individuals endured. (Boyd & Breeding Collection, Morton Museum of Cooke County.)

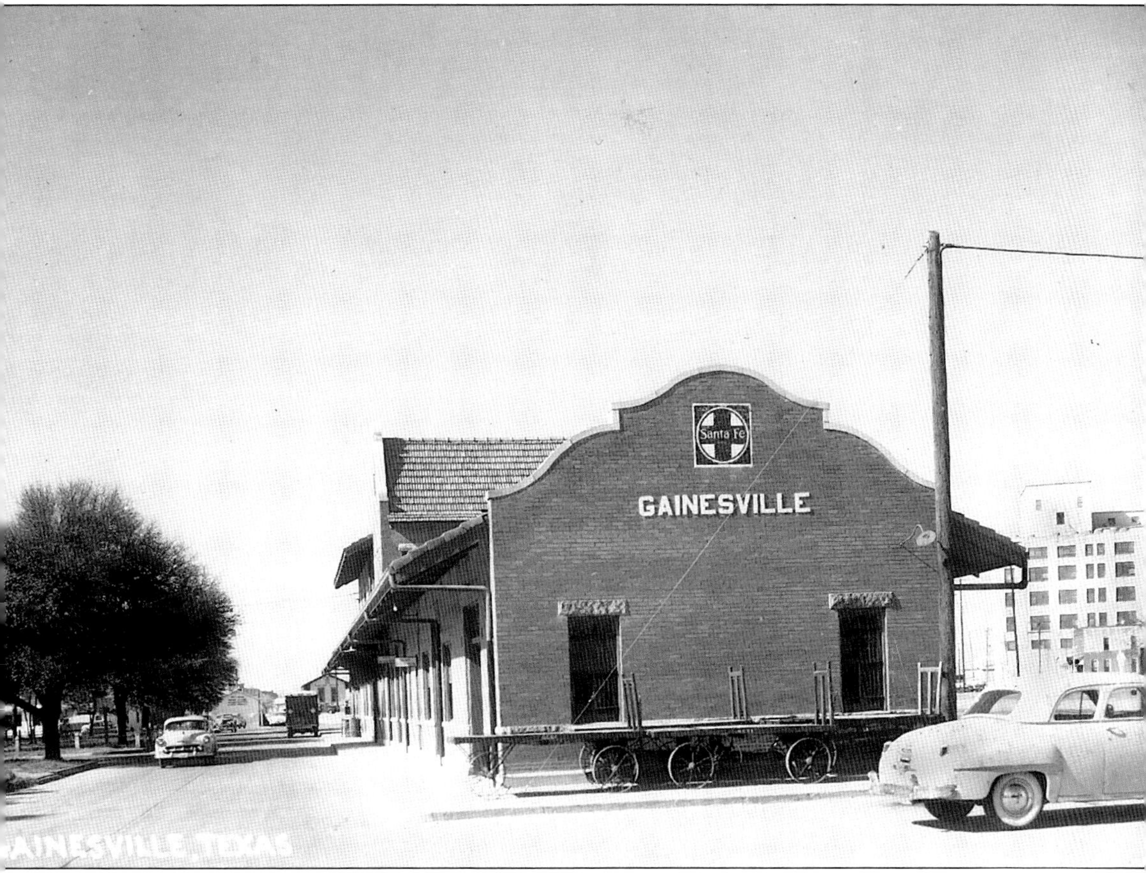

The Santa Fe railroad reached Gainesville in 1887. In 1902, the railroad erected this depot, replacing an earlier structure. The depot contained a Harvey House restaurant until 1931. Currently, the depot is undergoing restoration. (Donated by Mary McCain, Morton Museum of Cooke County Collection.)

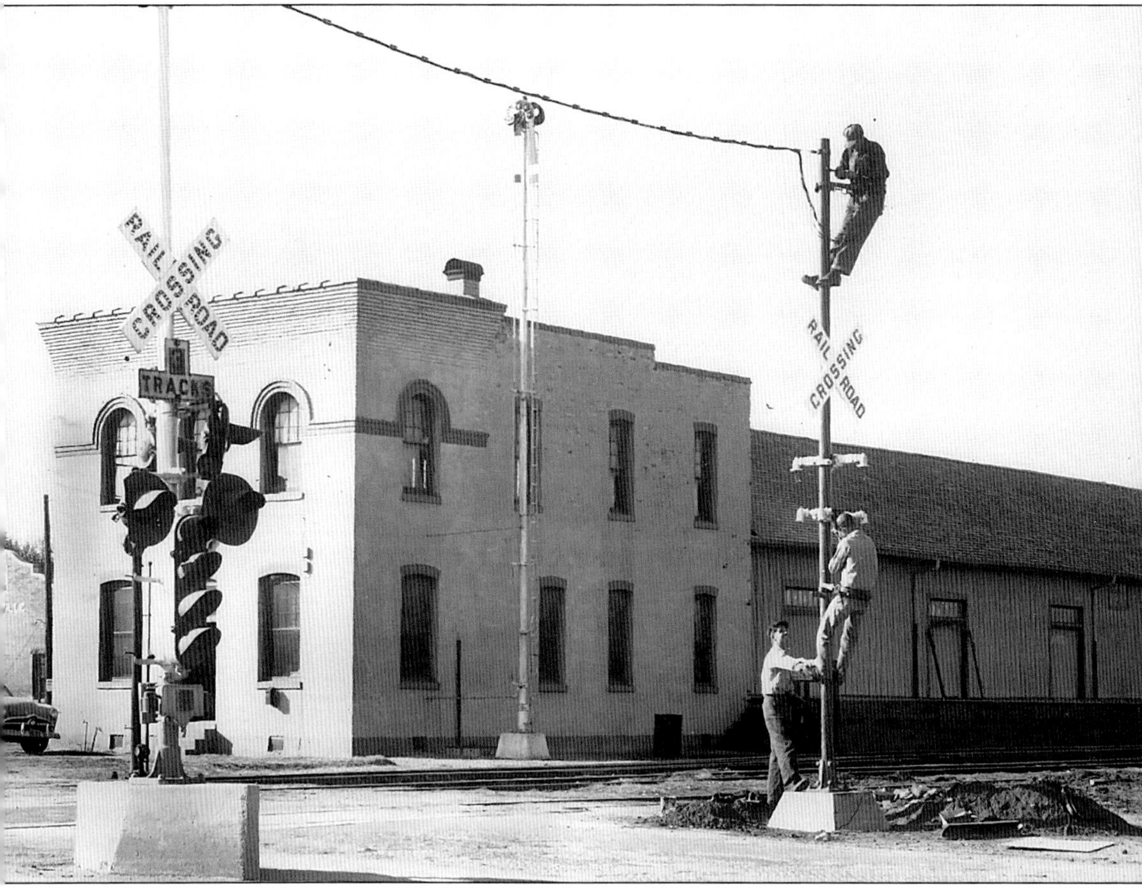

In 1956, the Katy line received new railroad crossings. In the background is the Katy freight depot, and at the edge of the photo a small section of the Santa Fe depot is also visible. (Boyd & Breeding Collection, Morton Museum of Cooke County.)

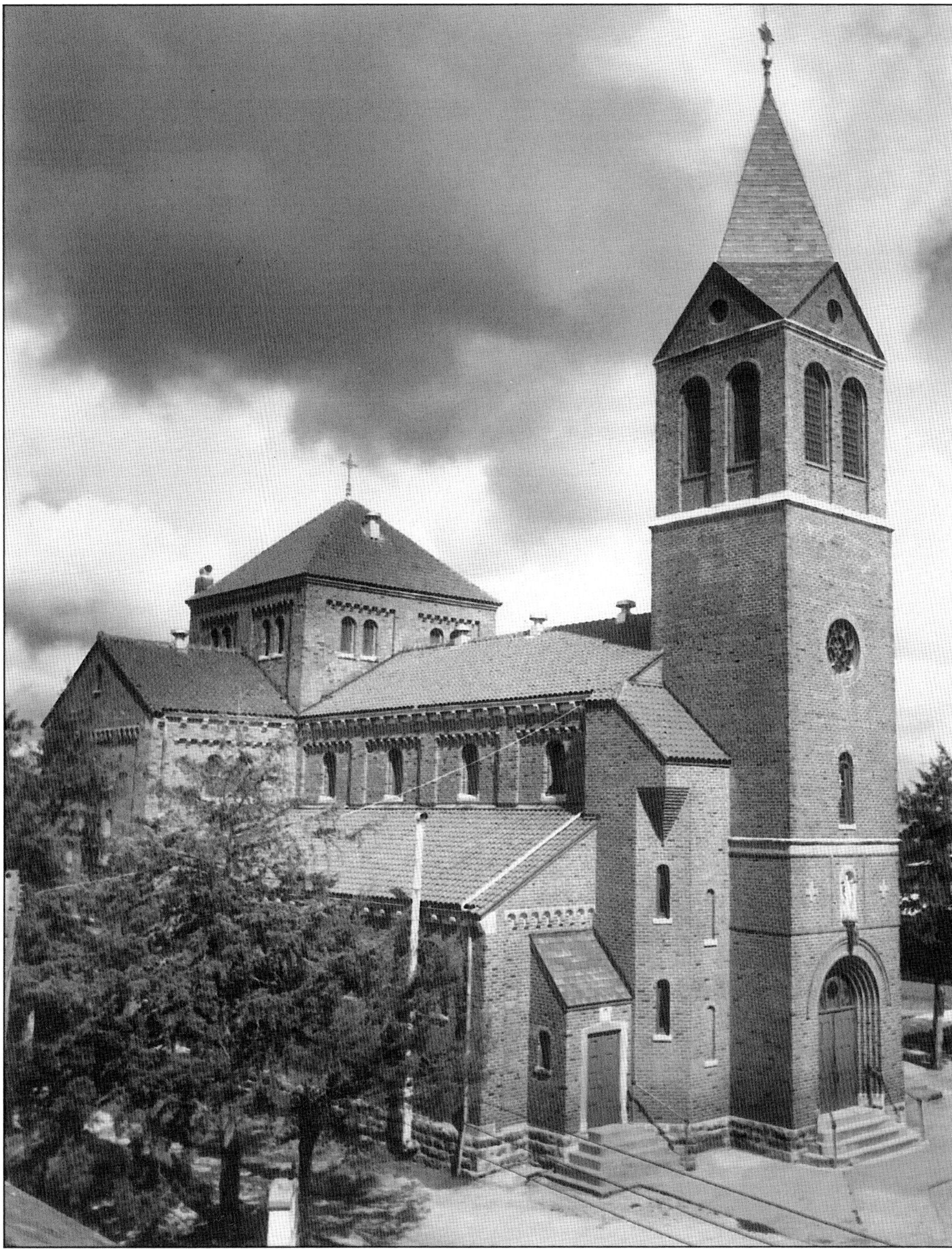

On March 31, 1918, the cornerstone of St. Peter's Catholic Church in Lindsay was laid. The interior of the church "is artistically decorated and attracts numerous visitors each year. In 1970, it was given a Texas historical marker." (Morton Museum of Cooke County Collection.)

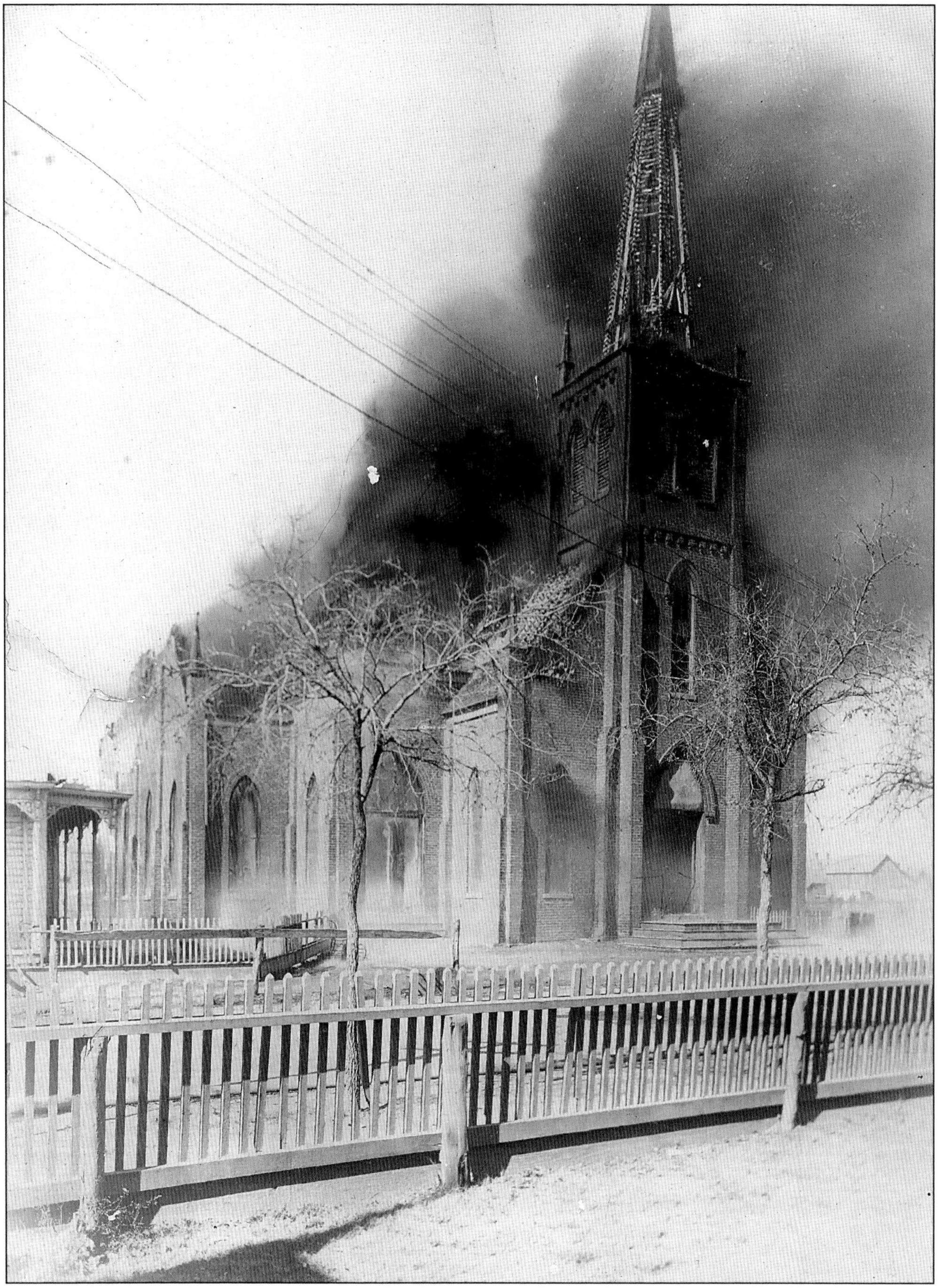

On February 13, 1898, the First Baptist Church in Gainesville was destroyed in a fire. "A defective furnace was blamed for the blaze which was discovered while the pastor, the Rev. W.S. Splawn, was reading a passage from the Bible." A new church was completed later in the year. (Morton Museum of Cooke County Collection.)

Ten

The Changing Face of the County

Time usually alters things. Historic structures may survive, but often face the threat of the wrecking ball; new inventions change our living arrangements; towns may develop the way the residents plan for them to, but sometimes find themselves controlled by outside forces, or occasionally even succumb and become ghost towns. Nothing stays the same for very long.

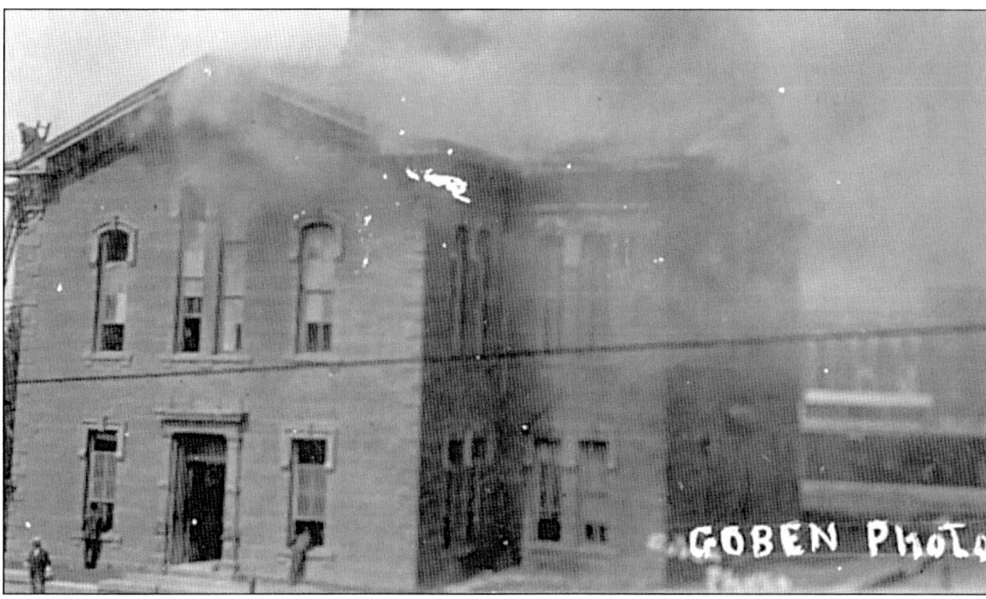

The 1878 Cooke County Courthouse was captured as it was burning in 1909. Construction of the new courthouse, which still stands, commenced in 1910. (Donated by Pauline McArdle, Morton Museum of Cooke County Collection.)

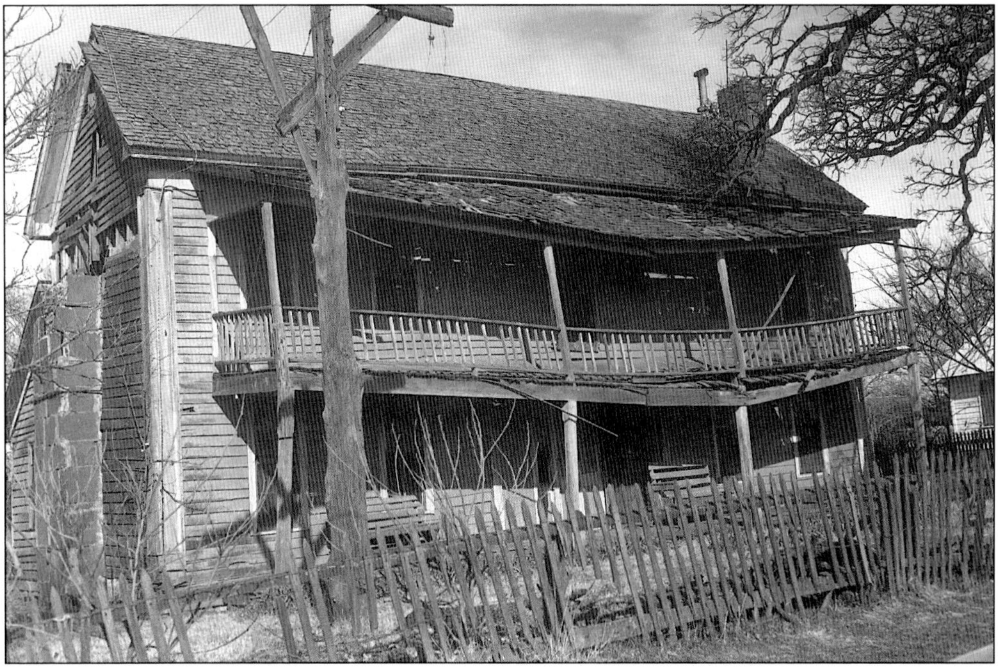

The Dexter Hotel once stood proudly in the thriving community of Dexter. But when the railroad, and later the highway, failed to come through the town, it slowly began to die out. The hotel started to deteriorate, as this photograph from the 1950s demonstrates, as fewer and fewer visitors came. Today, it no longer exists. (Boyd & Breeding Collection, Morton Museum of Cooke County.)

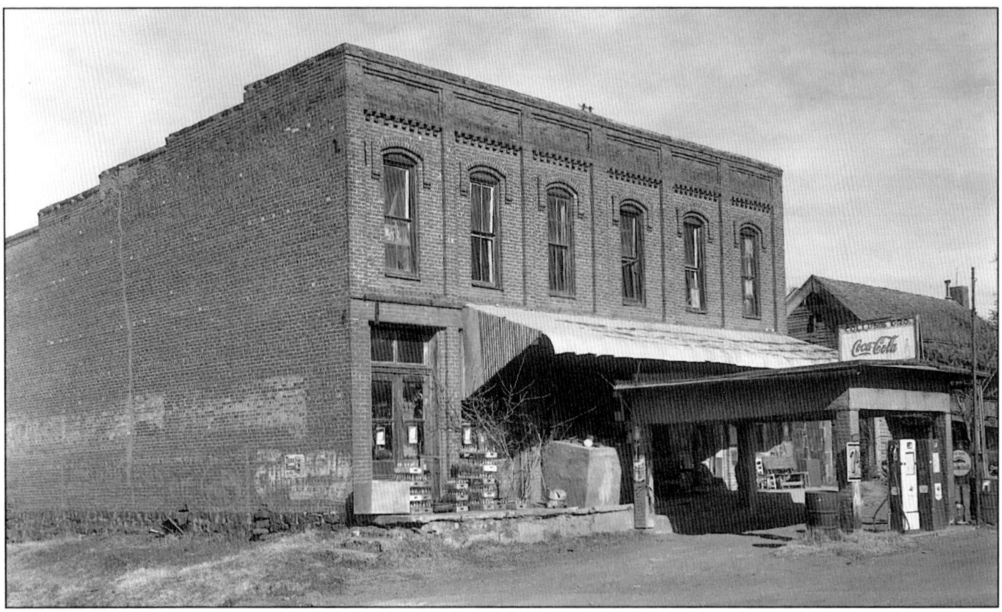

This building once housed the store in Dexter. It, like the hotel and the rest of the main street, began to decline as the years passed. This photograph was taken in the 1950s. The building no longer exists. (Boyd & Breeding Collection, Morton Museum of Cooke County.)

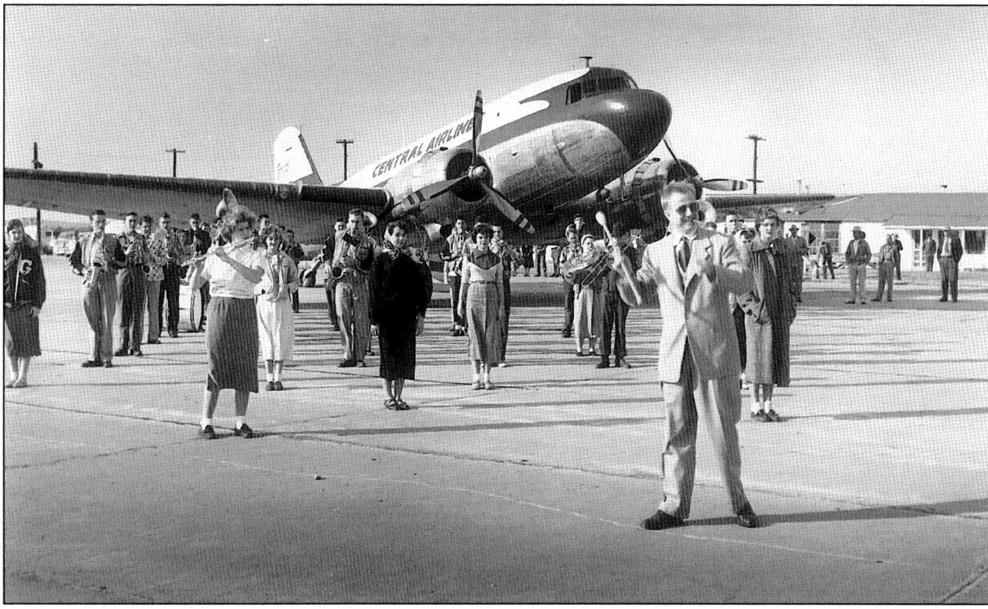

On November 7, 1950, two twin-engine Douglas DC-3 24-passenger airplanes on a flight to 15 cities serviced by Central Airlines landed at the Gainesville airport. The new aircraft would connect all points on Central's system with virtually any place in the world. Central Airlines would fly four flights daily through Gainesville. At the airport, Central Airlines executives were greeted with several musical numbers played by the Gainesville High School band. (Boyd & Breeding Collection, Morton Museum of Cooke County.)

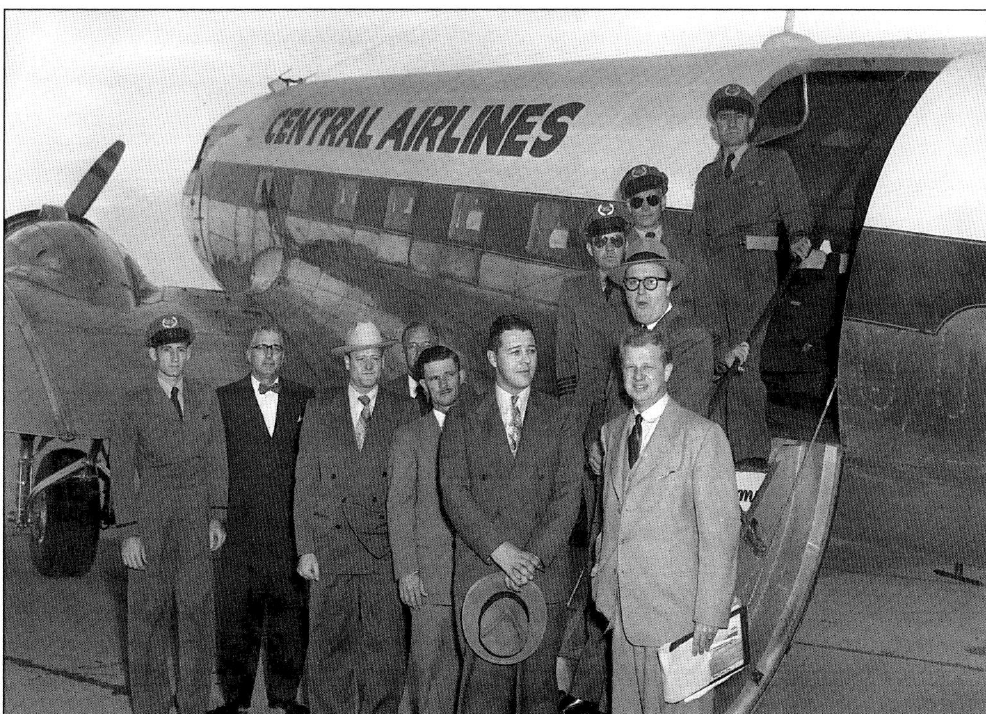

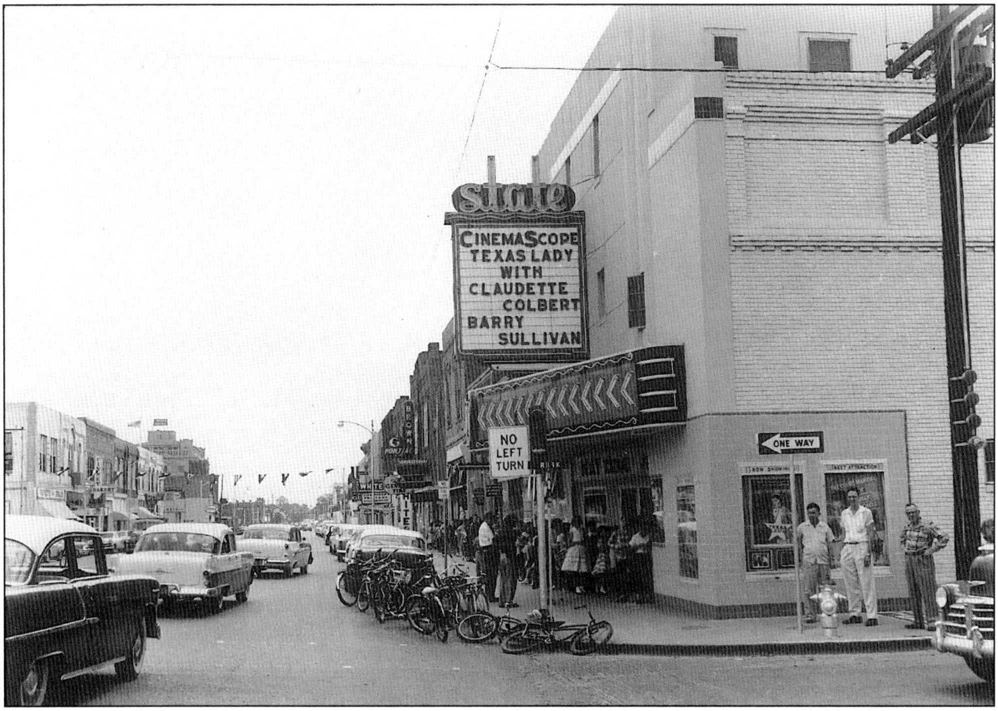

The last of what was once one of six downtown movie theaters in Gainesville, the State Theater was originally known as the Majestic Theater. This shot was taken on April 30, 1956. While the building still exists, the State Theater is no longer open. Currently, no community in the county has an operating movie theater. (Boyd & Breeding Collection, Morton Museum of Cooke County.)

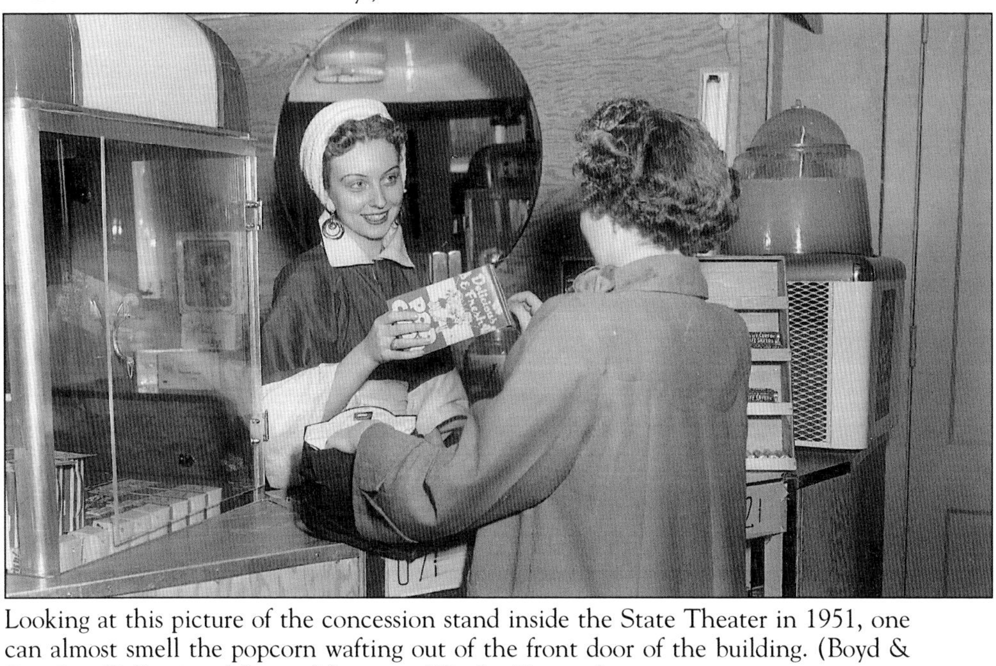
Looking at this picture of the concession stand inside the State Theater in 1951, one can almost smell the popcorn wafting out of the front door of the building. (Boyd & Breeding Collection, Morton Museum of Cooke County.)

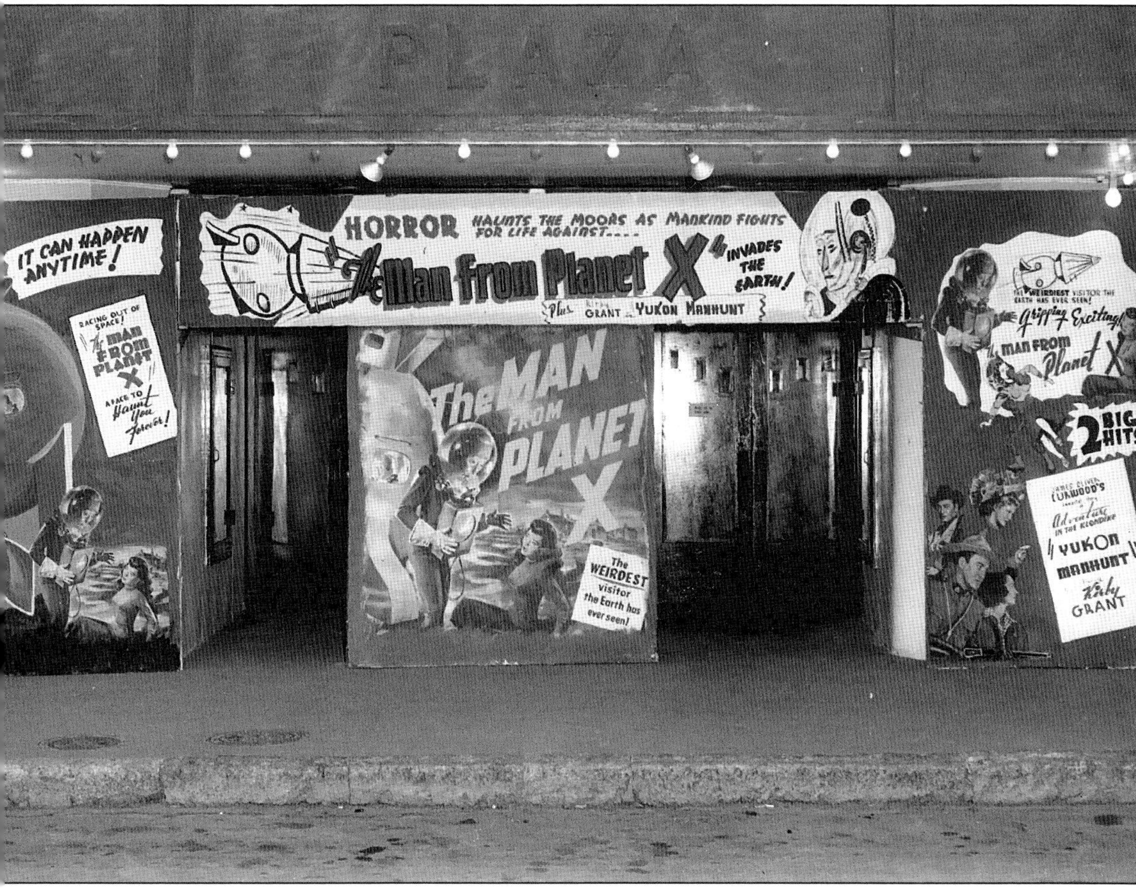

In this November 1951 photograph, the Plaza, one of the State's competitors, advertises its latest showings: *Man From Planet X* and *Yukon Manhunt*. Science fiction movies were becoming very popular by that time, and many people were interested in UFOs, space travel, and rockets. (Boyd & Breeding Collection, Morton Museum of Cooke County.)

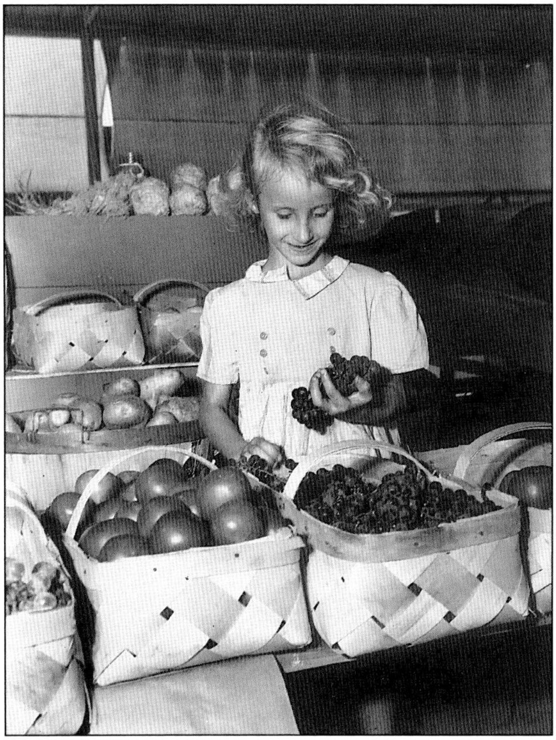

In these two scenes from the market square in Gainesville, Bobby Jean Allman thinks about eating the fruit in her hand and Henry Colwell checks out the vegetables. Note the Waples-Painter Lumber Company in the background. Farmers no longer sell their wares at the market square. (Boyd & Breeding Collection, Morton Museum of Cooke County.)

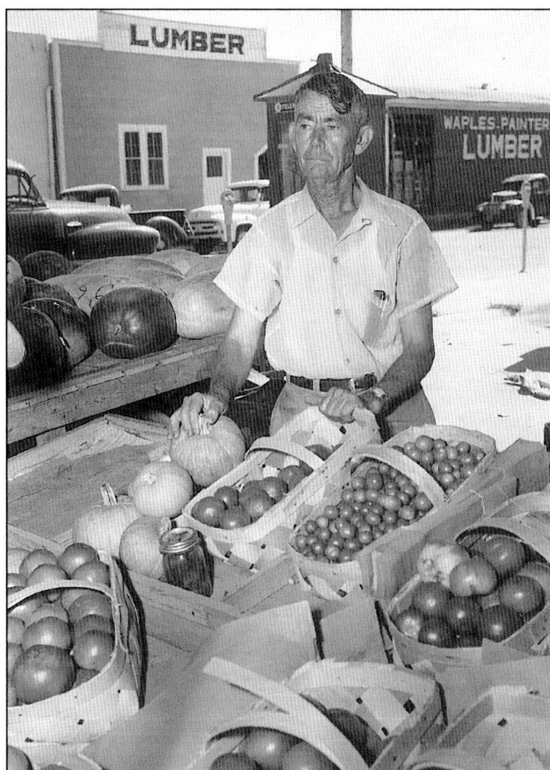

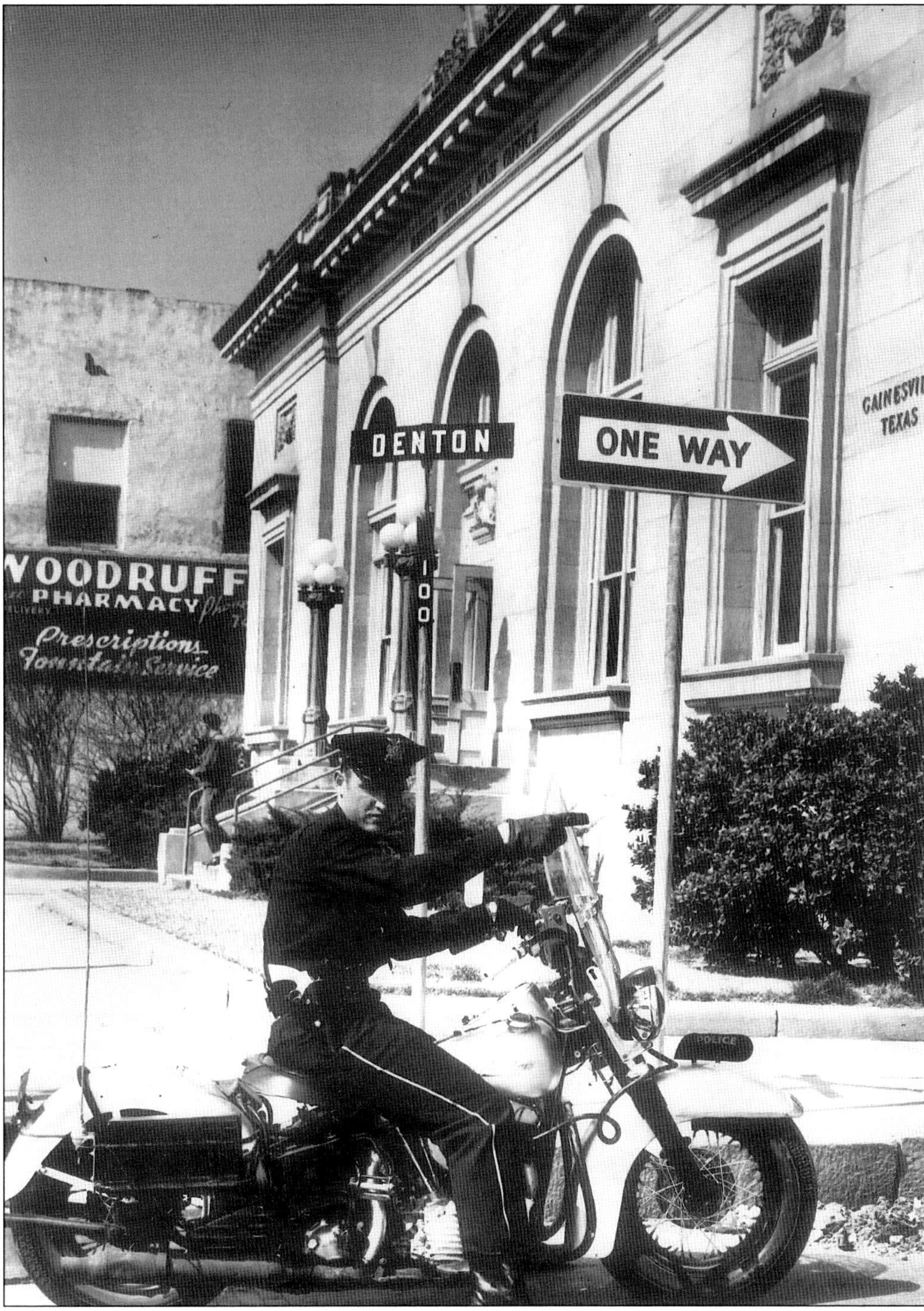

While Denton Street by the U.S. Post office in Gainesville remains a one-way street, very little else about this photograph remains the same. The post office shown in this photo no longer exists, nor does Woodruff Pharmacy. The brick street seen under the motorcycle has been covered. This photograph dates to the early 1950s. (Boyd & Breeding Collection, Morton Museum of Cooke County.)

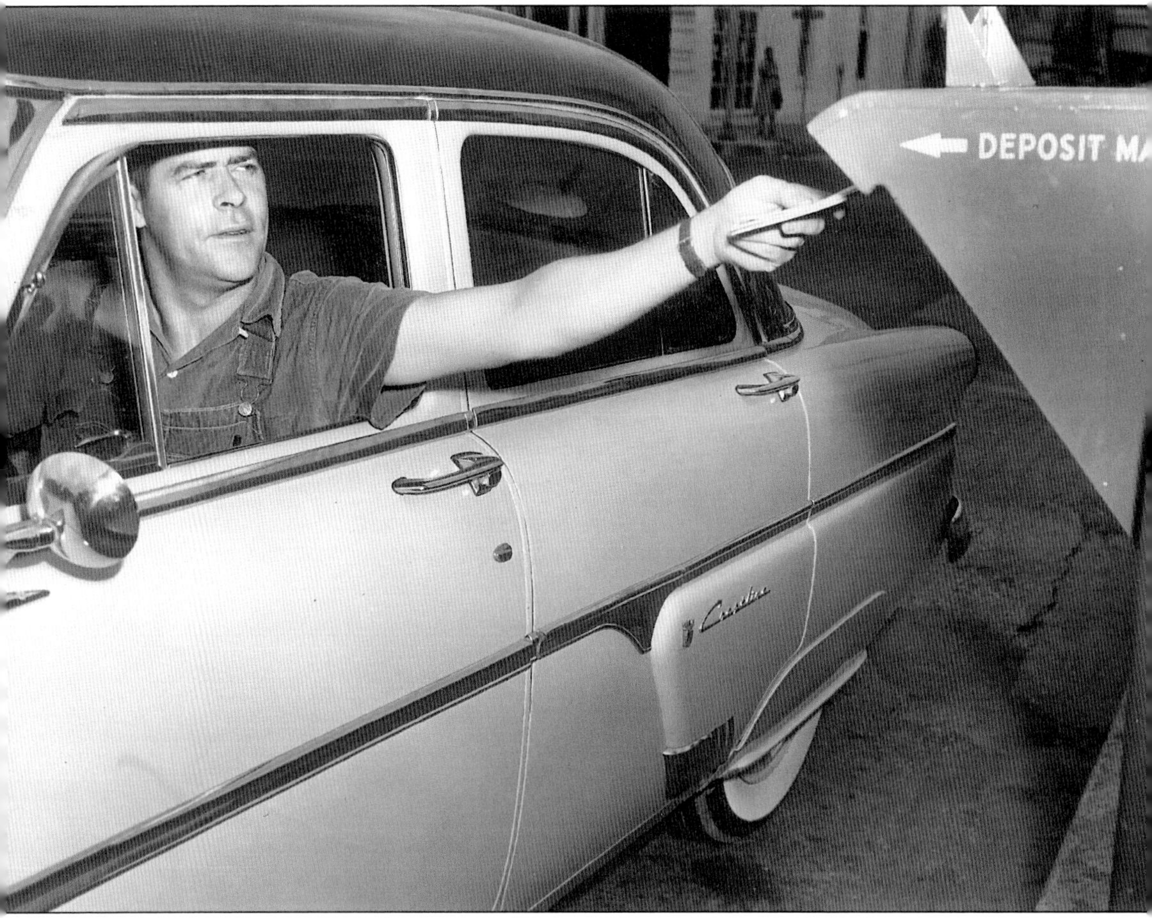

By the 1950s, the pace of life was quickening and people were looking for time-saving devices and convenience. One example of that appears in this 1955 photograph, as R.E. Faulkner placed his mail in the new drive-by box at the post office. (Boyd & Breeding Collection, Morton Museum of Cooke County.)

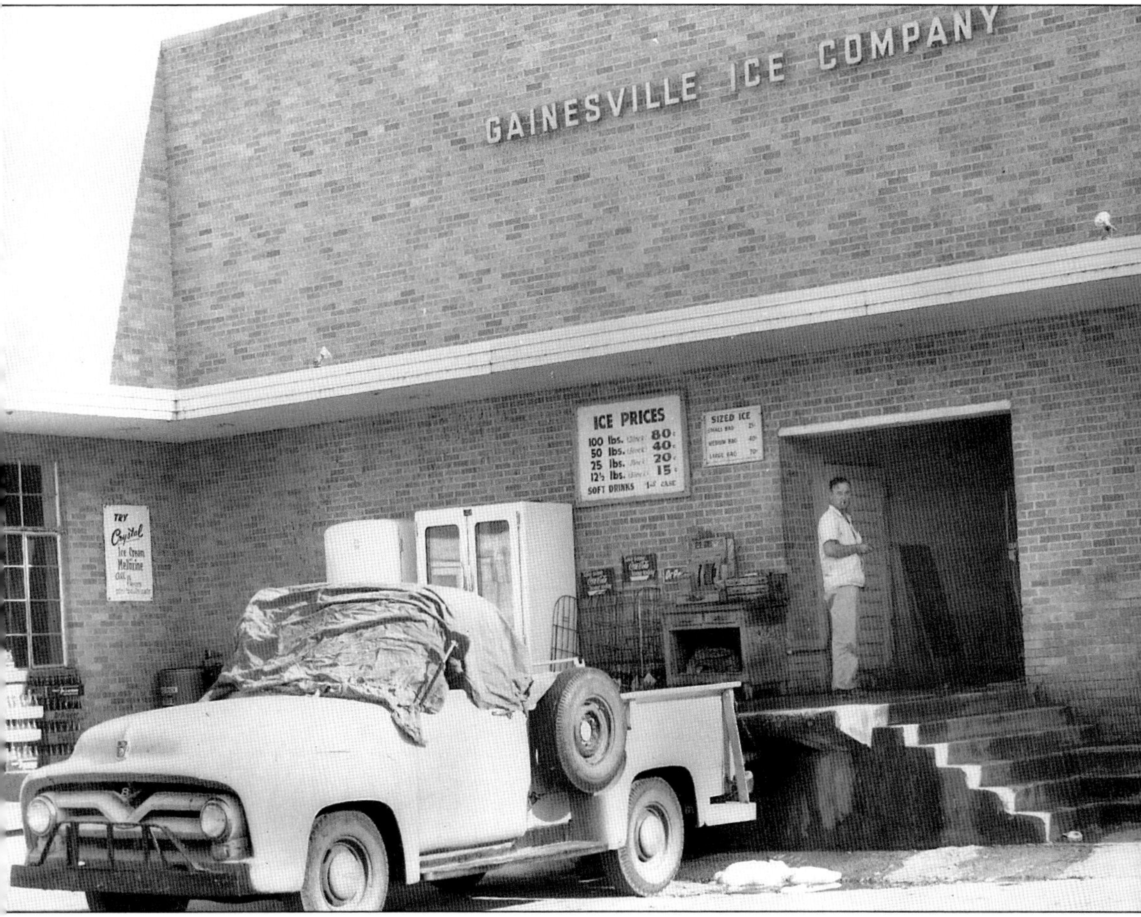

The Gainesville Ice Company was organized as a stock company in 1888 and began operations on August 1 of that year. Fifteen tons of ice was the day's output. Originally a frame structure, the plant was replaced by a brick building after a fire in 1909. In "the 1911 Labor Day parade, the Gainesville Ice company won first place for the best float, decorated with large cakes of ice into which were frozen watermelons, and other fruits and flowers. The company took over the Crystal Bottling Works in 1911 and began the manufacture of soft drinks in connection with its ice plant." The photograph was taken in August 1958. (Boyd & Breeding Collection, Morton Museum of Cooke County.)

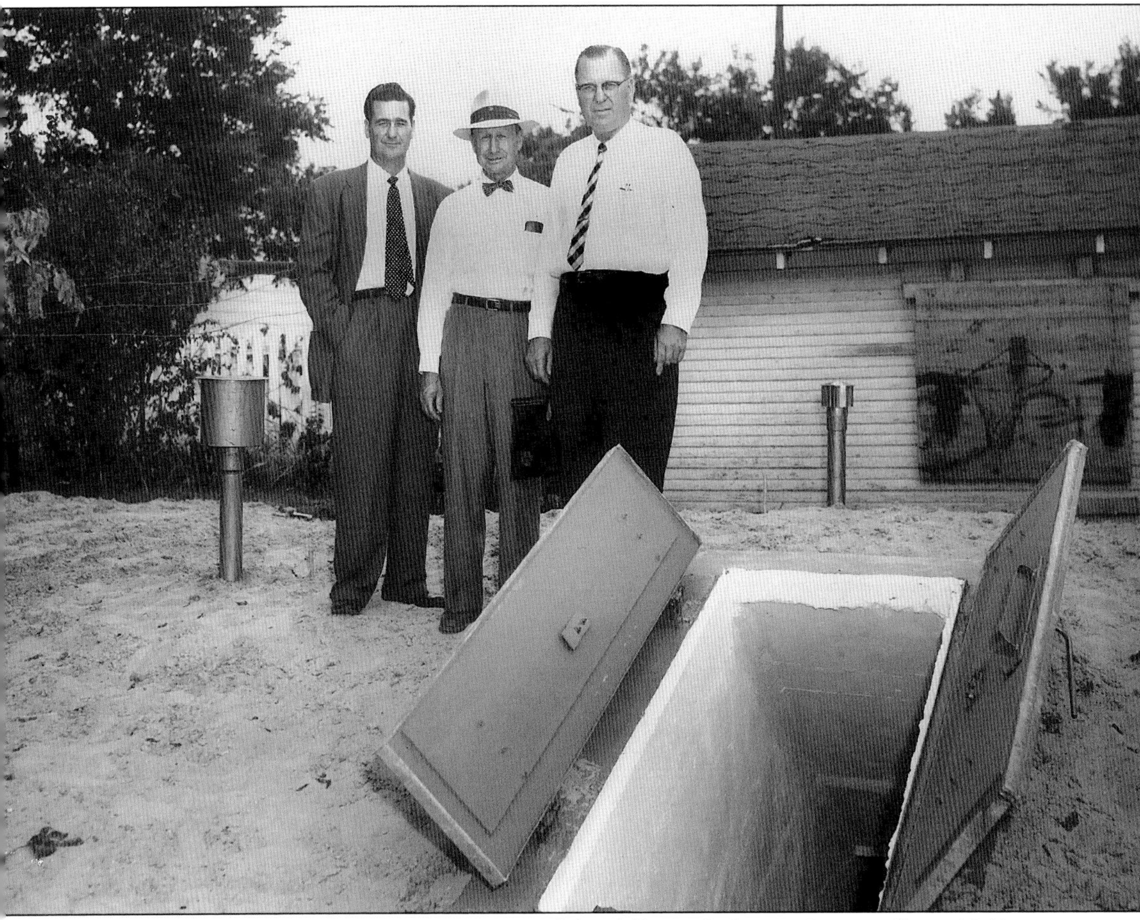

A sign of the times was the construction of this fall-out shelter in Gainesville in 1960, as more and more people grew concerned over the threat of nuclear war. (Boyd & Breeding Collection, Morton Museum of Cooke County.)

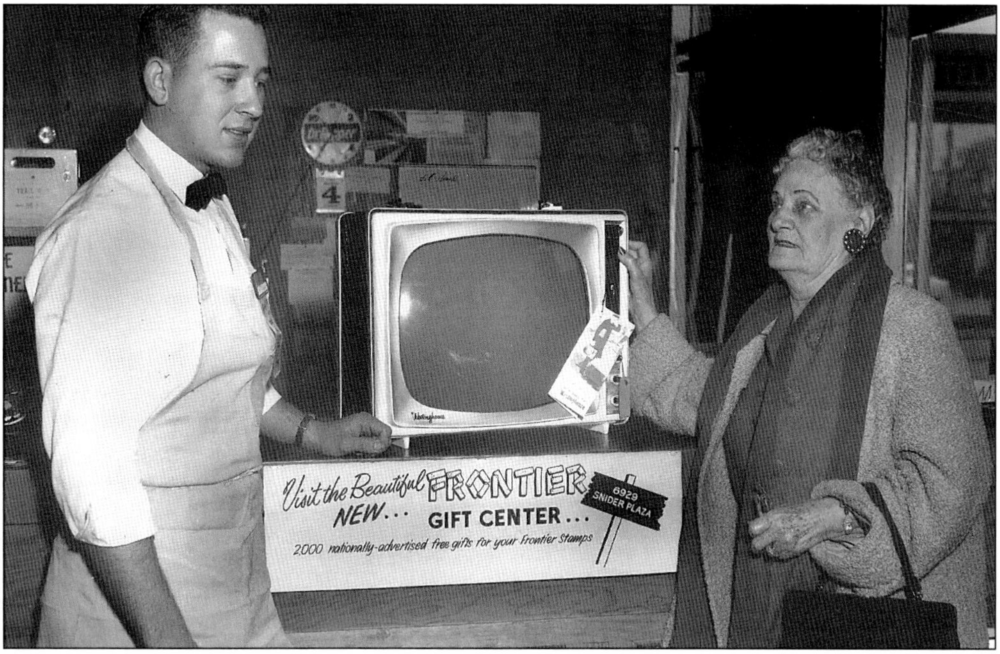

Times had certainly changed by 1960. A box known as a TV set was showing up in more and more homes and could now even be won in hometown contests. In this March 1960 photo a woman receives a television set at the Tom Thumb supermarket. A sign underneath the set advertises "Frontier Stamps," which may have been competing with "Green Stamps." (Boyd & Breeding Collection, Morton Museum of Cooke County.)

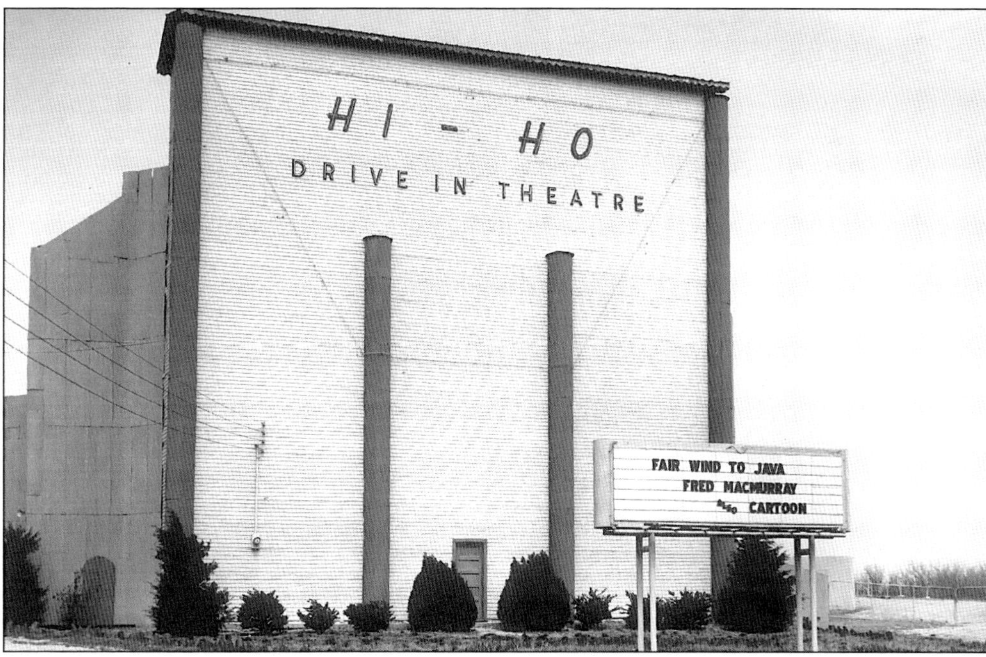

As outdoor drive-in movie theaters spread across the country, the Hi-Ho opened in Gainesville, becoming the only drive-in movie theater ever operated in the community. This shot shows the theater as it looked in 1954. (Boyd & Breeding Collection, Morton Museum of Cooke County.)

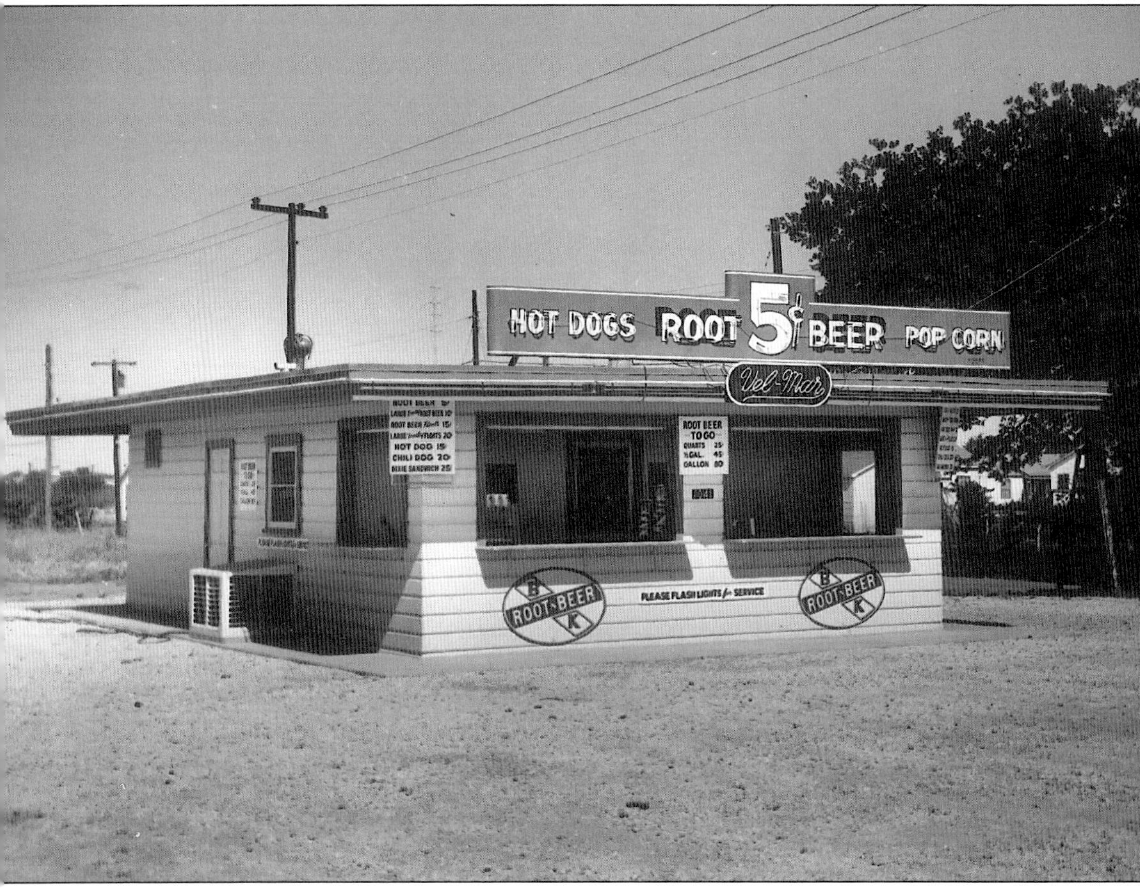

In 1953, customers who drove up to the Vel Mar Drive-In and flashed their headlights could then order, among other things, a chili dog for 20¢ and a root beer for 5¢. Cars were more prevalent, and drive-in restaurants would become more popular as the years passed. (Boyd & Breeding Collection, Morton Museum of Cooke County.)

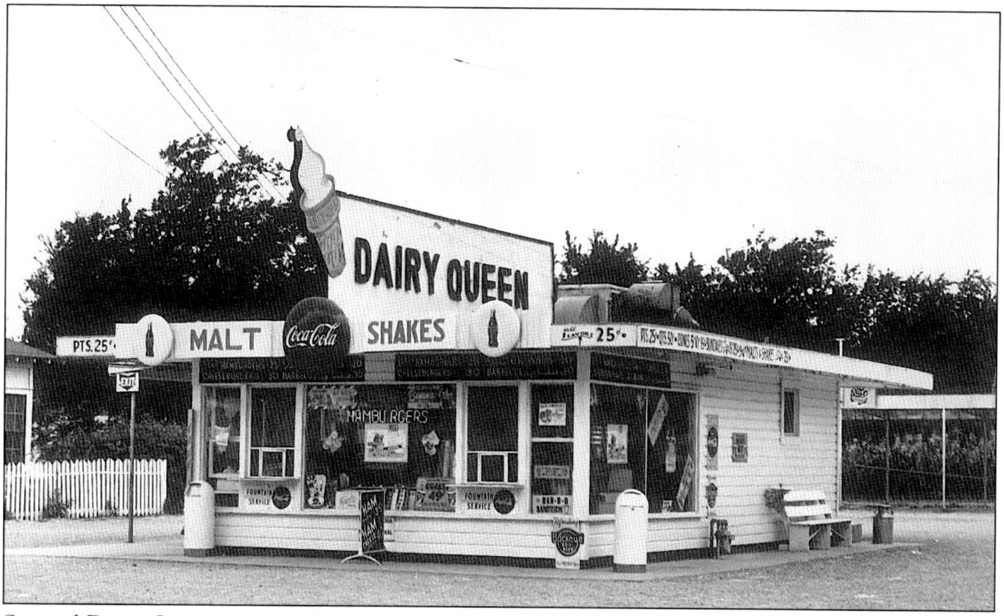

Several Dairy Queens once operated in Gainesville, but no longer. At this Dairy Queen, shown in 1955, customers could purchase hamburgers for 25¢ and cheeseburgers for 30¢. Currently, within the county, only Valley View residents enjoy a Dairy Queen inside their city limits. (Boyd & Breeding Collection, Morton Museum of Cooke County.)

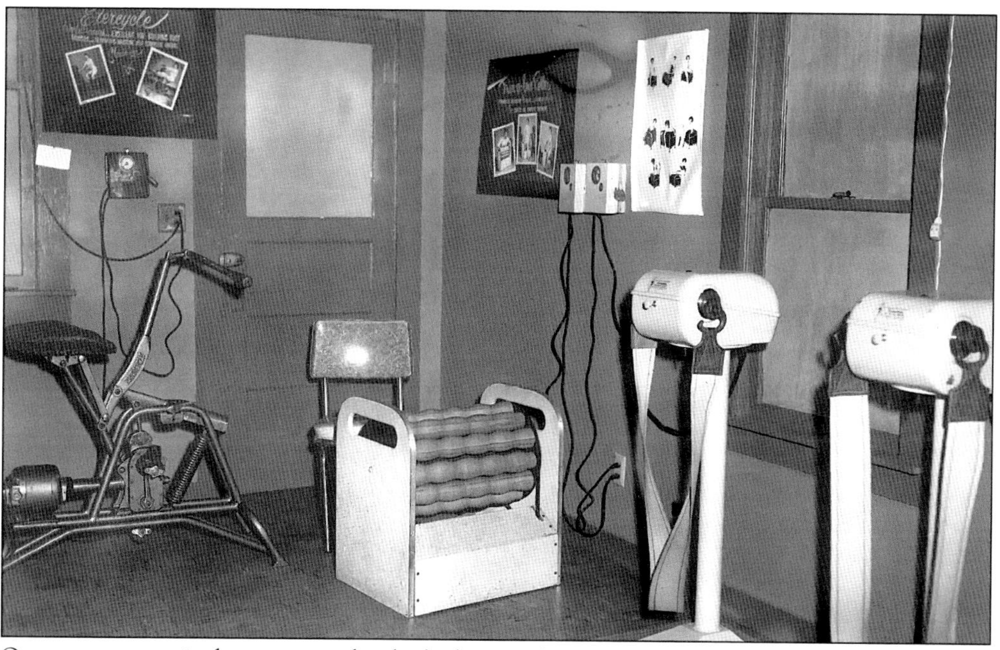
One common trait that many individuals share is the eternal "battle of the bulge." While the equipment in this "reducing salon" that operated on Grand Avenue in Gainesville in 1959 may look a little different from what people are accustomed to today, the goal in this salon was the same as it is today in gyms across the county. (Boyd & Breeding Collection, Morton Museum of Cooke County.)

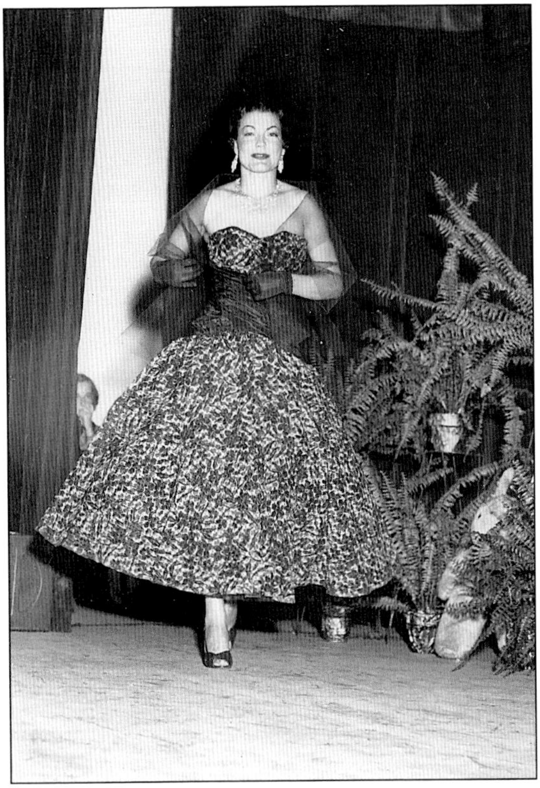

A frequently heard statement goes something like "Hold onto an outfit long enough and it will probably come back in style!" A fun aspect of history lies in examining fashions from different time periods. These dresses date to 1955. (Boyd & Breeding Collection, Morton Museum of Cooke County.)

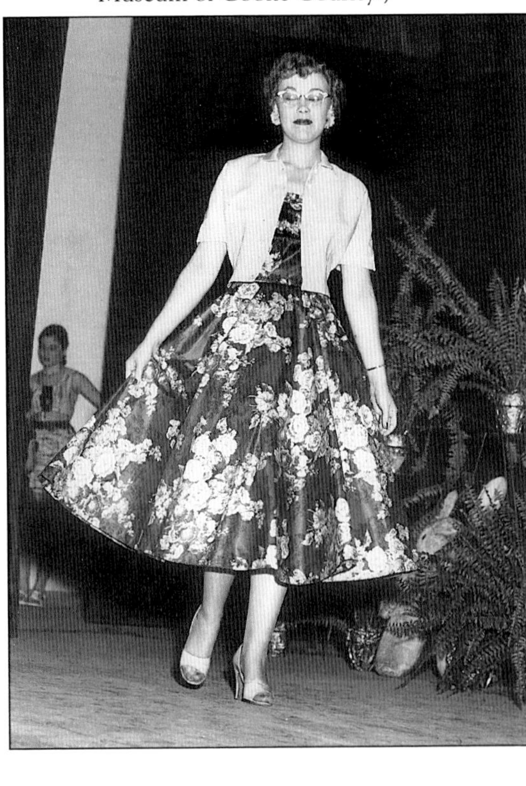